Page Intentionally Left Blank

Testimonials

"It's really a very good book."
-R.D., Full-Charge Bookkeeper

"It's good…, right-on and good."
-G.H., CPA & Controller

"It's fabulous (and I've taken a bookkeeping course)."
-C.D., A Former Bookkeeper

*"Wow. I'm impressed with the organization of it.
It's very well put together. I can't say enough."*
-R.N., Preschool Director

*"It's good. I think you really have something for the emerging business.
And I love the forms."*
-A.S., Business Owner

*"It's excellent! … It seems to be quite thorough,
which indicates a lot of hard work on your part, GOOD JOB!"*
-F.S., Engineer

*"You've done such a great job giving the step-by-step and providing practical
pointers that people would want to have… Very nice work overall!"*
-D.D., Attorney

*"I am a CPA in training… Your book on bookkeeping has been quite helpful…
It has cemented some of the core concepts I have learned."*
-C.H., **CPA in Training**

*"Hello, I recently got your full charge bookkeeping book and I LOVE it.
Thanks for making a great guide that's easy to follow
for even the most entry level bookkeeper."*
-M.J., Owner at a Bookkeeping Business

"P.S. - good job with the Bookkeeping manual!!"
-J.W., Accounting & Tax Business Owner

Full-Charge Bookkeeping
For the Beginner, Intermediate & Advanced Bookkeeper

Home Study Course Edition

by Nick J. DeCandia, CPA

Copyright © 2015
Den Publishing Company
All rights reserved.

ISBN-10: 1478162759
ISBN-13: 978-1478162759

Printed in the United States of America. 1 2 3 4 A C S 15 14 13 12

Websites: www.Full-ChargeBookkeeping.com
www.Full-ChargeBookkeeping.com/Certification

Email: CustomerService@DenPublishing.com

Table of Contents
Preface

1. Introduction .... pg. 8
   - What is Full-Charge Bookkeeping?
   - Getting Started and Organized When Hired
   - New Job Checklist
2. Tasks
   - Human Resource Administration .... pg. 10
   - Accounts Payable .... pg. 11
   - Accounts Receivable .... pg. 15
   - Collections .... pg. 16
   - Payroll .... pg. 18
   - Commissions & Bonuses .... pg. 23
   - Payroll Taxes .... pg. 24
   - Other Taxes .... pg. 28
   - General Ledger .... pg. 29
   - "Fixed Asset" Purchases .... pg. 31
   - Bank Reconciliations (Including Finding "Outages") .... pg. 32
   - Petty Cash .... pg. 34
   - State-Specific Tasks .... pg. 36
   - Financial Statements or Monthly Reports .... pg. 37
   - Year-End Items (W-2's, 1099's, Record Retention) ..... pg. 39
   - Corporate Taxes .... pg. 42
3. Authorities .... pg. 44
   - Frequently Used
     - IRS
     - State Specific Authorities
   - Other Authorities / Laws
4. Manual Bookkeeping .... pg. 46
5. Debits and Credits .... pg. 47
6. Computers .... pg. 49
   - Computer-Based Bookkeeping
   - What Else?
7. Insurance .... pg. 52
   - Health Insurance
   - Liability Insurance
   - Worker's Compensation Insurance
8. Industries .... pg. 54
   - Construction
   - Food & Beverage
   - Manufacturing
   - Retail
   - Service
   - The Non-Profit Sector
9. Dealing(s) with the CPA .... pg. 58
10. Bookkeeper as Management? .... pg. 60
11. A Word about Professionalism & Ethics .... pg. 63
12. A Word about 'Audits' .... pg. 64

Table of Contents (continued)

Appendices .... pg. 66
    A. Master Calendar (Schedule) .... pg. 67
    B. Chart of Accounts (Sample) .... pg. 69
    C. Financial Statement (Samples) .... pg. 71
        Income Statement .... pg. 72
        Balance Sheet .... pg. 73
    D. Accounting 'Basics' .... pg. 74
        Accounting Equations .... pg. 74
        Accounting Methods .... pg. 74
        Closing A Year .... pg. 74
        "Depreciating" Assets .... pg. 75
        "Draws" Taken by the Owner .... pg. 76
        Inventory and "Cost of Goods Sold" .... pg. 76
        Office Supplies (Expense?) .... pg. 79
        Relationship Between Financial Statements and
                the Chart of Accounts .... pg. 79
        "Retained Earnings" .... pg. 80
        "Writing-Off" a Receivable .... pg. 80
    E. Sample Forms .... pg. 81
        Collection Form .... pg. 82
        Commission Spreadsheet Form .... pg. 83
        Fax Cover Sheet .... pg. 84
        FUTA - SUTA Spreadsheet Design .... pg. 85
        HR - Employee Update Information Form .... pg. 86
        HR - Employee Request for Time Off Form .... pg. 87
        HR - Employee Warning Notice .... pg. 88
        Past Due Notice .... pg. 89
        Petty Cash - Receipts .... pg. 90
        Petty Cash - Change Order .... pg. 91
        Record Retention Form .... pg. 92
        Time Sheet for Employees .... pg. 93
        Travel Mileage Form .... pg. 94
    F. A Word about Career Advancement .... pg. 95
    G. "Career Resource Binder" Kept At Home .... pg. 97
    H. Resources & Bibliography.. pg. 98
Glossary.. pg. 100

STUDY OUTLINE - TEXTBOOK .... pg. 115
STUDY OUTLINE - APPENDICES .... pg. 155

TEST BANK .... pg. 161

Index .... pg. 183

Preface

Every small business should have a "full-charge bookkeeper".

Defined: a *full-charge bookkeeper* will perform all of the bookkeeping tasks of a small business, including payroll taxes and monthly financial statements, with little or no supervision.

Organization

You will notice that this book is comprised of many shorter chapters, because you will find in full-charge bookkeeping that no single task is all that complicated, buts that there are many tasks to perform. And whether you're studying Beginning, Intermediate, or Advanced Bookkeeping each chapter is carefully written with the beginner in mind, but complete in all aspects. Regarding the order of chapters in this book, Chapter 1 - Introduction defines full-charge bookkeeping and helps you get started, when hired. Beyond introductions, the first thing you realize about bookkeeping is all of the tasks to perform. Soon into tasks (like payroll taxes) you realize just how important authorities, such as the IRS, are to a bookkeeper. So, Chapter 2 covers "Tasks", and Chapter 3 discusses "Authorities".

I also found that bookkeeping progresses more naturally from manual bookkeeping to doing it on a computer. And, while much manual bookkeeping can be done without knowledge of debits and credits, computer bookkeeping may be troublesome without basic knowledge of debits and credits. So, I start with "Manual Bookkeeping", progress to "Debits and Credits", and then to "Computers" - in Chapters 4, 5 & 6. Then, I cover miscellaneous topics like "Insurance", some of the "Industries" out there, and "Dealing(s) with the CPA", in chapters 7, 8 & 9, to name a few.

Scope

This text covers bookkeeping for-profit sector businesses. Bookkeeping for non-profits is the subject of other books. Further, it is not within the scope of this book to research each state's specific tax requirements. As there are both federal and state taxes, I will discuss all federal taxes associated with full-charge bookkeeping, and the majority of the different state and local taxes you'll run into, as well as how you can uncover your own state's specific tax requirements. In fact, the Small Business Administration has put together a listing and links of each states' local tax authorities. However, again we do not claim completeness nor accuracy of any listing/s there, implied or otherwise. But, since the links typically lead to "General Tax Information & Forms", as well as State Unemployment Tax (SUTA)..., I do highly recommend using this state resource. It is available at: http://www.sba.gov/content/learn-about-your-state-and-local-tax-obligations; or: http://www.sba.gov/, > "Starting a Business" > "Establishing a Business" > "Taxes" > "Learn about Your State and Local Tax Obligations".

Additionally, this book is not about the specifics of any one year, for example: the current year's travel mileage reimbursement rate, but about how to do full-charge bookkeeping in general and knowing where to find the specifics of any one year. In this example, I would tell you which IRS publication to look at in order to obtain the current year's travel mileage reimbursement rate. Finally, it is within the scope of this book to define all new terminology. If you see a word in quotation marks (" ") that means I offer a definition for it, as it is probably new to you or particular to bookkeeping.

Readability

I've done a few things in this book to make it easier to read. First, as mentioned above, any and all new terminology is defined right there on the spot - within the text of the chapter. This way you won't have to stop and find a definition in the glossary, thus getting side-tracked. By the way, there is a full glossary as well. Second, I've tried to be good about dividing chapters into sections and sub-sections, with easily distinguished headings. A typical section organization would be like this:

Section Heading
SUB-SECTION HEADING
Further Sub-Section

You should also see that all "Notes" and numbered guidelines have the topic in *italics*, followed by the detail of that topic. Finally, you may notice some repetition within this text. Having said that, there is not a lot of it, it was done with significant deliberation and with good reason. For instance, the section on "Supervisory Situations" is included in both the "Bookkeeper As Management?" chapter and the "Career Advancement" appendix. You will notice a similar situation with the Corporate Tax information. It is included in both the "Tasks > Corporate Taxes" chapter and the "Dealing(s) with the CPA" chapter.

Preface (continued)

Breaking Into This Field - Of Money Handling

If you are looking to break into this field I have observed, basically, two avenues to do so: (1) v*ia a family business* - for instance, if your father or mother starts a business, and you offer or get to handle the books, and (2) a *more traditional route* - I, for one, had to gain cash handling experience through a retail sales job. Then, using that cash handling experience, I went to work for a bank - as a teller. From there, I moved to corporate accounting, taking a bookkeeping assistant position. This route may seem more difficult, but you do build an excellent foundation of experience and knowledge. *Note: I've decided to write something about my journey - at the end of certain chapter/s, called, "On a Personal Note".*

Certification

Give your career a boost with the title "Certified Full Charge Bookkeeper" (CFCB). The certification exam is a 100 true/false and multiple choice questions, open book, no time limit, but you must complete it in one sitting. A score of 70% achieves certification (60% achieves a "Course Completion Certificate"). Benefits include: (1) title, Certified Full Charge Bookkeeper, that gains instant respect; (2) certificate suitable for framing; (3) wallet card; (4) independent verification of your Certificate - for potential employers to verify, and more. For more information, visit: http://www.full-chargebookkeeping.com/Certification.html. Ready yourself and access the exam (administered by Class Marker.com) here: https://www.classmarker.com/online-test/start/?quiz=rfe558b929f5dd77.

Dedication

I would like to dedicate this book to five people:
Anne Shepherd, my high school English teacher, who inspired me to greater heights - in writing,
My mom, for all her levels of support; Nicholas Edward DeCandia, my father - an "eagle" among "nesters",
My brother, Don, whose (academic) achievements inspired me towards the same,
And my wife - for her very fine example as a full-charge bookkeeper!

Acknowledgments

Thanks the following people: Rita D. Newman, Camille & Ron DeCandia, Don DeCandia,
Frank Santoriello, Ann & Don Silva, and my wife - for her assistance.

About the Author

Nick established a national presence in 2001 with his ground-breaking article, "The New Face of the IRS" written for "Strategic Finance" magazine - January 2001 issue. He obtained a CPA License in 2007, and reached supervisory levels in both corporate and public accounting. Nick has a Business Degree, with concentrations in Accounting and Finance from the University of New Mexico, as well as an Engineering Degree from the University of Notre Dame. Having held various corporate accounting positions including: Bookkeeping Assistant, Intermediate, and Full-Charge - in addition to the supervisory level positions, Nick has written many accounting procedures for various employers. As Author and Founder of Den Publishing Company, Nick is currently pursuing a small business opportunity having written two textbooks, as well as maintaining a small tax practice.

Disclaimer

The information contained in this book is for general guidance only. It is provided with no guarantee of completeness, accuracy, timeliness, or of the results obtained from the use of this information. Furthermore, this book is provided without any warranty of any kind, express or implied, including any warranty of merchantability, performance or fitness for a particular purpose. While every effort has been made to make this book reliable, as to completeness and accuracy, there may be errors and/or omissions, both typographical and in content. It is sold with the understanding that the author and/or publisher are not, herein, engaged in rendering legal, accounting, tax, or other professional advice.

Since the application of laws can vary greatly, based on the specific facts and circumstances, this book should not be used as a substitute for consultation with professional accounting, tax, legal or other competent advisors. Furthermore, the author and/or publisher shall have neither liability nor responsibility to any person(s), or entity for any decision made or action taken in reliance on the information contained in this book. Finally, the author and/or publisher shall have neither liability nor responsibility to any person(s), or entity with respect to any loss or damage caused, or alleged to have been caused, directly or indirectly, by the information contained in this book.

Chapter 1 - Introduction

What is Full-Charge Bookkeeping?

A full-charge bookkeeper is one who can and does perform all of the bookkeeping tasks of any small business, including payroll taxes and monthly financial statements, with little or no supervision. About the only task needed to be "outsourced" is the corporate tax return (typically, to a CPA). That, in essence, is full-charge bookkeeping.

Defined: to *outsource* is to hire another company or individual to perform a task.

Getting Started and Organized When Hired

QUESTIONS TO ASK - DURING THE INTERVIEW, OR BEFORE TASKS
1. Defining the Position:
   Q: What exactly will I be responsible for?
   Q: Are there any tasks that will be outsourced?
2. Are there any areas we want to be doing differently / better, or paying more attention to?
3. Are there any areas/tasks that require more urgent attention?

WHERE TO START

Once you've clarified with the owner what he or she has hired you for, it's time to get to the business at hand. But, looking at accomplishing all of these tasks can be overwhelming; so where should you start? The first thing you should do is make sure you have a list of current employees, and their pay rates. Payroll may be soon, and you wouldn't want to be unprepared, or late with employees' checks. A good place to store the current list of employees is in an "Information" file-folder, close at hand, for payroll and other related areas. In addition to an "Employee Information Sheet", start a "Business Information Sheet" with things like tax identification numbers, phone, fax, address(es) and any company owner information you might need or acquire for credit applications.

While you're at it, and if the files are at your disposal, you may want to be sure that the human resource files are in order - "current" separated from "terminated" employees, and that each file has the proper documents: Forms W-4 & I-9 (reference: Chapter 2 - Tasks > Human Resource Administration). After preparing for payroll, the short list of things you should get a handle on is (1) the company bills (see Tasks > Accounts Payable). And, (2) review the company receivables to see where they stand (see Tasks > Accounts Receivable). That will get you started. For the complete "new job checklist", see below.

THE FILING SYSTEM

I must emphasize the importance of organization to a bookkeeper. Organized records not only make a bookkeeper's life easier, but also help those around the bookkeeper. For instance, what if the owner wanted or needed to find something on a day you were not there - perhaps a bill that needed to be paid, if a vendor called. You wouldn't want the owner to open your file drawers and find a mess. In fact, if you find the bookkeeper's files somewhat disorganized when you arrive, it might be to your benefit, and the company's as well, to organize them.

The typical file drawer organization should include approximately five file drawers as follows.
1. *Unpaid Payables* (defined below).
2. *Unpaid Receivables* (defined below).
3. *Paid Payables for Year 20xx* (the current year).
4. *Paid Receivables for Year 20xx* (the current year).
5. *Reports* (eg. Financial Statements, Payroll Tax Reports, Employee List).

Defined: *payables* are the bills that your company owes.

Defined: *receivables* are what customers owe your company.

The Unpaid Payables, Unpaid Receivables, and Reports file drawers should be closest to the bookkeeper's fingertips - for quickest access, when the boss asks for something. Previous years' paid payables and receivables should be stored in a box. For more information, reference Chapter 2 - Tasks > Year-End Items > Record Retention. Be sure to properly label the outside of the drawers.

Chapter 1 - Introduction (continued)

Getting Started and Organized When Hired (cont.)
I'd like to point out two more things regarding filing. The first is that in the business world, nearly everyone files the most recent documents to the front of folders, not the back. This way they will be easier to access. The second thing concerns filing for companies with proper names, for instance "John Smith Incorporated". Do not file this under Smith, but under John, because it is incorporated. Obviously, John Smith (not incorporated) would be filed under "Smith". Finally, you may get hired into a company with a file system, already in place, that is difficult to work with. You will have to "feel out" your place and relationship with the owner - to see if it is ok to make any suggestions or changes.

IS DAMAGE CONTROL NEEDED?
Do beware - the possibility exists that you get hired into a position which requires a certain amount of damage control immediately upon entering the position. For instance, if there hasn't been anyone in the bookkeeping position for six months. If you find yourself in this type of situation, you will need to start at the top, with the most important things - like payroll tax reports. Have reports been filed? Start with federal, then state and move on from there. You will also want to be sure there are not "shut-off notices" in the unpaid bills arena.

> Defined: a *shut-off notice* is a written communication, usually from a utility company (electric, water and/or gas company) that says the company you work for has an unpaid, overdue bill. It's telling you that your company is about to lose (utility) service.

New Job Checklist
1) *Job Responsibilities Clarification:* from interview and/or further discussion with company owner.
2) *Information File Folder:*
    a. *Employee Information Sheet:* list current employees and their pay rates, for payroll.
    b. *Business Information Sheet:* list tax ID numbers, phone, fax, address(es), any company owner information needed for credit applications.
3) *Stop Gap Check*:
    a. Payroll Tax Reports Filed?
    b. I-9's and W-4's for current employees?
4) *Start a Master Schedule (from Appendix A):* list pay-periods, payroll tax report due dates, etc.
5) *Files Organized / At Your Fingertips?*
6) *Payables Aging:* any potential costly shut-offs for unpaid bills?
7) *Receivables Aging:* any significantly old / outstanding invoices of customers that need to be contacted?
8) *Any Petty Cash?* Be sure to reconcile with the books and company owner upon entering the job.
9) *Bank Statements:* are there any that arrived and need to be reconciled to the books?
10) *Is it the End of the Month or End of the Year?* Reference those chapters to see what task to perform.
11) *Calendar:* be sure to add all items from your Master Schedule to your calendar!
12) *State-Specific Requirements:* be sure you gain / have gained and understanding of your state's specific tax requirements.

Note: *confidentiality* - it should go without saying that bookkeeping information is considered confidential, particularly payroll related information - pay rates and pay checks or amounts. Do treat it as such!

Chapter 2 - Tasks > **Human Resource Administration**

You may be a little surprised to see a chapter on human resource (HR) administration. There are two reasons it is here. One, if the company you work for is small, chances are there won't be too many administrative personnel around, other than yourself and the owner. So, tasks like HR administration may often fall to the bookkeeper. And, two, the bookkeeping tasks of payroll and payroll taxes *require* information contained on Form W-4 (defined below) like withholding allowances and the employee's social security number. So, it behooves the bookkeeper to be sure that form is filled out completely, when the employee is hired. Fear not, you can see this chapter is short.

> Defined: *Form W-4* is an IRS form entitled "Employee Withholding Allowance Certificate". It lists the name, address, social security number and withholding allowances for the employee.

Where to Start

As mentioned in Chapter 1 - Introduction, the first thing to do when entering a full-charge position, is to establish a list of the current employees' names, addresses and telephone numbers. Put it in a folder entitled "Current Employees List", and keep this folder in a drawer, close to you. It will help you do payroll, and you'll be able to have a quick reference if the owner needs a phone number, for instance. Chances are the human resource files will be kept in, or near your area. Be sure they are separated 'active' from 'terminated' employees, and both sections are alphabetized by employee last name. Keep the active section in front of the terminated section.

Are Human Resource Files in Order?

In order to be sure the human resource files are in order, check each current employee's file to see that there is a Form W-4 and Form I-9.

> Defined: *Form I-9* is the federal form entitled, "Employment Eligibility Verification". It's for immigration purposes, and if filled out correctly, indicates that the person is legally able to work in the United States.

Both forms (W-4 & I-9) are required by law. If any employee file is incomplete, make a short list and keep it on your desk to track down. Another useful document, in the employee files, is the original employment application, with starting pay rate and job title, initialed by the company owner. As stated above, Form W-4 is critical to a bookkeeper. It lists the number of withholding allowances, needed to do payroll - which determines how much tax is withheld. And, Form W-4 also lists an employee's social security number, which is needed to fill-out payroll tax reports.

Notes: 1. *Fielding phone calls* - if it is your responsibility to field phone calls regarding previous employees, be sure to check your state/local laws concerning privacy of information. For more information see Chapter 10 - Bookkeeper as Management? > If You Must Field Phone Calls...
2. *IRS forms* - are available on-line at www.irs.gov, by U.S. mail - calling 1-800-829-3676, or at your local IRS office.
3. *Form I-9* - is available from the U.S. Citizenship & Immigration Services at http://www.uscis.gov/ > FORMS > I-9.//

Chapter 2 - Tasks > **Accounts Payable**

Defined: *accounts payable* are the bills that your company owes.

Getting Organized

To get a handle on the company bills, start with your office, seeking all unpaid bills. You should be able to locate two file drawers of bills. One will be bills already paid. The other will be bills not yet paid, but entered into the system - computer or manual books. Both file drawers should be alphabetized by vendor name; and the paid files should also list the current year - example: "ABC Company, Paid Bills, Year 20xx". In the in-box should be bills that are both unpaid and not yet entered into the system. Bear in mind, there may be some bills in the owner's office.

In order to keep a handle on the payables, you, as the bookkeeper, will need to pay attention to the incoming mail. Perhaps you may even be in charge of retrieving it and/or distributing it. Paying attention to the mail - who receives it, is the best way to ensure that all bills make it to you. Basically, you collect incoming bills, also called "invoices", from the mail. But before entering them, you need to be sure your company received the product or service. You may also have to verify the price being charged. So, there are a couple of documents to be aware of - a packing slip and a purchase order (both defined below).

> Defined: an *invoice* is another name for a company bill (usually created from within a company). It can be either a bill you owe another company, or one that your customer owes you.

Packing Slips

> Defined: a *packing slip* is a form shipped with product (*not* services). So, it represents receipt of the goods by your company.

Note: *proof of receipt* - you should want to see a signature or initials of whoever, from your company, received the product - on the packing slip.

You should collect packing slips in a folder titled "Packing Slips". Alphabetize them by company name and match them up to bills, before entering bills into the bookkeeping computer system. Bills that don't match to any packing slips should be verified with the company owner, in order to ensure that the service or product was received. As mentioned above, you *may* also need to verify prices charged. That is where a purchase order comes into play.

Purchase Orders

> Defined: a *purchase order* (PO) is just that - an order or approval to purchase something. Purchase orders contain the price(s) agreed upon, and will be approved with a signature, by either the owner, or person authorized to approve a purchase.

Note: *smaller companies* - companies of less than ~$5 million sales per year typically will not use purchase orders.

You, as the bookkeeper - in a company that uses purchase orders, will need to have a copy, in order to know that the bills have the correct prices on them. Use pencil checkmarks when verifying prices. This will help you realize you've checked the prices on that invoice. When finished verifying staple the PO behind the invoice. Sometimes prices can be verified in the computer system - if the computers are networked.

If PO's are not used at your company, about all you can do is verify receipt of the product / service, and glance at the price, to make sure it's not completely outrageous. At that point, the price charged becomes the owner's or check signer's responsibility. And, for the record, I recommend that the bookkeeper not also sign the checks. You have enough responsibility, without that added burden.

Freight

Take a quick glance, down the bill (invoice) at the freight or shipping charge, just to be sure they're not charging you a ridiculous amount. I heard of one instance where the freight charge was $500. What was shipped were large catalogues, but the bookkeeper thought $500 sounded awfully high. She questioned it, and it turned out it should have been one third that amount. She ended up getting a $600 credit from similar previous charges. Better than ninety-nine times out of one hundred these types of charges will not be unusual, but if an amount strikes you funny or seems out of the ordinary, do question it. They will at least appreciate your diligence.

Chapter 2 - Tasks > Accounts Payable (continued)

Entering

After you have verified that the product or service was received and that the price is correct, you may then enter it into the system (i.e. computer bookkeeping program, like QuickBooks or Sage 50 (formerly Peachtree)). Checkmark or rubber-stamp the upper right hand corner, after you enter it - so you won't make the mistake of entering it a second time. The office supply stores have self-inking stamps with a variety of different words, like "Entered" in red ink, would make this unmistakable. Once entered, file the invoice by company (vendor) name, in your unpaid bills drawer.

Vendor Statements

Defined: a *vendor* is a company that sells a product or service to your company.

Defined: *vendor statements* list all outstanding or unpaid bills (aka: invoices), and are sent once per month.

Many, but not all vendors will send statements of account. You should balance to the statement - making sure that you have all invoices listed on it, and that they have applied all payments you have made. Obviously, if you mailed the check this morning, they will not have received it yet, so it will not have been applied to the statement in front of you. If there is an invoice listed that you don't have, try to find it. It may be somewhere within your company; else, call your vendor to get a copy of it faxed to you.

Do be on the lookout for finance charges on the statements. Typically vendors won't charge finance charges, unless you are quite *slow* in paying. Post them to that vendor's account, but be aware that some business owners object to paying finance charges - on business accounts. That becomes a matter between your boss and that vendor (you're just the middleman). Of course, after balancing to the statement, be sure to file it with that vendor's bills.

Payables Summary

So, here is the order of things.
1. *Incoming mail* - if you can't do them when they come in, file bills and statements in "Unentered Bills" folder you can keep in you In-Box.
2. *Match bills to packing slips* - verifying receipt of the goods.
3. *Compare bills to purchase orders* - verifying that the prices charged on the bill are the same as on the purchase order. Raise any 'material' discrepancies with the purchasing person.
4. *List any significant vendor communications* - like any "past due" or "shut-off notices" (defined below) - on a separate list. See "Does Your Company Pay Timely Or Not" below.
5. *Enter bills into the system* - glancing at the freight charge.
6. *Balance vendor statements to your books* - making sure you have all invoices listed, and that all payments have been applied. Post any finance charges.
7. *File bills and statements alphabetically* - by vendor name in an "Unpaid" or "To Be Paid" file drawer.

Defined: a *shut-off notice* is a written communication, usually from a utility company (electric, water or gas company) that says the company you work for has an unpaid, overdue bill. It's telling you that your company is about to lose (utility) service.

Should The Bookkeeper Be A Signer On The Checking Account?

I recommend against the bookkeeper being a signer for several reasons:
1. *You have enough to do.*
2. *Trouble with owner* - it will keep you out of trouble with the owner as far as approving payments on your own.
3. *"Segregation of duties"* - it will help maintain segregation of duties for security purposes. For more information, reference Chapter 10 - Bookkeeper As Management? > Does The Owner Want You To Sign Checks?

Defined: *segregation of duties* means to separate those tasks that, if not separated, could lead to undetected theft.

Accounts Payable Aging

Defined: an *aging* is a listing of companies, invoices, dates and dollar amounts (see example below).

Chapter 2 - Tasks > Accounts Payable (continued)

Accounts Payable Aging (cont.):
    As bookkeeper, your responsibility will be to maintain an accurate listing, or "aging" of the payables.

EXAMPLE – ACCOUNTS PAYABLE AGING
As of: 9/15/xx

Vendor Name	Invoice Date	0-30	31-60	61-90	Over 90 Days	Total
ABC Company						
Invoice # 123897	8/1/xx		$50			
Invoice # 123965	9/1/xx	$75				
Total, ABC Company						$125
XYZ Company...						

Does Your Company Pay Timely or Not?
    You will probably work for one of two types of companies. There are those who pay their bills on a timely basis / endeavor to do so, and there are those companies who don't - pay timely. For those that pay timely, you - as the bookkeeper, should work to take the two percent discounts offered for paying the bill within ten days of the invoice date. Look for "terms" in fine print, at the bottom of the invoice. "2/10, Net 30" stands for 2% discount if paid within 10 days, otherwise the invoice is due to be paid within 30 days. Two percent may not seem like a lot of money, but it adds up and is better in your pocket than theirs.

    If your company does not keep up very well with paying bills, you will probably receive communications from your vendors. A sample communication from a vendor is, "If you do not pay, we will stop shipping you product." It is your job to keep up with exactly what the vendors are communicating, and to communicate that to your boss, as needed. Vendor communications will come both over the phone and in the mail. Keep a telephone message pad, with carbon copy, on your desk to keep track of incoming calls. And, be sure to read all statements and letters from vendors, carefully. Sometimes the threatened action is in fine print.

Keep A List of Calls
    Keep a master list of requests, and photocopy it before giving it to the owner. As needed, give your list of requests to the owner so s/he knows what's going on with the vendors. That, in essence, is where your responsibility ends. It will be the owner's responsibility to decide what bills to pay. *And, it is ultimately the owner's responsibility to satisfy the vendors.* List should include dates, what vendors said, and dates of old invoices with dollar amounts.

    Typically, your boss will not want to be bothered every time the phone rings, in search of an unpaid bill. This causes you to keep a list. The only question is how often to give the owner the list. This is something you will have to gauge. I usually waited until the day I felt I'd be delinquent for not producing it - probably no longer than 10 to 14 days, or when I just couldn't stand it anymore.

    The only exception is when a vendor stops or threatens to stop a shipment that your company needs in order to operate. This would include a utility "shut-off notice". Then you would want to communicate with your boss that very day, and not wait. At this point, you will need to get familiar with the vendors, in order to have some idea of what is critical versus what is not. Realize that dealing with a slow paying owner / company is about as sticky as it gets, in bookkeeping.

Producing a Check
    When producing a check to pay a vendor, follow these guidelines.
1. *Include account number* - on the check or check stub.
2. *Pay oldest invoices first* - and include the invoice numbers on the check stub.
3. *If you are just paying a certain amount* - (e.g. $500) towards the account, be sure to ask your vendor to apply this money towards the oldest invoices first.

Credit Applications
    It is often the bookkeeper's responsibility to fill-out credit applications, in order to obtain accounts with new vendors. Fear not - it is the owner's responsibility to sign the credit applications, and provide the bookkeeper with the information needed to fill them out. Typically, companies create an information page that the bookkeeper uses, containing credit references, banking information, and perhaps some information about the company owners. Finally, don't be surprised if the credit applications ask for a "personal guarantee" from the company owner.

Chapter 2 - Tasks > Accounts Payable (continued)

"Factoring"
Defined: *factoring* means selling accounts receivable to another company, for say 80 cents on the dollar. The other company then owns and collects those receivables.

As a full-charge bookkeeper, you should be aware of factoring. Since some companies decide not to collect their own receivables, you in the payables department would be sending the check elsewhere. The way you will know is there should be a large stamp in red or black ink, on the front of the invoice, indicating that this invoice is now payable to this other company.

On A Personal Note:

At one point in my life, I was pursuing a Business/Finance degree, and working part-time at the bank (as a floating teller - moving from branch to branch on a weekly basis) in Albuquerque, NM. I knew that I wanted to stay in Albuquerque after graduation because all my family was there. So, I started looking at job postings inside the bank. But, all the jobs were so narrowly focused. I knew I wouldn't be happy - in one of those jobs. So, I started looking outside the bank, at smaller businesses - where I would have a broader view of what was going on. But the job ads were all bookkeeping-type jobs (not exactly college-graduate-typical).

Well, I had a decision to make. And happiness was (a large) part of that. I would pursue the bookkeeping route (which later led to an Accounting 2nd major & CPA after that). It was one of the best decisions I've made. I started in an A/P position (Assistant Bookkeeper - assisting the Accounting Manager). I was in that position for 3 years, before broadening my horizons from there! By the way (not to brag), but when they were advertising my position (when I gave notice), they had Controllers and such applying for that position. You see I had worked really hard at reducing a million dollars in payables down to about six hundred thousand. And, had good relationships with our vendors... It just goes to show - there's no small parts only small actors. So, do the best you can where ever you start - AND PEOPLE WILL NOTICE!

Chapter 2 - Tasks > **Accounts Receivable**

Defined: *accounts receivable* are what customers owe your company.

The key to good accounts receivable is keeping organized records. This way, you can answer the owner's questions, as to what customers owe, and accurate records provide a good starting point if collection activity is needed. The best way to organize your receivables is to file a copy of your company's invoice, alphabetically, by customer name in an "Unpaid Receivables" file drawer (with file folder entitled, "ABC Company, Unpaid Invoices"). If you file it by the month of the sale, as one company I worked for, it will be too difficult to find later. The paid invoices should then be filed in a different – "Paid Sales Invoices" file drawer, with the file folder label listing the current year. For example: "ABC Company, Paid Sales Invoices, Year 20xx".

Accounts Receivable Aging
It is a good idea to update your accounts receivable, by printing a detailed receivables aging, at least once per week. A receivables' aging is similar to a payables' aging. See example below. But, of course, a receivables aging will list customers, instead of vendors. It is also a good idea to review your receivables every week or two for unpaid and overdue invoices. At this point you will need to work on collections. Reference: Chapter 2 -Tasks > Collections - the next chapter.

EXAMPLE – ACCOUNTS RECEIVABLE AGING
As of: 9/14/xx

Company Name	Invoice Date	0-30	31-60	61-90	Over 90 Days	Total
A1 Customer						
Invoice # 123897	8/2/xx		$45			
Invoice # 123965	9/2/xx	$85				
Total, A1 Customer						$130
A2 Customer..						

Statements of Account
Defined: *statements of account* are typically sent once per month listing all outstanding invoices.

Once per month, at the beginning of the month, send out "statements" to your customers - listing unpaid invoices. This will help with collections, and help keep accounts between you and your customers straight. You may want to write a brief note, on some, saying something to the affect, "When might we expect payment?" But, be sure to consult with your boss before conducting any stringent collection activity.

A Word about Extending Credit
Before extending credit, it would be wise to employ the use of a credit application, for several reasons.
1. *To get a name* - of the accounts payable contact person.
2. *To get a signature* - agreeing to finance charges, should their account become overdue.
3. *To get a physical street address* - in case you need to "serve" a "legal complaint" (see glossary).
4. *To obtain credit references* - to find out how your customer has been paying some other suppliers.

As mentioned in Tasks > Accounts Payable, some typical credit terms you will hear are "2/10, Net 30" which means if you pay the invoice within 10 days, take 2% off the invoice amount. If not, the invoice is due 30 days from the invoice date, regardless. The most effective credit policy I've seen is a 60-day cut-off policy. In other words, if or when your customer's bills reach 60 days old, either they pay, or you don't ship (product or service) to them. It also helps to let them know in a kind way, that you *had* to cut them off - that it was *not* personal, but rather your company's policy - in order to survive. Of course, this is something only your boss should decide to enforce.

Factoring
As mentioned in the Accounts Payable chapter, you should be aware of "factoring receivables". Some companies decide not to collect their own receivables. Instead, they sell their receivables to another company, for say 75 or 80 cents on the dollar. The other company now owns and collects those receivables. This type of arrangement can be useful because you receive your money, upon shipment of your product, by wire transfer the next business day.

Chapter 2 - Tasks > **Collections**

Defined: *collections* means collecting accounts receivable from customers who are not paying timely.

As you might think, accounts receivable and collections go hand in hand, and even overlap at times. As mentioned above in Chapter 2 - Tasks > Accounts Receivable, "Statements of Account" are a good start on the collection road. They do a couple of things. First, they keep balances straight between you and your customers. Second, they let your customers know, without actually asking for payment, that you have attention on how much they owe you. Finally, they are a place on which to jot a note like, "When might we expect payment?" or use a "Past Due" stamp on the statement.

Beyond simple Statements of Account, the best place to start collections is with your boss. Be certain the company owner has approved any collection activity you would like to undertake. Your boss, the company owner, may not want to bother certain customers or may have made arrangements with certain customers, in order to close a sale/s.

Start Softly

After you have secured the boss' blessing, start softly. In other words, you might want to start with a phone call to the customer, stating that you just wanted to check on the status of a bill. They may have already mailed the check. For some, a soft call is all they will need to get moving - they may have lost your invoice, for instance. Do, however, document your activity, using the "Collection Form" in Appendix E. Probably the biggest misconception about collections is that you have to start out by being overbearing. Get in communication with them first. Find out what their issues are, and what might be holding up payment. I think you'll find much of accounts receivable can be collected this way!

The Next Approach

If a soft approach is not fruitful, more collection action will be needed. Continue to pursue it, by telephone with *steady determination*. Maintain your professional demeanor. What if you can't get through via the telephone? For instance, you get the idea they are giving you the run around, not calling you back, or the person you need is always "out of the office", mailing a "Past Due Notice" (Appendix E) may be an option. Be sure to document your actions and their responses, using the Collection Form in Appendix E. If you're still not getting anywhere, then go to your boss regarding the next approach. Show your boss the collection activity on this customer - the collection form filled out, to convince your boss that you're having trouble getting through. Suspending service may need to be discussed. If they are no longer customers, they might have little reason to pay, other than avoiding legal action.

Suspending Service

If they are a repeat customer, your steps will need to be a somewhat delicate. You will need direction from your boss, but suspending shipments/services should probably be part of the discussion. They might want you to work with them, and you/your boss should be prepared for that framework. Know what plan is acceptable, but ensure your customer keeps to the plan. A standing company policy could be helpful to have in place. For example, don't ship to customers over 60 days out. See "A Strong Credit Policy" below.

Documenting, Communicating and Follow-Up

Documenting your collection activity is the best way to keep on top of collection activity. This way you will have a record of the time and date you called (or mailed any notice), with whom you spoke, and their response. Note on the collection form a place for "follow-up action". This is important, because you cannot depend on your customer to do what they said they would do, necessarily. Remember, it is equally important to keep your boss apprised of your activity and results - both positive and negative. Positive results reflect on the effectiveness of your work, and negative results will lead towards stronger collection activity or approaches.

Legal Remedy

If all else fails or they are no longer a customer, you may be forced to pursue legal remedy. Laws do vary by state, or locality (city/county) on this topic. But know that an attorney is *not* always necessarily needed to go down this avenue. For instance, in New Mexico, if the claim is less than $5000, you may file a "legal complaint" at the local courthouse, and then "serve" that complaint to your un-paying customer. The bookkeeper or business owner is fully capable of filling out this complaint. And "process servers" can typically be found at the courthouse, via their business cards.

Chapter 2 - Tasks > Collections (continued)

Legal Remedy (cont.)
    Defined: a *legal complaint* is a document you file in your local courthouse to pursue a legal remedy, e.g. against an un-paying customer.

    Defined: to *serve* is to officially give a "legal complaint" to the person or entity (company) being complained about. "Process servers" are often used for this.

    Defined: *process servers* are people who serve complaints for a small fee.

A Strong Credit Policy
    If your customer knows you have a strong credit policy, they may be more apt to pay. As mentioned in the Accounts Receivable chapter, the most effective credit policy I've seen is a 60-day cut-off policy. In other words, if or when your customer's bills reach 60 days old, either they pay, or you don't ship (product or service) to them. It would also help here to let them know in a kind way, not with a mean spirit that you have to cut them off. That is to say that it is not personal, but your company's policy - in order to survive.

Notes: 1. *Best days to call* - you may find Tuesday, Wednesday and Thursday to be the best days to place calls. Mondays and Fridays people are more often out of the office.
          2. *Construction work* - if your company does construction work, "materialsmen liens" are a more powerful legal remedy for collecting. Reference: Chapter 8 - Industries > Construction > Materialsmen Liens.
          3. *Uncollectable* - if an accounts receivable becomes uncollectible, for example - your customer goes out of business, then you will need to "write-off" the receivable. Reference: Appendix D - Accounting 'Basics' > "Writing-Off" a Receivable.
          4. *Collection letters* - it's been my experience that "collection letters" (standardized form letters) are mostly ineffective.

On A Personal Note:
    After working my way up to a FCB position, I got hired as a Bookkeeping Supervisor for a local popular Mexican food supplier in Albuquerque. I was to oversee 3 data entry clerks along with some other rather menial tasks, related to purchasing and collections - in fact. (The only problem was the person who hired me was not forth-right in letting me know about the collection activity, when I interviewed. And, I asked very specifically about my tasks in that position.) At any rate, they did have another collections guy. So I let him carry the majority of that burden and observed. He did very well in that position - just getting in SIMPLE, HONEST COMMUNICATION with our customers. It was pretty neat to behold. Oh, and by the way - he got noticed as well - by the President of the company! Nice, right?

Chapter 2 - Tasks > **Payroll**

Payroll should begin with a list of current employees and their pay rates. You'll see that I've organized this chapter into "Payroll - Via A Computer" and "Payroll - Manually". Chances are, you'll be doing payroll via a computer bookkeeping program, but you should know how to do payroll manually, regardless. Before doing any payroll, there are a few things you will need to know.

What You Need to Know Before Doing *Any* Payroll
Bookkeepers need to be aware that national law, specifically the Fair Labor Standards Act and Fair Minimum Wage Act requires payments of a *minimum wage, payment for overtime*, and *record keeping* (source: http://www.dol.gov/ > page down to the bottom, >A to Z Index > W > Wages).

MINIMUM WAGE
Beginning on January 1, 2015, 20 states increased their minimum wage rate, bringing the total to 29 states that have rates higher than the federal minimum wage rate. Ref.: http://www.dol.gov/whd/minwage/america.htm. And, for states (or cities) that have higher rates than the federal, the higher (local state or city) rate applies! In the other 21 states, where their rate is either the same or lower (or they have no stated rate), the federal minimum wage rate (of $7.25) applies. Reference: http://www.dol.gov/dol/topic/wages/minimumwage.htm.

For instance - Santa Fe, New Mexico has a minimum wage of $10.84 (effective March 1, 2015). Since this is higher than the federal minimum wage, this higher rate applies to jobs in Santa Fe. So, before beginning payroll, you will need to determine if your state or local minimum wage is higher than the federal rate, and if so what exactly is your local minimum wage. Reference the site/s listed above, and your local Department of Labor will also be of assistance, here. Finally, federal minimum wage information is also available by calling 1-866-4-USWAGE.

Note: *food & beverage industry* - if working in the Food & Beverage industry, waiters and waitresses (making at least $30/month in tips) have a minimum wage of $2.13/hour, as long as their tips make up the difference to get to the federal hourly minimum wage. Some states have a higher base wage. Source: U.S. Dept. of Labor http://www.dol.gov/dol/topic/wages/wagestips.htm (or www.dol.gov; >A to Z Index >T >Tips).

PAYMENT FOR OVERTIME
Federal law requires that any hours worked over 40 in a seven-day period be paid overtime, not less than time and a half. Source: http://www.dol.gov/dol/topic/wages/overtimepay.htm. Please note, I have not uncovered any state overtime laws, but I don't rule out that possibility. So be sure to check the laws in your state regarding the payment of overtime.

RECORD KEEPING
For hourly employees, federal law requires companies to keep records of at least the following.
1. *Identifying information* - about employees, for example: name, address, social security #'s.
2. *Days and hours worked* - as well as wages earned, and deductions made.
   Source: http://www.dol.gov/dol/topic/wages/wagesrecordkeeping.htm .

Payroll - Via A Computer
SET-UP:
1. *Payroll module:* be sure the payroll module in the computer is up and running.
   a. *NOT a new computer:* see if you can open the payroll module and can start to do payroll. If you are taking over the bookkeeping position from someone else, the payroll system should be set-up.
   b. *New computer:* if this is a new computer, refer to the owner's manual to be sure both the federal and any state tax tables are loaded.
2. *Employee information:* check employee information to be sure it is current and entered.
   a. *Names & current addresses:* current addresses are important to mail W-2's at the end of the calendar year.
   b. *Pay rates:* if uncertain, look in the HR file or check with the business owner.
   c. *Withholding(s):* verify the number of exemptions or withholding allowances from Form W-4, in the personnel file, to ensure the correct amount is withheld.

Chapter 2 - Tasks > Payroll (continued)

Payroll - Via A Computer (cont.)
   DOING IT:
1. *Collect timesheets:*
   a. *Have all of them?* Verify that you have all timesheets by comparing against the list of current employees.
   b. *Timesheets Signed?* They should be signed by both the employee and the employee's supervisor. You will not want to pay an employee based solely on his or her signature, only to find out your employee lied, and you paid an incorrect amount. The supervisor's signature covers you.

   Note: *salaried employees* - it is required by law in some states to have a record of hours worked. Some companies use sign-in / sign-out sheets located near the entrance, if you have difficulty getting your salaried people to fill out a timesheet. Salaried employees are also known as "exempt" employees because they are not paid for overtime.

2. *Complete math on timesheets:* calculating and indicating regular hours, of 40 or less in a 7-day period, and indicate those hours over 40, also known as "overtime".
3. *Any commissions?* Be sure you've paid any commissions due to your sales people. Also, realize that some employers may prefer to have a separate commission check.
4. *List deductions:* on the timesheet list any special deductions including:
   a. *Medical insurance:* if there is a medical insurance deduction or retirement savings plan deduction (eg. 401-k), because these benefits are exempt from taxes, these need to be deducted from gross wages, <u>before</u> any taxes are taken out. Reference: IRS Publication 15-B, "Employer's Tax Guide to Fringe Benefits" > Accident and Health Benefits (Table 2-1).
   b. *Any garnishment.*

   Defined: a *garnishment* is a legal order or judgment to deduct wages from a person, and send those wages to a government agency. Examples include child support, alimony and back taxes due.

   c. *Any employee advance:* like if your company loaned an employee $100 to get to pay day.
   d. *Any other state specific tax.* For example, New Mexico has a Worker's Compensation Administration Tax of $4 per quarter.
5. *Enter hours:* begin entering hours, and any special deductions into the computer. Put a check mark in the upper right hand corner after entering a timesheet. Be sure to label deductions properly, so employees won't question you, when they see it on the check stub.
6. *Review:* after entering all timesheets, review each entry in the computer to be sure things are correct. Put a second check mark in the upper right hand corner, to indicate that it was verified.
7. *Print checks:* be sure to use "duplicate check stub" mode, even if you get your canceled checks back, so that both the employee and employer-bookkeeper have a record of all *deductions* taken. If you are unable – your computer bookkeeping system doesn't have duplicate mode, then simply photocopy the checks and deductions.
8. *Flip through checks:* to be sure they look ok - printed legibly: no zero or million dollar checks.
9. *Prepare for signature:* paperclip timesheets to the back of the checks.
10. *Get checks signed.*
11. *Remove:* bookkeeper's stub or photocopy if you don't have a bookkeeper's stub - in case of a question.
12. *Print a payroll register:* or payroll journal from the computer bookkeeping software, which ever report will best serve you. Store payroll report in the file drawer with the other reports printed monthly.
13. *Distribute:* checks only to the employees being paid.

Note: *paycheck "picked up"*- if an employee wants his or her check picked-up, require a note – signed by the employee, indicating who will pick it up. And, when that person shows up, look at his or her ID - before giving out the check. Keep the note, and file it in the employee's HR file.

14. *Store:* put a rubber band around all timecards and check stubs or copies, for the pay period and save them in a file drawer for the year, as *confidential* information.

Chapter 2 - Tasks > Payroll (continued)

Payroll - Manually
   SET-UP: If you're doing payroll manually, there are a few things you will need to gather.
1. *List of current employees'* - names and pay rates.
2. *Tax tables:* listed in IRS Publication 15 (Circular E), "Employer's Tax Guide".
3. *Calculator or adding machine.*
4. *W-4's:* to give you the number of exemptions claimed - in order to use the tax tables, in Circular E.

Note: *one list* - I suggest that it will be helpful to have one list of current employees' payroll information. The list should contain their current pay rates, and the number of exemptions. This will provide a handy reference when doing payroll manually. Keep this information confidential!

   DOING IT:
1. *Collect timesheets:*
   a. *Have all of them?* Verify that you have all timesheets by comparing against the list of current employees.
   b. *Timesheets Signed?* They should be signed by both the employee and the employee's supervisor. You will not want to pay an employee based solely on his or her signature, only to find out your employee lied, and you paid an incorrect amount. The supervisor's signature covers you.

   Note: *salaried employees* - it is required by law in some states to have a record of hours worked. Some companies use sign-in / sign-out sheets located near the entrance, if you have difficulty getting your salaried people to fill out a timesheet. Salaried employees are also known as "exempt" employees because they are not paid for overtime.

2. *Complete math on timesheets:* calculating and indicating regular hours, of 40 or less in a 7-day period, and indicate those hours over 40, also known as "overtime".
3. *Any commissions?* Be sure you've paid any commissions due to your sales people. Also, realize that some employers may prefer to have a separate commission check.
4. *Calculate Gross Wages* = (Regular Hours x Regular Wage Rate) + (OT Hours x OT Wage Rate).
5. *Calculate Deductions:*
   a. *FICA* = 7.65% x Gross Wages,   where % translates to: 0.0765 x Gross Wages
      Social Security = 6.2%
      Medicare   = 1.45%
       FICA total   = 7.65%

   Defined: *FICA* = Federal Insurance Corporation Act; the means by which the federal government collects social security and Medicare for the elderly.

   b. *Federal Tax Withheld:* go to tax tables in Circular E, using the number of withholding allowances for each employee.
   c. *Any state income tax withheld:* you will need to contact your own state's Department of Taxation or the like - to find out if your state has an income tax, and if so to get a hold of the tax tables.
   d. *Medical insurance:* if there is a medical insurance deduction or retirement savings plan deduction (eg. 401-k), because these benefits are exempt from taxes, these need to be deducted from gross wages, <u>before</u> any taxes are taken out. Reference: IRS Publication 15-B, "Employer's Tax Guide to Fringe Benefits" > Accident and Health Benefits (Table 2-1).
   e. *Any other state specific tax.* For example, New Mexico has a Worker's Compensation Administration Tax of $4 per quarter.
   f. *Any employee advance.* Like if your company loaned an employee $100 to get to pay day.
   g. *Any garnishment* - legal order or judgment to deduct wages from a person.
6. *Calculate Net Wages* = Gross Wages minus all Deductions.
7. *List separately* - on the pay stub:
   a. Regular and Overtime Hours
   b. Gross Wages
   c. All Deductions - list and label each one separately.
   d. Net Wages

Chapter 2 - Tasks > Payroll (continued)

Payroll - Manually (cont.)
8. *Fill out checks* - using Net Wages calculated.
9. *Review your work* - and be sure you've prepared a check for every employee.
10. *Prepare for signature:* paperclip timesheets to the back of the checks.
11. *Get checks signed.*
12. *Photo copy checks and stubs* - to have a record of what was paid and deducted.
13. *Distribute checks* - only to the employees being paid.

Note: *paycheck "picked up"*- if an employee wants his or her check picked-up, require a note, signed by the employee indicating who will pick it up. And, when that person shows up, look at his or her ID - before giving out the check. Keep the note and file it in the employee's HR file.

14. *Store:* finally, put a rubber band around all timecards and check stubs or copies, for the pay period and save them in a file drawer for the year, stored as confidential information.

Notes: 1. *Tips* - when your employee reports tips in the Food and Beverage Industry, you are required to collect tax (federal withholding, social security and Medicare) on those tips, as well as deduct it from your employee's base pay or wage. Reference: IRS Publication 15 > chapter entitled "Tips".
2. *Garnishments* - you should keep a ledger of wages garnished, for audit purposes and for good record keeping. The ledger should contain the beginning balance or amount owed the state. This will come from a letter in the mail. The ledger should also contain: dates, check numbers, and amounts remitted to the state, with a running balance so you know when to stop garnishing.
3. *Reimbursements* - if you need to reimburse an employee, for any reason, *always* do a separate check for that. It will keep taxes out of the picture, which it should be, and keep your accounting straight.
4. *Business miles driven* - the IRS publishes "standard mileage rates". To find out how much to reimburse an employee for business miles driven (not commuting), reference IRS Publication 15-B, "Employer's Tax Guide to Fringe Benefits" > What's New > Cents Per Mile Rule. Realize that this rate does include gasoline.
5. *Check date* - the check date determines the tax quarter of a payroll, not the pay-period ending date.
6. *Required poster* - note employers are required by federal law to display certain information regarding employees' rights. This is something that your employer has most likely taken care of sometime before your arrival. But, you should be aware, and if your employer has not, here is the web-site where you can print the required poster / information (free of charge) www.dol.gov > page down to the bottom, >A to Z Index > P > Posters.
7. *High income individuals* - if you have any high wage earners (wages above $200,000) an additional 0.9% Medicare Surtax is due. See IRS Publication 15 > Medicare Taxes > Additional Medicare Tax Withholding.

Independent Contractors
As the bookkeeper, you may run into "independent contractors", aka: "contract labor".

Defined: *independent contractors* are people who are doing work for your company, but are self-employed - not employees of your company. They pay their own (payroll) taxes. So, you pay them straight wages, without any taxes deducted.

Example: the most common example of an *independent contractor* is in the construction industry, where they're known as subcontractors - an electrician or plumber, for instance.

Even though you aren't deducting taxes, they still owe the government taxes, and you must help report their income. You report their income by filing a Form 1099-MISC, at the end of the year. Reference: Chapter 2 - Tasks > Year-End Items > Form 1099 MISC.

Defined: *Form 1099-MISC* is an IRS form entitled, "Miscellaneous Income". It is required to be filed by the bookkeeper to indicate amounts paid to independent contractors - in excess of $600 per contractor, per year (less than $600 and Form 1099 need not be filed for that contractor, that year).

Chapter 2 - Tasks > Payroll (continued)

REQUIREMENTS TO BE CONSIDERED AN INDEPENDENT CONTRACTOR

Fulfilling the requirements to be considered an independent contractor is tougher than it ever has been. Requirements include "behavioral control" issues, "financial control" issues, and "relationship" issues. Reference: IRS Publication 15-A, "Employer's Supplemental Tax Guide" > Chapter entitled, "Employee or Independent Contractor?" available @ www.irs.gov.

The IRS is cracking down in order to ensure receipt of all taxes due. Penalties can be huge and levied to the employ*er*. Yes, it would be safer to err on the side of employee rather than independent contractor. If, however, you would like the IRS to make a determination for you, you may request that via IRS Form SS-8, "Determination of Worker Status for Purposes of Federal Employment Taxes and Income Tax Withholding".

IF YOU HAVE AN INDEPENDENT CONTRACTOR WORKING AT YOUR COMPANY

If you do have an independent contractor doing work for your company, you should make sure you have both a Form W-9 and a certificate of worker's compensation insurance from his or her insurance company on file. Without Form W-9 you will not have the independent contractor's Taxpayer Identification Number needed to issue a 1099 at year-end. And without his/her certificate of insurance, your insurance company will require you to list him/her on *your* bill, dramatically raising your insurance cost.

If you do have an independent contractor, start a file labeled, "Contract Labor", in which to store W-9's, certificates of insurance, 1099's and copies of payments to the independent contractor. If you have more than one contractor, start separate files for each. When entering that person into the computer bookkeeping program, be sure to check mark the appropriate box, indicating contract labor. Otherwise, your computer program will not know who is contract labor, come the end of the year. And don't be surprised if you need to enter them in the "Vendors" module, not the "Employees" module.

Chapter 2 - Tasks > **Commissions & Bonuses**

Defined: if unfamiliar, *commissions* are pay earned by a sales person on sales he or she made, while a *bonus* is extra money given to an employee usually for a particular reason - like for Christmas.

Depending on your company, you may or may not have any commissioned employees. In other words, your company may not have any sales people, other than the owner, or they may be straight salaried sales people. But, if you do have an employee who earns commissions, you must be sure you know the exact percentage(s) agreed to, between the owner and commissioned employee. It would even be a good idea to have a copy of the commission agreement on file for reference. If there is no *written* agreement (a situation I ran into – there was just an oral agreement) take a moment to type the percentage(s) in simple wording and get both the owner's and the employee's signature. That way it covers what you're doing!

Calculating Commissions
SINGLE % SITUATIONS
If you have a single percentage situation - the same percent commission for all sales, or you are *un*able to use a computer for some reason, you can easily calculate commissions manually. If you'd like, you can use ledger or columnar paper. Below is an example of a single percentage situation, and how to display it.

Example: say Charlie earned 12% commission on *all* sales. If Charlie sold $2500 worth, his commission would be = 0.12 x 2500 = $300.

Pay-period				
Beg. Date	End Date	Sales for the Period	% Commission	Commission this Period
xx/xx	xx/xx/xx	$,$$$	%	$$$

MULTIPLE % SITUATIONS
It is possible your commissioned employees / sales people may earn different commission rates depending on to whom or how much they sell. In this case, it will be easier for you to use a computer spreadsheet program, like Microsoft Excel, to calculate and display commissions. I've also created a form you may use to calculate and display commissions. Reference: Appendix E - Sample Forms > Commission Spreadsheet Form.

Example: say Betty earned 15% on the 1st $1000 in sales, and 10% for everything above that. If Betty sold $3000 worth, her commission would be = (1000 x 0.15) + (2000 x 0.10) = $350.

Commissions & Bonuses are Fully Taxable
Know that commissions and bonuses are fully taxable. You will need to deduct federal withholding and FICA (social security and Medicare) from all commission and bonus checks. And, commissions and bonuses are also subject to Federal Unemployment Tax. Finally, they should be included on your employee's W-2 at year-end. Reference: IRS Publication #15 > Supplemental Wages.

One Paycheck or Two?
Although you/your boss may want to cut a separate check for commissions, rather than including it with an employee's regular pay, if they receive both, my suggestion is to write only one check for both regular pay and commissions. But, identify them separately on the check stub. This way you'll be more likely to withhold the proper amount of tax, should commissions push the employee into a higher tax bracket. Do be sure to note also on the paycheck stub - the pay period of the commission, and attach a copy of the commission calculation.

Storing Commissions
Keep a separate folder or binder for each commissioned employee, in which you should have at least the commission spreadsheet and check number, which paid that commission. A two-inch binder can provide a good place to store each pay period's commission spreadsheet and agreement. Label the spine of the binder "Joe Salesperson's Commissions", and keep it near your desk, but in view for your boss to access. If doing commissions manually, beware of keeping your only commission spreadsheet in a binder that the owner accesses. Store a copy elsewhere, should your boss accidentally misplace it.

Chapter 2 - Tasks > **Payroll Taxes**

Defined: simply put *payroll taxes* are taxes that arise because of payroll.

Payroll taxes consist of both federal and state specific payroll taxes. As mentioned in the Preface, it is not within the scope of this book to research each state's specific tax requirements or to give you all the specific dollar amounts of any one particular year. Instead, it is the purpose of this book to teach you not only how to do full-charge bookkeeping, but where to find both state specific requirements and the dollar specifics of any one year. Having said that, it would be a good idea at this point to obtain and have next to you, a copy of the current year's version of IRS Publication #15 (Circular E) "Employer's Tax Guide" – as this is the 'bible' for payroll taxes, available at www.irs.gov. You may just want to print the first half of it for easier reference, less the "Tables" in the back.

Federal Payroll Taxes
All federal (payroll) taxes are paid to the IRS. There are three things to do with federal payroll taxes: *deposits*, *quarterly reports* and *annual reports*. To help you keep track, reference Appendix A - Master Schedule, to keep track. In order to make deposits, you will need to use your company's federal "Employer Identification Number" (EIN). You will find it on previous payroll tax reports filed. If this is a new business, file IRS Form SS-4, "Application for Employer Identification Number", to obtain a federal ID number for your business. You may also have a state taxpayer identification number. A good place to record these numbers for referencing, is on the inside cover of your "Current Employees" or "Master Schedule" file folder. Then they are close at hand.

DEPOSITS
Defined: federal payroll tax *deposits* are made after payrolls to pay taxes withheld from pay checks, plus taxes due from the employer. These are called #941 payments (an IRS number).

Basics
You will notice when doing payroll that you withhold taxes from each employee. The federal taxes you withhold are federal income tax, and FICA - Federal Insurance Corporation Act. "Social security" and "Medicare" are the two components of the FICA tax, at 6.2% and 1.45% of gross wages, respectively. The federal government wants you to pay those taxes fairly soon after you withhold them, and for the federal government you do this by making these payroll tax deposits.

Amount
In addition to the FICA you withheld from each *employee*, the *employer*, or company you work for, must match that FICA amount. Therefore, the amount of the deposit is equal to the federal income tax withheld, plus employees' FICA (7.65% of gross wages), and employer's "matching" FICA (7.65% of gross wages). As a result, the total amount to remit equals 15.3% of gross wages + federal income tax withheld.

Deposit Amount = (0.153 x Gross Wages) + Federal Income Tax Withheld

If using a computer bookkeeping program to do payroll, there should be a report to print providing the totals needed. You would be wise to re-check by hand the computer's calculation. It won't take long. If doing payroll manually, use your check stubs or copies - to run an adding machine tape to get a total for gross wages and federal income tax withheld.
The only hitch in the amount is that Social Security (the 6.2%) has a "wage base" or maximum wages per employee, on which you'll calculate that 6.2% portion. Any wages above the limit for an employee during the year will not be taxed the 6.2%. They will only be taxed 1.45% (the Medicare portion). The wage limit is quite high though. It changes each year - typically goes up, and is close to $100,000. To get the exact dollar amount, reference IRS Publication 15 > "What's New" > "Social Security and Medicare tax [for 20xx]". Yes, it may be unlikely or rare that you would reach the wage limit for any employee you'll be paying, but you need to be aware it exists.

When to Deposit
How often you are required to deposit, depends on the amount of payroll taxes your company paid in the past. The IRS has two schedules, "monthly" and "semi-weekly"; $50,000 in payroll taxes for a year has typically been the dividing line. If a company reported $50,000 or less it would be a monthly depositor. If it reported more than $50,000, in a look-back period, in taxes, then it would be deemed a semi-weekly depositor. Refer to IRS Publication 15 > "Depositing Taxes" > "When to Deposit" to see where your company fits in.

Chapter 2 - Tasks > Payroll Taxes (continued)

Federal Payroll Taxes (cont.)

How to Deposit

There was once a time when all payroll taxes were remitted through your local bank. Well, the IRS has jumped on the electronic bandwagon, and now requires companies to deposit electronically. Again, refer to IRS Publication 15 > "Depositing Taxes" > "How to Deposit". The IRS electronic system is entitled, "Electronic Federal Tax Payment System" (EFTPS). To get information about EFTPS / enroll, visit http://www.eftps.gov, or call 1-800-555-4477. See "Note" below for certain low tax payment amount instances (like less than $2500 in total tax liability for the quarter..). Do pay particular attention to the proper tax type, quarter and year, when depositing electronically, and reference IRS Publication 966, "Electronic Choices to Pay All Your Federal Taxes".

Note: *liability less than $2500 in a quarter* - if your company's payroll tax liability is less than $2500 for the current quarter or preceding quarter you may make payment with the 941 quarterly report, rather than making deposits. Reference: IRS Publication 15 > "Depositing Taxes" > "Payment with return".

QUARTERLY REPORTS

Defined: the *federal quarterly payroll tax reports* are: (1) Form 941 entitled "Employer's Quarterly Federal Tax Return", and (2) *payment* of Federal Unemployment Taxes (FUTA).

Only payment of FUTA is due quarterly because the FUTA tax return is due annually. All payroll taxes use the calendar year: January - December. Federal taxes are further divided by quarters. Form 941 and payments of FUTA are due at the end of the month following the quarter. Note that the *check date* determines the tax quarter of a payroll, not the pay-period ending date.

	Months	Due Dates of Reports	
1st Quarter:	January, February & March	April 30	(Post-Marked By)
2nd Quarter:	April, May & June	July 31	
3rd Quarter:	July, August & September	October 31	
4th Quarter:	October, November & December	January 31	

Form 941, "Employer's Quarterly Federal Tax Return"

If all of your payroll tax deposits were made, there will not be any payment needed - just Form 941 to fill out and mail to the IRS, at the end of the quarter. And if you are using a computer accounting program, like QuickBooks or Sage 50, it should have Form 941 capabilities - form can just be printed out, already completed. Reference: IRS Instructions to Form 941. Finally, there is no *annual* Form 941, just the four quarterly reports.

Payment of Federal Unemployment Taxes (a.k.a. FUTA)

There are no quarterly Form 940's to file - just payment is due, each quarter. As mentioned above, Form 940 is an annual form. Furthermore, federal unemployment taxes are generally *reduced* by the amount of "State Unemployment Tax" (SUTA) paid, so do calculate SUTA first, then FUTA. For help with this calculation, I've designed a form. See FUTA - SUTA Spreadsheet in Appendix E.

Note: *commissions & bonuses* - be sure to include all commissions & bonuses when calculating Federal Unemployment Tax. Reference: IRS Publication 15 > "Supplemental Wages".

The current FUTA tax rate is 6.0% of gross wages - actually just the first $7000 of gross wages paid in the year - which is called the "wage base". And the maximum credit for State Unemployment Taxes paid is 5.4%. If your company receives the full credit, that would leave just 0.6% in FUTA taxes owed, or 0.006 x wage base. Reference: IRS Publication 15 > Federal Unemployment (FUTA) Tax > Computing FUTA tax.

As mentioned above, I've designed a spreadsheet to help facilitate calculations (Appendix E - Sample Forms > FUTA - SUTA Spreadsheet). And refer to Publication 15, or IRS "Instructions for Form 940", when making calculations. Since Federal Unemployment Taxes are based on each employee's first $7000 of wages, for the year, you will probably pay your FUTA taxes within the first or second quarters, for full-time employees.

Chapter 2 - Tasks > Payroll Taxes (continued)

Federal Payroll Taxes (cont.)

Finally, *"If your FUTA tax liability for any calendar quarter is $500 or less, you do not have to deposit the tax. Instead, you may carry it forward and add it to the liability figured in the next quarter to see if you must make a deposit. If your FUTA tax liability for any calendar quarter is over $500 (including any FUTA tax carried forward from an earlier quarter), you must deposit the tax by EFT."* Reference: IRS Publication 15 > Federal Unemployment (FUTA) Tax > Depositing FUTA tax.

When to Do Form 941 and Calculate FUTA

You should fill out Form 941 and calculate FUTA just as soon as the quarter ends. Even though payments are not due until the end of the following month (see "Due Dates of Reports" above) it will be smart to complete these tasks as soon as possible after the quarter ends. Quarterly payroll tax reports should be copied to the business owner (and the CPA - with owner's approval). Of course, make a copy of all payroll tax reports filed and keep them filed with your other monthly reports. Label file folder: "Payroll Tax Reports - Year 20xx".

ANNUAL REPORTS
Form 940

The only federal, annual, payroll tax *report* is Form 940, "Employer's Annual Federal Unemployment Tax Return" (FUTA). *[Form 941 is a quarterly report.]* Form 940 is due January 31, and if $500 or less is due in the fourth quarter, for your company's FUTA deposit, you may pay that amount with your Form 940 return. If you owe more than $500, you must deposit it electronically and mail the Form 940 return separately. Source: IRS Publication 15 > "Federal Unemployment (FUTA) Tax".

Notes: 1. *annual report for Form 941?*- "Employer's Quarterly Federal Tax Return" is due each quarter, and does *not* have an associated annual report.
2. *Form 944* - don't make the mistake of thinking you can use Form 944, Annual.. in place of Form 941. The maximum wage in order to use Form 944 is only ~$4000 ($1000 maximum tax liability including both employer & employee's portions of FICA, as well as federal withholding). Not to mention that the IRS requires special request and approval in order to use Form 944.
Reference: IRS Instructions for Form 944.

State Payroll Taxes

As I mentioned in the Preface, it is not within the scope of this book to research each state's specific tax requirements. And, each state is different. So, you will need to investigate your own state's payroll tax requirements. Below is a discussion of the typical state payroll taxes you will find, *State Unemployment Tax, state income tax*, and *ways to uncover your state's payroll tax requirements*. Know that some states don't have income tax - Florida, for example. And finally, as the bookkeeper, you will probably run into state sales tax also, but strictly speaking that is not payroll related. It is covered in Chapter 2 - Tasks > Other Taxes.

STATE UNEMPLOYMENT TAX

State Unemployment Tax (SUTA) is generally filed in conjunction with Federal Unemployment Tax (FUTA). Often, the amount paid in State Unemployment Taxes may be taken as a credit towards the amount of Federal Unemployment Taxes owed. So, the bookkeeper should first calculate any State Unemployment Taxes due, and then federal. As mentioned above, I've created a spreadsheet to help facilitate calculations (ref: FUTA - SUTA Spreadsheet in Appendix E - Sample Forms). Also, be sure to reference your state's instructions for filling out any State Unemployment Tax forms. In New Mexico, State Unemployment Taxes are paid quarterly (like FUTA), to the N.M. Department of Labor.

Note: *State Unemployment Tax Agencies* - the U.S. Department of Labor maintains a list of State Unemployment Tax agencies here: http://www.workforcesecurity.doleta.gov/unemploy/agencies.asp.

Chapter 2 - Tasks > Payroll Taxes (continued)

State Payroll Taxes (cont.)
    STATE INCOME TAX
        The other typical state payroll tax is state income tax. You should be aware that some states don't have income tax - Florida, for example. Again, you'll have to research your state's taxing authorities to know how, when and where to remit state income taxes that have been withheld from employees. In New Mexico, we remit State Income Tax withheld to the N.M. Department of Taxation and Revenue, on a monthly basis. Take note - you may be required to file both monthly and quarterly reports in your state. As mentioned above, in New Mexico we remit State Income Tax on a *monthly* basis, but State Unemployment Tax is remitted *quarterly*.

    WAYS TO UNCOVER YOUR STATE'S PAYROLL TAX REQUIREMENTS
1. *Search* - the bookkeeper's files for previous tax reports.
2. *Search* - on-line, requesting:
        "(your state's) Taxation Department" or "Treasury Department"
        "(your state's) Department of Labor"
        "(your state's) government" or "payroll tax requirements".
3. *Look in* - the government pages of your local phone book and make some calls.

Note: *payroll taxes* - by far the most complex thing a FCB has to do is payroll taxes. If there is one IRS form, instruction or publication to reference it is Publication 15. In fact, the IRS even set-up their own Pub. 15 website: http://www.irs.gov/uac/About-Publication-15 (listing the most current Publication 15, any recent developments..).

Chapter 2 - Tasks > **Other Taxes**

Defined: *other taxes* are the typical taxes a bookkeeper would run into that aren't covered in the payroll tax and corporate tax chapters.

Do be aware that there is no such thing as a national or federal sales tax, or "gross receipts tax" - defined below. Although other taxes vary by state, the typical ones a bookkeeper will run into are state sales tax, property tax, and a business license fee. Finally, I'll say a word about some lesser know taxes "tangible" and "intangible property taxes", also defined below.

State Sales Tax

Defined: if unfamiliar *state sales tax* is generally levied on retail sales - of just products sold, and is paid to, for instance the Department of Taxation & Revenue as in the case of New Mexico.

There are a few things to be aware of. First, some states tax *services* in addition to products. When taxing both, it is often referred to as "gross receipts" tax.

Defined: *gross receipts tax* is levied by states, typically on products *and* services sold, as opposed to "state sales tax" - levied on just products sold.

Second, you should be aware that some transactions might not be subject to sales tax - within a particular state. For example, in New Mexico "Non-Tax Transaction Certificates" exist to exempt certain groups from paying sales tax, like non-profit organizations. You will have to research your state's laws in this area. First, try contacting your state's Department of Taxation. Finally, know that state sales tax probably will not be billed to your company. You will have to report it.

WAYS TO DETERMINE YOUR STATE'S TAX REQUIREMENTS
1. *Search* - the bookkeeper's files for previous tax reports.
2. *Search* - on-line, requesting:
    "(your state's) Taxation Department" or "Treasury Department"
    "(your state's) Department of Labor"
    "(your state's) government" or "tax requirements".
3. *Look in* - the government pages of your local phone book and make some calls.

Property Tax

Defined: *property tax* is levied by local authorities, typically the city or county on land and/or buildings, based on their assessed value. The higher the assessed value the higher is the tax.

In New Mexico, such taxes are assessed by and paid to the county treasurer. Half is due in December and the other half is due in May of the following year. This bill should show up in the mail.

Business License Fee

Defined: a *business license fee* buys a right, or permit, to operate a business within the city or county lines.

In New Mexico, for example, the city of Albuquerque levied approximately $35 per year, to each business, in order to conduct business within the city limits. If it's a new business you will have to file with the city for the first year, and then should receive a bill in the mail for subsequent years.

Intangible or Tangible Property Tax

Defined: *intangible property tax* is levied on an intangible asset – like Accounts Receivable, while *tangible property tax* is levied on business personal property - like office equipment.

Very few states levy these types of taxes. Kentucky for instance has levied approximately one and a half cents per $100 on intangible business property rights, like accounts receivable. To be sure your county or state does not impose Tangible or Intangible Property Tax, search on-line at "(your state's or county's) Tangible Tax" and "(your state's or county's) Intangible Tax". //

Chapter 2 - Tasks > **General Ledger**

Defined: the *general ledger* is the place where all transactions (or debits and credits) get posted.

Note: *knowledge of debits and credits* - is needed in order to properly deal with the general ledger. So, be sure to study Chapter 5 - Debits and Credits, before proceeding here.

Since manual bookkeeping with debits and credits is a thing of the past, this chapter will focus on the general ledger as it relates to computers. As a full-charge bookkeeper, there are a few things you will need to do with the general ledger. First, you will need to put "journal entries", defined below, into the computer for some transactions. Second, you will need to be able to print "transaction listings" (also defined below). Third, you will need to maintain the "chart of accounts" (defined below, and reference Appendix B - Chart of Accounts), and finally you *may* need to balance the general ledger - if you have a particularly older version of bookkeeping software.

Journal Entries (a.k.a. General Journal Entry)
Defined: a *journal entry* is debits and credits "in balance" describing a transaction, where: "in balance" here means the total of all debit dollars equals the total of all credit dollars.

Most transactions, entered into the computer, will automatically post to the general ledger. For instance, if entering bills, printing sales invoices or issuing payroll checks *through the computer,* the debits and credits that need to be posted will automatically post to the general ledger. There are, however, some transactions that would not hit the GL, unless entered manually. And this is where a bookkeeper really earns his or her keep - keeping up with transactions that are occurring but are not hitting the computer.

"Petty cash" (defined below) is an example of this. If you're using petty cash, your computer bookkeeping system would have no way of knowing this unless you enter it, manually. Fortunately, the computer bookkeeping systems have a place designated just for these types of situations. It is called entering a journal entry or general journal entry. Say, for example, you want to start a petty cash account. Below is the journal entry you will need to enter into the computer bookkeeping system.

Defined: *petty cash* is a small amount of cash, kept on hand - preferably in a locked box, for incidental items (example: buying pizza for lunch).

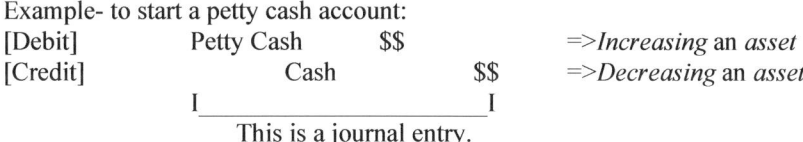

Journal entries will access what's called the "chart of accounts" (defined below). Cash and Petty Cash are examples of accounts in the chart of accounts. If you have access to a computer accounting program, take a moment to practice manually posting a journal entry, using the chart of accounts. There are more examples in the debit & credit chapter. So, you need to be on the watch for transactions that are not going through the computer. In these cases, you will need to post manually to the general ledger. I often found it useful to write out on scratch paper, my journal entry, before going into the computer to do it.

Producing a Transaction Listing
Defined: a *transaction listing* lists all of the transactions - debits and credits, for selected accounts over a specified period of time.

Occasionally, you will need to produce a transaction listing for a particular account. One example would be if you needed to research something - like how much has been spent on the point-of-sale system. You could print a summary transaction listing providing just beginning and ending balances over the specified period of time. Or you could print a detailed transaction listing providing dates and amounts of *all transactions* for the selected time period, along with beginning and ending balances. Generating transaction listings is mostly self-explanatory, once you find that area in the bookkeeping program - often within the General Ledger module. You will usually select an account from the chart of accounts, and a time period (or beginning and ending dates).

Chapter 2 - Tasks > General Ledger (continued)

Maintaining the "Chart of Accounts"
    Defined: the *chart of accounts* lists every account in the general ledger. Reference: Appendix B - Chart of Accounts.

    Most computer bookkeeping programs, including QuickBooks and Sage 50 Accounting, have preloaded charts of accounts. If, however, you find those charts lacking, you will be able to add and delete accounts to create a chart that best suits your company. Do beware however, if you are not the person setting up the accounting system, you probably will not and should not do too much changing of the chart. In fact, you will not be able to delete any accounts that have transactions posted to them, and a few that are used as defaults within the bookkeeping programs. On the other hand you *should* add an account whenever a situation arises that warrants keeping a separate account. For instance, your company decides to invest in a "point-of-sale system" (defined below). You, as the bookkeeper, should add an account to the chart by that name, in order to keep track of moneys spent for it!

    Defined: a *point- of-sale system* is a computer program tied into the cash registers that updates inventory levels after every sale.

Balancing the General Ledger (In Select Instances)
    Defined: *balancing the general ledger* means that all debits equal all credits posted for the month.

    Fortunately, these days computer bookkeeping programs, including QuickBooks and Sage 50, won't allow a journal entry to be posted that is not in balance. So, the general ledger will balance automatically at the end of the month. If, for some reason, you run into a bookkeeping program that does not balance automatically, you will need to run a "trial balance".

    Defined: a *trial balance* is a detailed listing of all debits and credits posted to the general ledger for a certain period of time. It will display two totals at the bottom, one for all debits and the other for all credits posted. If the trial balance balances, the total for debits will equal the total for credits.

    If your trial balance does not balance, you will have to hunt for the out of balance transaction/s and correct it. Correcting it involves going back to the original transaction or document, to find and reenter the correct amounts. If you're having trouble finding the transaction, reference Chapter 2 - Tasks > Bank Reconciliations > Finding "Outages". Once the general ledger is balanced, and all data for the previous month is entered, you should be ready to print financial statements.

Note: *changing accounting periods* - some may consider changing to the next accounting period or month, part of GL tasks. Please see Chapter 2 - Tasks > Financial Statements - because I've listed changing accounting periods there.

Chapter 2 - Tasks > **"Fixed Asset" Purchases**

Defined: *fixed assets* are another name for "Property, Plant & Equipment" (PP&E). Where fixed assets are listed on the Chart of Accounts (Appendix B), PP&E are listed on the Balance Sheet (Appendix C). Examples include: land, buildings, vehicles, furniture, fixtures and equipment.

As you can see from the short length of this chapter, the task of fixed assets is not a very complicated one, but it is certainly an important one. As a full-charge bookkeeper, it will be your responsibility to track any/all fixed assets purchased during each calendar year, post those assets to the general ledger, and communicate this information to the CPA at the end of the year.

Tracking

The best way to track fixed asset purchases is to maintain a file-folder named, "Fixed Assets". Within this folder you should have a hand-written ledger in which you record the date, short description of the asset, and price paid. You should also make a photocopy of the invoice from the company, and attach or store the invoice copy behind your asset list. This will provide audit-ready documentation and a convenient reference for your CPA.

The only thing you will need to consider/decide with the owner and/or CPA is the dollar amount above which a purchase is "capitalized" (defined below) versus expensed. Land, buildings, vehicles, furniture or fixtures are rather obvious. They always get treated as fixed assets. Equipment can sometimes present the temptation to expense it, rather than capitalize it. It's my experience that it is best to consider all equipment over a certain dollar amount (like an expensive adding machine) as a "fixed asset". You may want to set up a dollar limit of say $50, above which you list the item as an asset and below which you expense it in the current period (like office supplies). Reference: Appendix D - Accounting 'Basics' > Office Supplies (Expense?).

Defined: to *capitalize* is to treat or record an item as an asset and then "depreciate" (defined below) it, as opposed to treating it as an expense.

Defined: to *depreciate* is to treat as an asset, being "used up" over time. Reference: Appendix D - Accounting 'Basics' > Depreciating Assets.

Posting & Communicating

Note: *knowledge of debits and credits* - is needed in order to post fixed assets. So, be sure to study Chapter 5 - Debits and Credits, before proceeding here.

Posting fixed asset purchases will amount to a journal entry similar to the following:

| [Debit] | Equipment | $$ | | =>*Increasing* an *asset* |
| [Credit] | | Cash | $$ | =>*Decreasing* an *asset* |

Obviously, it will not always be the "Equipment" account to debit. If buying a vehicle, debit that vehicle. Communicating fixed asset purchases to the CPA should take place only once per year – at the end of the year. More likely than not the CPA will want only your detailed listing of assets purchased for the year, and not need to see the actual invoice copies. Regardless, cover yourself and do make those copies. The one time you don't, will be the one time people will want to see them. Since there are other things to do for/with your company's CPA at year-end, please reference: Tasks > Year-End Items, Tasks > Corporate Taxes and Chapter 9 - Dealing(s) with the CPA.

Chapter 2 - Tasks > **Bank Reconciliations**

Don't let a corporate bank reconciliation scare you. If you are able to reconcile your own personal bank account, then you are able to reconcile a corporate one. The methods are the same - corporate is just larger. If you are unfamiliar with the method, or have used an unconventional method to reconcile, you should familiarize yourself with the backside of most bank statements. They usually provide a form with which to reconcile - listing "outstanding checks" and "deposits in transit".

Paper Trail

Defined: a *paper trail* is records showing how things were done, or that they were done correctly.

In order to leave a proper and adequate "paper trail" (defined below) you, as bookkeeper, should use this conventional approach and actually fill out the form. This way anyone who may follow you, either in the bookkeeper position or not, will be able to see what you did. If the form does not provide enough space, you may use a spreadsheet program, like Microsoft Excel, and make a form that gives enough space. Use it every month and be sure to staple it to the bank statement. Filling out a paper reconciliation is a sound approach even if you have a computer bookkeeping program - with a bank reconciliation module. After you have completed the reconciliation on paper, it should then be easy to enter that data into any computer program. If you skip the paper reconciliation, and head straight for the computer, you may find yourself befuddled.

Bank Statements and Credit Cards

Typically, corporate bank statements are cut from the bank on the last day of the month. I recommend trying to complete the bank reconciliation the day it arrives in the mail. If you are unable to do it then, set yourself a deadline of, say, within three business days of receiving it. If the bank returns company checks or if you have transaction receipts, a convenient way to store your statement (and reconciliation) is in the envelope in which it was mailed. Just write the month and year on the outside of the envelope. And file them in a file folder, named "Bank Reconciliations - Year 20XX", to make them easy to find.

If credit cards are involved your reconciliation maybe a bit more challenging. The credit card companies often aggregate or batch figures together. One solution, here, might be to photocopy the bank statement and highlight off (with a highlighter) the easiest figures first. If you get stuck, don't be afraid to start over with a clean copy.

Finding "Outages"

Defined: an *outage* is an out of balance situation, or an amount that you're out of balance.

There is one point I'd like to make here. Obviously, one endeavors and should balance bank reconciliations and the like, to the penny. But, that doesn't mean I would advise spending three days looking for one penny, on *any* 'outage'. Whether balancing a bank reconciliation, a cash drawer, petty cash or any other out of balance situation, the method for locating the outage is essentially the same. You must first use your analytical powers, and come up with one or two places to look. You will want to start in the place that either most likely contains the outage (in your mind), or the place that is the easiest to search through. For instance, a bank teller would probably recount the cash drawer, first.

You should continue in this fashion, analyzing and then recounting until you've left no stone unturned. Even if you think to yourself that it is certainly not in *that* place. Be sure to recount that place as well. It's been my experience that this method proves effective better than 95% of the time. As stated above, obviously, one endeavors and should balance bank reconciliations and the like, to the penny. But, that doesn't mean I would advise spending three days looking for one penny, on *any* outage. Note: if you repeatedly find a cash register $10 or $20 short at the end of the day, when a certain employee closes, it would be your duty to report that connection, after the second or third occurrence to the business owner!

There's a couple of "finding the outage" tips, I need to pass along.

Divide by nine tip: if the amount you are "out of balance" divides evenly by nine, you likely have a transposition error!

Defined: a *transposition error* is one where you reversed the order of two numbers - causing an out of balance situation. Example: $954.00 (the correct amount) was entered as $945.00 (reversing the order of the 5 and 4). Transposition errors always divide evenly by nine!

Chapter 2 - Tasks > Bank Reconciliations (cont.)

Note: it will only divide evenly by nine (and it may be nine dollars or nine cents) if the only error you have is a transposition one. If you have more than one including a non-transpositon error, your "out of balance situation" will not divide by nine.

Divide by two tip: if the amount you're out of balance is not found right away, divide the out of balance amount by two, and look for that figure. What can happen is you've added when you should have subtracted. That will double the amount (out of balance)!

On A Personal Note:
In the following example, I'm not trying to brag - but just trying to illustrate the importance of taking the due diligence steps to hunt for (& find) your outages, not to mention the due diligence when performing your reconciliations. When I was at the CPA firm, one of the partners (& actually a corner office partner) called on me for some work at a car dealership. Their bookkeeper had passed away, and they were behind a year or so on, among other things, their bank reconciliations.
Well, I was just a "staff auditor", but I had done similar-type "clean-up" work for Accountemps in Albuquerque. And, this partner had already sent a manager (~from our firm) to try to get them caught up, but he was "painting with very broad strokes" - leaving at least one bank reconciliation some $3000 out of balance. Well, of course that type of work (from our manager) did not amuse the new Accounting Manager at the car dealership. Mind you - these bank reconciliations were ~40 pages long - of transactions, each. I spent weeks (probably longer, on and off), there - tediously and meticulously working to balance those reconciliations. And still, more than half the time, I would have to find some one thing or another that caused my own reconciliation to not balance the first time. In the end, I did balance each to the penny (~praise to the Lord~). And that Accounting Manager (not to mention the partner) ~loved me. [Note: that was an unusual situation, to say the least - that was best handled in balancing everything, if at all possible.]

Should The Bookkeeper Be A Signer On The Checking Account?
    I recommend against the bookkeeper being a signer for several reasons.
1. *You have enough to do.*
2. *Trouble with owner* - it will keep you out of trouble with the owner as far as approving payments on your own.
3. *Segregation of duties* - it will help maintain segregation of duties for security purposes. For more information, reference Chapter 10 - Bookkeeper As Management? > Does The Owner Want You To Sign Checks?

Chapter 2 - Tasks > **Petty Cash**

Defined: *petty cash* is a small amount of cash, kept on hand - preferably in a locked box, for incidental items (example: buying pizza for lunch).

Part of your duties as bookkeeper may include handling petty cash. You will find some businesses use petty cash - perhaps extensively (as one business I worked for). Other businesses may not use petty cash at all. In either case, you should know the full extent of handling it. Ironically, something so small or seemingly insignificant can be rather involved, as evidenced by the length of this chapter.

One might think that you could just put all petty cash expenses to, say, office supplies, for the year. And if your company's petty cash amounts for the year are immaterial (say, less than one hundred dollars all year) then that *may* be ok. But, when you get to the financial statement for the year, you'll look at the office supplies account and say to yourself, that account is not right. That is why we take pains throughout the year to categorize petty cash amounts. The areas a bookkeeper will be concerned with, regarding petty cash, are controls, refunding the box and what to do at the end of the month.

Note: *knowledge of debits and credits* - is needed in order to properly handle petty cash. So, be sure to study Chapter 5 - Debits and Credits, before proceeding here.

Controls

If you just started at the company, be sure that the cash you inherit - in the box - equals what the General Ledger account entitled Petty Cash says you have, in the computer. If they don't equal each other, see the company owner immediately!

DAY TO DAY CONTROLS

Each company may have its own procedures for dealing with petty cash, but, in all cases, the proper controls need to be in place. As mentioned above, petty cash should be kept in a locked box, and at most only the bookkeeper and the company owner accessing the box, for control purposes. That is the best way to be sure money is not leaving the box, without your knowledge. Remember the company owner will, ultimately, hold you responsible for the accounting of that cash, regardless of the amounts.

Typically, if something is to be purchased out of petty cash, it will require the owner's approval (verbal OK for small amounts). And always petty cash receipts should be used, to keep track of who is receiving the cash and for what purpose. When I was a full-charge bookkeeper, I created and used the Petty Cash Receipts found in Appendix E - Sample Forms > Petty Cash - Receipts. Do keep blank petty cash slips inside the box, as a reminder to use them.

When giving out the cash, be sure to get their signature on the petty cash slip. This proves that they received the cash. Also, be sure to remind the employee to bring back the change and sales receipt. Put the change in the box, and staple the sales receipt to the filled-out petty cash slip. If you feel the need for an added control, keep a sheet of ledger paper inside the box, depicting amounts subtracted, added and a running balance.

Refunding The Box

Of course, you can't always just take from the box. Every so often, you will need to refund money to it. Usually, a company check is cashed at the bank in various denominations and coins, as needed. Reference: Appendix E - Sample Forms > Petty Cash - Change Order. When funding or refunding petty cash, the entry should be as follows:

[Debit]	Petty Cash	$$		=>*Increasing* an *asset*
[Credit]		Cash	$$	=>*Decreasing* an *asset*

BUSINESSES WITH CASH REGISTERS

If your business involves the use of a cash register, there is probably no need to use a petty cash box. But you will still want a paper trail - slip of paper indicating cash was removed, by whom, and for what purpose. And the bookkeeper will need to make a journal entry, of whatever that particular expense was, into the accounting system (see Tasks > General Ledger > Journal Entries).

Chapter 2 - Tasks > Petty Cash (continued)

End-of-the-Month
At the end of the month you will need to balance petty cash, "post" to the general ledger, and store receipts.

Defined: *post* means to enter (or record) debits and credits into the bookkeeping system.

BALANCING
Balancing petty cash means that the beginning amount of cash in the box, minus your petty cash receipts for the month, will equal what cash is left in the box, at the end of the month. One can see here as well, that a ledger of petty cash can be helpful. If for some reason you are not balancing, you should make every effort to determine where you are off, without spending three days looking for one penny. For additional help on balancing, reference Chapter 2 - Tasks > Bank Reconciliations > Finding Outages.

POSTING
After balancing petty cash for the month, you will need to post it to the general ledger. But first you will need to "code" all of the petty cash slips.

Defined: to *code* is to indicate which account, from the Chart of Accounts, a particular expenditure belongs to. It simply means putting the chart of accounts account number at the top of the petty cash slip.

Coding
To code, you will pull out your Chart of Accounts (reference: Appendix B - Chart of Accounts). Look on the chart to determine what account each expenditure belongs to. For example: #5220 - Meals & Entertainment would be for pizza. After determining which account, write the corresponding account number(s) on each petty cash slip. It is quite possible to have more than one account number per slip, if more than one item is purchased, and they are for different accounts. After you code all petty cash slips, sort them by account number and run adding machine tapes to total each account. Label the top of each tape with the account number. Now you're ready to make your journal entry for the month.

Entering
You will enter petty cash into the general ledger, through a journal entry. See Tasks > General Ledger > Journal Entries. Your journal entry will look something like this:

[Debit]	Meals & Entertainment	$$		=>*Increasing* an *expense*
[Debit]	Repairs & Maintenance	$$		=>*Increasing* an *expense*
	…	$$		"
	…	$$		"
	…	$$		"
[Credit]	Petty Cash		$$	=>*Decreasing* an *asset*

Finally, find the area in the computer bookkeeping program where you are able to enter a journal entry. It's usually through the general ledger module. The area should look similar to the above entry - with a place for debits and a place for credits. You will choose accounts from the chart of accounts, and then enter the dollar amounts. Remember each general journal entry needs to balance.

STORING
After balancing and entering, store your receipts for the month, including petty cash slips, sales receipts, and any ledger, in a manila envelope, labeled "Petty Cash - January 20xx" (make sure all receipts are stapled to their corresponding petty cash slips).

Final Word On Petty Cash
This may seem like an awful lot of work, just for petty cash. And that very thought will probably cross your mind every month, as you do petty cash. But remember it's your duty, and small amounts each month multiplied by twelve months can add up to substantial amounts - that we endeavor to be correct.

Chapter 2 - Tasks > **State-Specific Tasks**

Defined: *state-specific tasks* are those required by, or reported to the state in which you live, not including state payroll taxes (see Tasks > Payroll Taxes).

As I mentioned earlier, smaller companies do not have many administrative personnel working for them, so any state-specific tasks, such as the one common to all states – listed below, will typically fall upon the bookkeeper. However, recall that it is not within the scope of this book to list out all states' requirements. Having said that, it's been my experience that there are not too many state-specific tasks out there, but you should be aware that they are possible, and that there is one common to all states.

State-Specific Requirement Common to All States
The U.S. Congress enacted this state-specific task in 1996. It's called the "Personal Responsibility and Work Opportunity Reconciliation Act" (PRWORA). You can Google it. The act requires employers in all 50 states to report new-hires and re-hires to a "state" directory. This is to help facilitate child support payments, for parents who change jobs frequently. Even though PRWORA is a federal law, it involves state forms and a state directory, for reporting. You will probably find your state's "new-hire directory", by searching on-line, "[your state] new hire directory". I found New Mexico's there. And, Florida's site is: https://newhire.state.fl.us/SitePages/home.aspx.

Example of a State-Specific Task
Within the New Mexico Department of Labor, is a department entitled the "Worker's Compensation Administration". They require all companies in New Mexico to pay approximately four dollars - per employee, per quarter (to cover their printing costs - I was told). Two of those dollars may be deducted from the employ*ee*'s payroll. But the other two dollars the employ*er* must pay. The Worker's Compensation Administration also has a form to fill out each quarter, called the "WC-1".

Ways To Uncover State-Specific Requirements
Here is how you may determine your state's specific requirements.
1. *Previous reports* - search the bookkeeper's files for any previous reports that may have been filed.
2. *Documentation* - read all documentation received from your state's authorities.
3. *Search on-line* - requesting "(your state's) business requirements".
4. *Phone book* - look in the government pages of your phone book for business related agencies like the department of labor, and make some calls - if needed.
5. *Mail* - finally, paying attention to the incoming mail, and attending any conferences or workshops put on by your state or local authorities are great ways to learn about state's requirements.

Chapter 2 - Tasks > **Financial Statements or Monthly Reports**

First of all, don't let the words financial statements scare you. I've included a sample "Income Statement" and a sample "Balance Sheet" (both defined below) in Appendix C. These are the only two financial statements used in small businesses. Also, computer bookkeeping programs, including QuickBooks and Sage 50 Accounting, have financial statements built-in or pre-programmed that you can use. Note that some business owners may have other reports they want to see on a monthly basis, but the typical reports are listed below. Before printing any reports, you must finish entering the month's information.

>Defined: an *Income Statement* subtracts expenses from revenues to give how much income you had for the period - month or year. It is one of the two main financial statements - the other is the "Balance Sheet".

>Defined: a *Balance Sheet* lists assets, liabilities, and "owner's equity", as of the last day in the period. It is one of two main financial statements - the other is the Income Statement.

>Defined: *owner's equity* equals assets minus liabilities. It is a measure of any extra an owner has in the business.

Enter All Data
As mentioned above, before printing any monthly reports, you should be sure you have entered all relevant information into the computer bookkeeping program - QuickBooks or Sage 50 for example. So, businesses typically delay printing until after the first few days of the month (or even a week, in some cases) to be sure all of last month's bills have been received and entered.

If you hand write checks be sure all checks written last month are entered. Enter all invoices for payables and receivables. Do your journal entry for petty cash. Wait for and balance the bank statement. Corporate bank statements typically cut on the last day of the month. You may think that whether a check has or has not cleared the bank does not affect your reports for the previous month. There are two reasons to balance the bank statement *before printing reports*: (1) bank service charges that you wouldn't have known about, and (2) in case the company owner carries around some blank checks and decided to use one. Once you are confident you have everything you need entered for the month, you are ready to print the monthly reports.

You should no longer need to balance the general ledger before printing reports, unless you're working with quite an older version, because current versions of bookkeeping software won't allow you to post a journal entry unless it's in balance (debits = credits). If you do need to balance an older version, see Chapter 2 - Tasks > General Ledger > Balancing the General Ledger.

Print Reports
The bookkeeper should print reports at the beginning of every month, after all data is entered. Print both an income statement and balance sheet, for the previous month. Every company is different and therefore may require additional reports, but the typical reports to print are as follows. The company owner may also want to see, what's called "year-to-date" information.

>Defined: *year-to-date (information)* is information from January 1, through today's date, whatever date today is.

<u>Typical Monthly Reports</u>
*Financial Statements: Income Statement & Balance Sheet
*Check Register (for each account)
*Aging of Accounts Receivable (detailed)
*Aging of Accounts Payables (detailed)
*General Ledger Transaction Listing (can be summary if detailed is too lengthy).

Note: *payroll reports* - should be printed after each payroll. Reference: Chapter 2 - Tasks > Payroll > Payroll - Via A Computer > DOING IT > Step #12.

Chapter 2 - Tasks > Financial Statements (continued)

Print Reports (cont.)

Year-to-date information pertains *only* to the income statement. For instance, if you printed financial statements for the month of April, the income statement will show what happened, as far as revenues and expenses, just for April. But the owner may want to know how the company has done, so far, for the entire calendar year. So, you would print an income statement for the period from January 1 through April 30. This is called year-to-date. The balance sheet, on the other hand, shows the balances in the assets, liabilities and owner's equity accounts *as of* a certain date - not for a period of time. For example: as of April 30th there is $1000 in the checking account.

Note: *fiscal year* - some companies operate in a twelve month period other than the calendar year (January 1 - December 31) known as a "fiscal year" (example: July 1 - June 30).

Obviously, reports should be copied to the business owner, as well as put in a binder or folder, labeled "Monthly Reports for 20xx". Remember, at the end of the year you will want to print financial statements for both the month (December) and the year.

Change to the Next Accounting Period / Month

Gone are the days when *every* computer bookkeeping program required you to close the current month, before being able to enter any data into the next month. It will depend on the program, but typical scenarios include not closing any month at all, to having open 24 months at a time.

Defined: *closing an accounting period* involves bringing income statement accounts (revenues & expenses) to zero balances in order to start counting from zero - in the next accounting period. Otherwise, your next month's sales would include the previous month's sales. Current versions of bookkeeping software typically no longer requires you to close the period, but will reset those income statement accounts automatically back to zero.

How does this impact a bookkeeper? First, it becomes more convenient to be able to enter six months of data at a time. But, on the other hand, if you're printing reports every month, running into an old invoice can pose a problem. Of course, as mentioned above, be sure you have entered all relevant data before printing reports!

Prior Period Amount Missed

Defined: a *prior period* is a month or year prior to the one you are currently working in.

Here's the old invoice scenario: a bill never made it through the mail, and that company doesn't send monthly statements, so you never knew about it until they called. You might consider the cost versus the benefit of entering say an $8 invoice, in a prior period and having to reprint, copy, distribute and file all of those reports again. Since your financial statement amounts will be far greater than $10, this invoice is what's called "immaterial".

Defined: *immaterial* means not material or irrelevant.

If you're asking yourself when or at what amount would it be relevant? There really is no set dollar amount or even a set percentage. The basic answer to that is when the included amount (or previously missed amount) could potentially change a decision makers mind about what's in the financial statements. Since that is also "grey", it's sometimes better to choose a dollar amount above which you'd not be happy to not include the invoice or bill (like say $50 or $100).

If it's small enough to not run reports again, then pencil in today's date / the date you received it - on the invoice, and enter it into the computer for this (today's) date. Eight dollars, in this case, is not going to make that much difference in the scheme of things. If, for some reason, you really need to enter additional information in a "prior period", be sure to reprint those reports. Obviously, the best idea is to try to avoid having to reenter and reprint reports, for any of the prior periods.

Chapter 2 - Tasks > **Year-End Items**

At the end of the year, you will need to do several things, in addition to payroll tax reports, financial statements and the corporate tax return (covered in their own chapters). First, you will need to print and mail Form W-2's and perhaps some 1099 Forms. Second, you will need to store last year's files, and create new ones for this year - known as "record retention". And finally, you will need to start to gather year-end reports for corporate taxes. Reference: Appendix A - Master Schedule, to help you keep track of all of it.

Form W-2
> Defined: *W-2's* are the forms mailed by companies at the end of the year, indicating each employee's wages and taxes paid, for the calendar year.

WHEN?
Actually, W-2's need to be done after all payroll checks are generated for December. So, January is the time to do them. In fact, the deadline for mailing them is January 31st. But, get started as soon as you can in January, to give yourself enough time.

Note: *commissions and bonuses* - be sure they are included in your employees' totals on their W-2. Reference: IRS Publication #15 > Supplemental Wages.

HOW?
These days computer bookkeeping programs, such as Sage 50 and QuickBooks, have Forms W-2 & 1099 generating capabilities. You'll typically find these forms in the "Reports" Module, under the areas of Payroll for W-2's and Accounts Payable for 1099's. Also, be sure to do the fourth quarter payroll taxes before the W-2's. This way you can make sure the wages of your four payroll tax reports, for the year (add together the four quarterly reports by calculator) equal the wages of your W-2's. If your computer bookkeeping program does not have a report titled "W-3" - which is for totals, print a payroll journal or payroll register to compare totals.

You can even print to screen or your monitor, to see if the totals match. If they do not, then print to the printer to compare reports. When these balance, you will have confidence that your totals are correct and you'll be prepared, should your company ever be audited. If there are discrepancies, print any detailed reports you may need to find and correct mistakes (reference: Tasks > Bank Reconciliations > Locating Outages). For information on forms, see the sub-section below entitled, "Blank Forms on Which to Print W-2's and 1099's".

In addition to mailing W-2's to the employees, you are required to mail what's called the 'transmittal'. The transmittal is nothing more than a copy of each W-2 (they print in multiple copies at a time) and Form W-3, "Transmittal of Wage and Tax Statements" - which lists the total of all the W-2's. This transmittal gets mailed to the Social Security Administration, not the IRS. Although this transmittal is not due until the end of February, I find it better to mail it out with, or soon after, mailing the W-2's. I also suggest looking into e-filing W-2's at: http://www.socialsecurity.gov/employer/.

WHAT ELSE?
Finally, along with the owner's W-2, you will probably need to print a list of "draws" the owner has taken during the year. Reference: Appendix D - Accounting Basics > "Draws" Taken by the Owner.

> Defined: a *draw* is a removal of cash from the business, beyond the owner's salary (a.k.a.: a dividend).

The owner would use the list in order to include the draws as part of his or her income for the year. Be sure to put a copy of your report to the owner, in a folder labeled "Draws to Owner" in order to maintain a good "paper trail" (defined below) for audit purposes. You should be able to print a report of all transactions for a single general ledger account, like "Draw - Owner" Reference: Chapter 2 - Tasks > General Ledger > Producing a Transaction Listing.

> Defined: a *paper trail* is the files or records showing how things were done, or that they were done correctly. An example is copies of payroll tax reports.

Chapter 2 - Tasks > Year-End Items (continued)

Form 1099-MISC
    Defined: *Form 1099-MISC* is an IRS form entitled, "Miscellaneous Income". It is required to be filed by the bookkeeper to indicate amounts paid to "contract labor".

Contract labor is just what it sounds like - labor under contract. They are not employees of your company, so do *not* have taxes taken out when paid. They are self-employed, but still owe the government payroll taxes just the same. So, the government requires companies paying them to issue 1099's, to keep track of wages paid to contract labor.

Notes: 1. *Wages Less Than $600 Per Year* - no 1099 is required to be issued, if the wages were less than $600 for the year. This is the only exception, introduced to keep paperwork down.
          2. *Designating A 1099 Recipient* - you will need to have designated this person (contract labor) as a 1099 recipient - in the computer. Typically you will check a box when entering that person's name, etc. But, don't be surprised if you need to do this in the Vendors not Employees section.

Bookkeepers need to mail 1099's in January for the preceding year. There are several different types of 1099's. The 1099-MISC (miscellaneous) is the one for contract labor. They are simple one-page forms, which most computer bookkeeping programs will print in the correct places, once the blank forms are loaded into the printer (see "Blank Forms on Which to Print W-2's and 1099's" below). If your computer bookkeeping program does not print 1099's, blank forms from the local IRS office and a typewriter will do. Be sure you retain a copy for your bookkeeper's file - to give you a paper trail.

If you *do* need to submit 1099's for contract labor in any given year, use Form 1096 to transmit them. Form 1096 is an IRS form entitled, "Annual Summary and Transmittal of U.S. Information Returns" - used to transmit totals. Instructions are printed on the form and it can be found at IRS's web-site www.irs.gov. Finally, if you find you do not have a contractor's social security number (aka: Taxpayer ID Number) which is needed to complete Form 1099, send that contractor a Form W-9, "Request for Taxpayer Identification Number and Certification", and keep it on file. I've even sent W-9's "return receipt" to show proof that I'm not a party to tax evasion.

Blank Forms
    As far as blank forms on which to print, the IRS can provide a few. QuickBooks and Sage 50 parent companies should sell blank forms. Contact their customer service departments, listed in Appendix H - Resources. And the office supply stores typically carry the blank forms you need. Because I had many more W-2's to produce than 1099's, I used to purchase blank W-2's, but get my 1099's from the local IRS office. You will want to purchase these forms before January 1st. In fact, I used to receive advertisements from Sage 50 or QuickBooks for these forms and next year's tax tables, in November. So, that's when I put it on the Master Schedule - Appendix A.

When obtaining blank W-2's be sure they have at least four copies - one copy for your bookkeeper file and three copies for your employee (federal, state, and a copy for the employee to retain). Understand that most computer bookkeeping programs (Sage 50 and QuickBooks included) will print in the correct places, once the blank forms are loaded into the printer. To see for yourself do a small test run (~2 employees) on plain white paper, and see if it lines-up with the blank forms you've acquired, or take the test run with you when acquiring forms.

Note: *window envelopes* - often sold with the forms, would be helpful. The W-2's have addresses on them, so you wouldn't have to re-address the envelopes, in order to mail them.

Record Retention
    Defined: *record retention* includes storing last year's files and starting new ones for the upcoming year.

Realize that it is very important to save records – for reference and 'audit' purposes (see Chapter 12 - A Word about Audits). Some companies may want to keep all records indefinitely, and that is fine, if you have the room for storage. Other companies may create their own schedule, for how long to save which records. That is fine as well. Remember you work for them. If you need to establish a schedule at your work place, below is a typical one that you may use or augment for your needs.

Chapter 2 - Tasks > Year-End Items (continued)

Defined: *record retention schedule* is a plan for how long to store which types of documents.

RECORD RETENTION (SAMPLE) SCHEDULE

File Type	How Long to Retain
Accounts Payable - Paid	3 - 5 Years
Accounts Receivable - Paid	3 - 5 Years
Commissions	7 Years *
Time cards / Timesheets	7 - 10 Years *
General Ledger Reports	10 Years *
Payroll Tax Reports	Indefinitely
Bank Statements	Indefinitely
Financial Statements	Indefinitely
Corporate Tax Return	Indefinitely

* Note: if reports contain $'s, you may want to shred them - when disposing.

It will be helpful to maintain a list each year of what you put into boxes, to be saved. Use a form (ref: Appendix E - Sample Forms > Record Retention Form) to list boxes, contents, and dates. Keep each year's list, along with your record retention schedule, in a folder titled "Record Retention". Be sure to clearly label the outside of boxes, with the box number and brief description of contents! Keep in mind that a list will be particularly handy when you need to look for something, or if your company is ever audited.

As far as payables and receivables go, only "paid payables" and "paid receivables" need to be stored. "Unpaid payables" and "uncollected receivables" should be kept in the bookkeeper's current file/desk drawer(s). When it's time to "dispose", some just toss the boxes into the dumpster. Others may take more precautions and go through the trouble of actually shredding - particularly the more sensitive documents, like G/L reports, commissions and any payroll records showing dollars.

STARTING NEW FILES

Typing labels often makes for a much more professional looking file system and is easier on the eyes the whole year through. The office supply stores sell a variety of labels for just this purpose. So, the company's shopping list for record retention for a year should include some boxes to store last year's files, a box of manila folders, and some blank labels.

Gather Year-End Reports for Corporate Taxes

As mentioned earlier corporate taxes are the only task to outsource. And as part of year-end items, you should also start to gather reports to be ready to send to the CPA - in order to produce the corporate tax return/s (see Chapter 2 - Tasks > Corporate Taxes). Reports should include: financial statements, check register/s, as well as an employee payroll report - listing amounts paid to each employee for the year, along with copies of payroll tax reports (both federal and state). Do not send them right away. Instead, hold them in a file labeled "Reports for CPA". You'll need to hold these for the moment because you will be adding additional things the CPA will need to produce the corporate tax return/s. There is a more complete list in the next chapter.

Realize that the CPA's review of your tax and other reports should help on multiple levels. First, the business owner should feel more comfortable knowing his or her CPA is checking or verifying the company's important tax / bookkeeping reports. Second, this will add to your confidence, knowing a CPA has verified your work. And finally, the CPA will ultimately feel more comfortable with you producing tax reports, and therefore should have positive things to say about you to the business owner.

Note: *corporate taxes* - are part of what a full-charge bookkeeper will need to deal with at the end of the year, but it is a big enough topic to warrant its own chapter. Please see Chapter 2 - Tasks > Corporate Taxes.

Chapter 2 - Tasks > **Corporate Taxes**

Defined: *corporate taxes* are a tax on the income of the business for the year.

Note: *fiscal year* - some companies operate in a twelve month period other than the January 1 - December 31 calendar year, known as a "fiscal year" (example: July 1 - June 30).

As mentioned in Chapter 1 - Introduction > What is Full-Charge Bookkeeping?, corporate taxes are about the only task not expected to be completed by a full-charge bookkeeper. Businesses, both large and small, typically use a Certified Public Accountant (CPA) to prepare their corporate tax return/s. As a full-charge bookkeeper, your job will be gather information for the CPA, and to make any "quarterly estimated tax payments" (defined below).

Gathering Information for the CPA
As far as gathering information, there will certainly be a federal tax return, and there may be a state return as well. The CPA should be knowledgeable about any state return. Finally, in addition to gathering information for the returns, you may want (or your company's owner may want you) to take this opportunity and send a few other items to the CPA for review.

FEDERAL RETURN
After you complete the "year-end items" - in January, come February you will need to contact the CPA to see what documents s/he will need in order to produce the federal corporate tax return, due March 15th. Here, I will give you some idea of what to expect regarding the CPA. The typical items the CPA will need are listed below.

Typical Corporate Tax Items for the CPA
*Financial Statements: Income Statement & Balance Sheet
*Check register(s)
*Summary Agings of Payables & Receivables
*General Ledger - Summary Transaction Listing

Defined: a *transaction listing* lists all of the transactions - debits and credits, for selected accounts over a specified period of time.

Note: a *summary GL listing* - might suffice as long as you provide detailed listings for the "Additional Items" listed below.

Additional Corporate Tax Items (May Include)
*"Fixed Asset" accounts: there maybe more than one (defined below).
*Computer Equipment Asset or Expense Account
*"Draws" Taken by the Owner Account (defined below).
*Charitable Contributions/Gifts Account   Reference: Appendix B - Chart of Accounts

Defined: *fixed assets* is another name for "Property, Plant & Equipment" (PP&E). Where fixed assets are listed on the Chart of Accounts, PP&E are listed on the Balance Sheet. Examples include: land, buildings, vehicles, furniture, fixtures and equipment.

Defined: a *draw* taken by the owner is a removal of cash from the business, beyond the owner's salary (aka: a dividend).

OTHER REPORTS
Along with documents to produce the corporate tax return, the owner may also want you to send the CPA: copies of payroll tax reports - both federal and state, and an employee payroll report [listing amounts paid to each employee for the year]. You should have started a folder, entitled "Reports for CPA" from your Year-End work (previous chapter). Go ahead and add the corporate tax documents you've collected above - to this folder. Before presenting it to the CPA, you will need to 1) review the reports for accuracy - see below, and 2) let your company's owner know you have this file prepared for the CPA.

Chapter 2 - Tasks > Corporate Taxes (continued)

Before presenting your reports to the CPA, you will need to review them to be sure they look accurate. For instance, the Typical and Additional Items listed above you will want to scan down the amounts to see if they appear reasonable (no gross errors) - given your strong knowledge of the company. Scan the general ledger summary transaction listing - to be sure the amounts posted to your company's accounts appear reasonable.

STATE RETURN & GETTING COPIES BACK

Some states will have a corporate income tax. New Mexico is one. But, your CPA should be aware of this and produce that return as well. Typically, information you provided to the CPA for the federal return is sufficient to produce the state return as well. At any rate, the CPA will let you know if there is any additional information needed! It will behoove you to know your state's requirements, for your benefit and the benefit of your company. Search on-line, at "[your state's] corporate income tax".

As far as getting copies of the corporate tax return/s back from the CPA, he or she should be providing copies to the owner of your company. You, the bookkeeper, may or may not see / get copies back for the bookkeeper's files. At any rate you *may* want to check with your company's owner, a month or so after the tax return is due, to see if your owner received copies, and if not, if s/he wants you to follow-up with the CPA. This would involve lobbing a call over there to check on the status of the return/s. Note: by no means - at this point, should you call the CPA on your own - without your boss' specific direction!

Quarterly Estimated Tax Payments
> Defined: *quarterly estimated tax payments* are installments of corporate income tax due. Contact your company's CPA for more information.

Note: *exempt* - certain types of corporations (S-Corporation or Professional Corporation) are generally exempt from estimated tax payments. You may want to confirm that your company is not "exempt" with your CPA.

You will need to contact the CPA no later than the first day of the month that installments are due. See "Tax Due Dates and Contact Dates", below. Be sure to ask your company's CPA for the payment amount.

Tax Due Dates	Contact CPA Dates	
April 15th	April 1st	Reference: Appendix A - Master Schedule,
June 15th	June 1st	for all tax due dates and contact dates.
September 15th	September 1st	
December 15th	December 1st	

As far as method of payment, the IRS requires deposits to be made electronically using the EFTPS (Electronic Federal Tax Payment System). Reference: IRS Instructions to Form 1120-W > Method of Tax Payment. You can enroll @ https://www.eftps.gov/eftps/ or by calling 1-800-555-4477. //

Chapter 3 - **Authorities**

Defined: *authorities* include those government agencies, at both the federal and state levels, responsible for either collecting taxes or administering laws (example: the IRS).

You will find that fairly early on, in doing bookkeeping tasks, you will need to look up something like when to make your payroll tax deposit. That's why authorities play a major role in bookkeeping, and follow tasks in this book. I've divided this chapter into "Authorities Frequently Used", and "Other Authorities / Laws".

Authorities Frequently Used
The most frequently used authorities you will find are the IRS, and state-specific ones.

INTERNAL REVENUE SERVICE (www.irs.gov)
The IRS will be the only federal authority you will use, frequently. They collect all federal payroll taxes, and federal corporate income tax. Below is a short list of tasks and associated IRS Forms / Publications. For a longer list reference Appendix H - Resources.

Task	IRS Forms & Publications	Some Specifics
Payroll	Publication 15 (Circular E), "Employer's Tax Guide"	Withholding Tables
Payroll Taxes	Form 941 & Circular E	Federal Income Tax Withholding
	Form 941 & Circular E	FICA: Social Security & Medicare
	Form 940 & Circular E	Federal Unemployment Tax
Corporate Income Tax	Deposit Electronically.	The CPA to determine amount.
Human Resource Administration	Form W-4	Withholding Allowances
	Form I-9 *	Immigration Form

* Recall that Form I-9 is also used in human resources, but is not an IRS form. It is available from U.S. Citizenship & Immigration Services @ http://www.uscis.gov/i-9-central.

IRS Forms & Instructions May be Obtained (Source: IRS Publication 15 > "...Tax Products")
1. *On-line* - at http://www.irs.gov/.
2. *From your local IRS office.*
3. *Over the phone* - by calling 1-800-TAX-FORM (1-800-829-3676).

STATE-SPECIFIC AUTHORITIES
State unemployment tax, state sales tax, and state income tax are the main reasons for the state authorities. Your state may have one or all of these state taxes. And the possibility exists that there will be more than one state-specific authority you will need to use. For example, in New Mexico, there are two main authorities used frequently - the N.M. Department of Taxation & Revenue for state income tax & state sales tax, and the N.M. Department of Workforce Solutions for State Unemployment Tax. As mentioned earlier, it is not within the scope of this book to list each state's specific tax authorities, but here is how you may determine yours.

Ways to Determine Your State's Tax Authorities
1. *Search* - the previous bookkeeper's files for prior tax reports.
2. *Search* - on-line requesting:
    "(your state's) Taxation Department", "Treasury Department" or "Department of Labor"
    "(your state's) payroll tax requirements"
3. *Look in* - the government pages of your phone book, and make some calls.

(continued next page - is "Other Authorities / Laws" a FCB should be aware of)

Chapter 3 - Authorities (continued)

Other Authorities / Laws

The following is a list of some other laws and authorities I've run into over the years, that have a bearing on full-charge bookkeeping:

Law	Bookkeeper Impact	Authority
Fair Minimum Wage Act	~ Raises the federal minimum wage. On 7/24/09 the federal minimum wage became $7.25. Source: http://www.dol.gov/ > A to Z Index > M > Minimum Wage.	U.S. Department of Labor
Fair Labor Standards Act	~Requires payment of a minimum wage & overtime (for over 40 hrs in 7 days). ~Requires display of "minimum wage poster", and another for employers of workers with disabilities. The posters can actually be printed off the U.S. Dept. of Labor's website: http://www.dol.gov/ > A to Z Index > P > Posters.	U.S. Department of Labor
Health Insurance Portability and Accountability Act (HIPAA)	~Requires "plan administrators" (maybe the bookkeeper) to provide terminated employees, who had health insurance, a certificate of prior health coverage. Note: some health insurance companies will provide this certificate for you, but you will need to check with your insurance provider to find out, or to see about obtaining blank certificates to issue. Source: www.dol.gov > A to Z Index > H > Health Insurance Portability & Accountability Act (HIPAA).	U.S. Department of Labor
Personal Responsibility and Work Opportunity Reconciliation Act (PRWORA).	The act requires employers in all 50 states to report new-hires and re-hires to a state directory. This is to help facilitate child support payments, for parents who change jobs frequently. Search on-line: "[your state's] new hire directory".	State Agencies
Public Law 91-596	Requires companies to track workplace injuries & illnesses.., using pre-designed forms. Many industries are exempt. Visit http://www.osha.gov/ > A to Z Index > R > Record Keeping.	U.S. Department of Labor (Occupational Safety & Health Administration)
American Disabilities Act	~Awareness: requires businesses serving the public to have a structure(s) that can accommodate the handicapped. Source: http://www.ada.gov/.	U.S. Department of Justice

Notes: 1. For companies with *20 or more employees* COBRA comes into play. See Chapter 7 - Insurance > Health.
2. For companies with *50 or more employees* the "Family and Medical Leave Act" comes into play. Reference: http://www.dol.gov/ > A to Z Index > "F" > Family and Medical Leave Act.//

Chapter 4 - **Manual Bookkeeping**

What's the point of learning "manual bookkeeping" - when computers can help us with so much? Well, I believe it's important to learn, for instance, journal entries (debits and credits), from a manual perspective first. That way you know what the computer is trying to do, or supposed to be doing. And we will cover debits and credits in the next chapter, followed by computers - in the chapter after that. So, short of debits and credits and computer bookkeeping, what does manual bookkeeping look like? Well, it looks very much like what an entrepreneur or one man owner/operator might be doing!

Without Debits and Credits or a Computer

Imagine you start a business and can't be bothered with a computer, or debits and credits. Funds, of course, are limited so you decide to try to do as much, of it, yourself, as you can. Besides, doing the books yourself is a good way to keep control of the finances, and keep good track of how you're doing. So, let's see what you can get done on your own.

Here's what you can accomplish without a computer, or debits and credits:
*Maintain a checkbook, and therefore pay bills.
*Do payroll, using tax tables provided by the IRS.
*Calculate and pay payroll taxes (using IRS Publication #15, "Employer's Tax Guide").
*Keep track of what customers owe you (on regular paper).
*Calculate and pay any commissions.
*Calculate and pay "other" taxes (like: state sales tax).
*Reconcile the bank account/s.
*Do any human resource administration (applications, I-9's & W-4's).

What's Left?

Looking at the list above, what haven't you accomplished yet? The answer is surprisingly little - monthly reports or financial statements, and corporate taxes. As far as financial statements, I believe many do-it-yourself business owners are more concerned with surviving - making enough sales to meet payroll and pay bills. If there's something left in the checking account at the end of the month, then maybe that's all they need to know. As far as corporate taxes, even those using computer bookkeeping programs (with debits and credits) should contact a CPA to get that done.

Next Steps

Of course, some of the tasks above would be accomplished more easily by using a computer - *not* a computer bookkeeping program that uses debits and credits, but a spreadsheet program like Microsoft Excel, for example. A spreadsheet program is fairly simple to grasp (does not use debits and credits) and would make it much easier to track what customers owe you, to keep track of commissions, and to calculate any sales tax owed to the state, not to mention helping you generate all of your monthly totals.

As the business grows, financial statements might then become of interest. The business owner could continue to do most of the bookkeeping, but give an outside accountant whatever s/he needed (monthly check registers, sales for the month, etc.) in order to generate an income statement, and perhaps a balance sheet. Finally, if the owner got tired of doing all the bookkeeping and could afford one, a full-charge bookkeeper, using a computer and debits and credits, would be the final step.

Chapter 5 - **Debits and Credits**

Q: Why do you need to know debits and credits?
A: 1. You need to know debits & credits to be able to make journal entries, for entering things like petty cash and depreciation - into computer bookkeeping software.
   2. Debits & credits will help you produce and understand financial statements.
   3. Trying to do the books through a computer bookkeeping program may prove problematic without debits and credits.

Introduction

The first thing that comes to mind when one hears "debit" and "credit" are the layperson definitions - where a credit increases an account and a debit decreases an account. In the accounting world, debits and credits have different meanings.

Defined: *debit* simply means the left side of a ledger, and *credit* means the right side of a ledger.

Debits & credits are used in a "dual entry" system.

Defined: a *dual entry system* means that every transaction affects two accounts. For example, when you buy equipment, your cash account will decrease, but your equipment account will increase. Reference the Chart of Accounts - Appendix B, to be familiar with which accounts are assets, liabilities, owner's equity, revenues and expenses.

In order to do debits and credits you really only need to know three facts.

Fact 1: Assets - Liabilities = Equity of the Owner *or*
   Assets = Liabilities + Owner's Equity   (This is called the Basic Accounting Equation).

   Defined: *owner's equity* equals assets minus liabilities. It is a measure of any extra an owner has in the business.

Fact 2: All debits must equal all credits, in a journal entry (aka: the journal entry balances).

   Recall: a journal entry is nothing more than debits and credits, in balance, describing a transaction (see Example 1, below).

Fact 3: To increase assets, debit them. Notice assets are on the left / debit side of the accounting equation.

The rest of debit and credit usage can be derived from these three facts. But, you will need to focus and study this chapter quite intently. First, we'll start with assets, liabilities and owner's equity. Then we'll cover revenue accounts and expenses.

Assets, Liabilities and Owner's Equity

Recall Fact 3, above: *to increase assets, debit them*. We can derive from this, using opposites:
*Since debiting increases Assets, crediting decreases them.
*Liabilities and Owner's Equity are on the right side of the Basic Accounting Equation, so to increase them credit them.
*Since crediting increases Liabilities and Owner's Equity, debiting decreases them.

Brief Review:
Assets	=	Liabilities	+	Owner's Equity (Fact #1)
left side		*right side*		
Debit to Increase (Fact #3)		Credit to Increase		
Credit to Decrease		Debit to Decrease		

Chapter 5 - Debits and Credits (continued)

Assets, Liabilities and Owner's Equity (cont.)
Let's look at some examples:

Example 1- You buy equipment for cash:
    [Debit]   Equipment $$ =>*Increasing* an *asset*
    [Credit]   Cash $$ =>*Decreasing* an *asset*

Example 2 - You pay a bill:
    [Debit]   Accounts Payable $100   =>*Decreasing* a *liability*
    [Credit]   Cash $100 =>*Decreasing* an *asset*
    |_____|
    A 'journal entry' - in balance (Fact #2)

Notes: 1. *Help* - I usually find ways to "cheat" in figuring out the journal entry. For instance, if cash is involved I'll figure out the cash side first and then balance the entry with the other account on the other side.
            2. *Conventions* - not all journal entries consist of just one debit and one credit. You can have as many of either, just as long as the total debit $'s equals the total credit $'s. It is customary, however, to list all debit(s) first and then all credit(s).

Revenues and Expenses
We've just covered assets, liabilities and owner's equity. The only things left are revenues and expenses.

REVENUES
The way I remember revenues is to think of a sales transaction. When you make a sale, you increase cash (an asset), so debit cash. To balance the entry, you must credit sales. But you are also increasing sales. So to increase a revenue account, credit it.

Example 3 - You make a sale:
    [Debit]   Cash $500   =>*Increasing* an *asset*
    [Credit]   Sales $500   =>*Increasing* a *revenue account*

Note: *rules* - you probably noticed that journal entries don't have to have a revenue account offsetting an expense account, or asset offsetting a liability. There are no particular rules in the area of what is allowed to offset what.

EXPENSES
Here is how I remember expenses. When you pay an expense you decrease cash, or credit it. To balance the entry, you must debit the expense - incurring or increasing that expense. So to increase an expense, debit it.

Example 4 - You repair your car:
    [Debit]   Automobile Expense $150   =>*Incurring* an *expense*
    [Credit]   Cash $150 =>*Decreasing* an *asset*

Conclusion
For the record, I don't consider debits and credits something you read and say to yourself, "Oh - I get that now" and never need to look at again. More likely, myself included, it is something you will need to "put there" in your mind, each time you have to journalize a transaction. And, to put it there, I say to myself, "To increase assets, debit them." I then find everything starting to flow from there. Yes, you may need to go over this chapter a couple of times, if this stuff is new to you. But don't be afraid to refer back to this chapter, and try working some examples, on your own - make up scenarios.

Chapter 6 - **Computers**

As far as bookkeepers are concerned, computers can be sub-divided into the topics of bookkeeping via a computer and everything else. If you haven't had a chance to become computer literate, and are looking to enter this field, I would suggest that now is a good time to start learning about computers. It will improve your chances of finding employment and can assist you, in the long run, with other tasks - whether at work or at home.

Bookkeeping Via A Computer

As mentioned earlier, all computer accounting (or bookkeeping) programs will be based on debits and credits, so knowledge of debits and credits is important to mastering any computer bookkeeping program. Be sure to go through, at least the debits and credits chapter, prior to going through this chapter. It would also be helpful to go through the manual bookkeeping chapter, as a natural progression to computer bookkeeping.

Q: Why are debits and credits needed for computer bookkeeping?
A: Debits & credits will enable you to make journal entries to the general ledger for things like petty cash and depreciation - needed for financial statements.

COMPUTER ALREADY IN PLACE

If your company has a computer bookkeeping program already in place, it will be your job to get to know the software they are using. There is a good chance it's either QuickBooks or Sage 50 Accounting. In any case, if you're not familiar with the program, or if it's a different version from the one that you know, go through the tutorial(s), provided with the program.

It is not my intention to teach computer accounting programs in this chapter. Each program has a fine tutorial built into the software. And, I strongly suggest going through them. If, for some reason, the version you're working with is older, and does not provide a tutorial, fear not. All programs these days are menu driven, and self-explanatory. All you have to do is take your time to find what you need. And if you get really stuck, break out the instruction manual or call their customer support line.

NEW COMPUTER

If you're going to initiate a new computer bookkeeping system at your company, QuickBooks and Sage 50 are probably your best bets. However, you may want to shop for another suitable program out there. Bookkeeping software can be found online, as well as at the major office supply stores - like Office Depot / Office Max, and Staples.

Most bookkeeping programs do the majority of the same things. But, do spend some time examining any interface pictures or examples you can find - to see which software provider will suit your tastes the best. And, also know that each software provider will have several versions of their program out there, depending on what specifically is included (like QuickBooks vs. QuickBooks Pro). So, also spend some time comparing the different versions to find the particular version best suited to your company's needs (including any potential growth). Sometimes the areas included in the bookkeeping software are referred to as "modules".

Defined: a module is a section or feature of a computer bookkeeping program (eg: tracking inventory).

All the program versions will have the payroll module, but each version lists all of what's included on the box, or on the web-site. So, think about your company and study the different versions - on the web-sites or stand in the office supply store reading the back of the box, to be sure you obtain the program version that has what your company needs. Once you set up the computer, be sure to go through the tutorials provided. And, if your state has income tax, be sure the appropriate state tax tables are loaded. Often state tax tables are pre-loaded, but do refer to the owner's manual to be sure.

The phone numbers and websites for QuickBooks and Sage 50 Accounting (formerly Peachtree Accounting) are as follows:

QuickBooks (Intuit Company): visit: http://quickbooks.intuit.com/ or call 1-877-683-3280.
Sage 50 Accounting: visit: http://na.sage.com/us/sage-50-accounting or call 1-877-495-9904.

One final note: a lot of these bookkeeping software providers are really pushing you to sign up for their online monthly "subscription service". If you have the option to get the computer disc for the program (like from the

Chapter 6 - Computers (continued)

Bookkeeping Via A Computer (cont.)
    NEW COMPUTER (cont.)
local stores) for a desktop computer, that is the route I recommend - for more than one reason. First of all, you don't have to pay their monthly fee, from now until the end of time. Secondly, for security purposes, I recommend against the "cloud-based" services. There have been many, many large company breaches of the online information - your proprietary information! And, finally, you won't have to worry if or when they are "updating their system" - keeping you from getting to your data / information / work tasks that need to get done. Period.

    POSTING TRANSACTIONS & SETTING-UP CUSTOMER / VENDOR ID #'s
        Remember that most transactions will post to the general ledger automatically. For example, when posting bills to the Accounts Payable module, behind the scenes the computer bookkeeping program is posting to the general ledger. The same is true when printing payroll checks through the payroll module. However, things like petty cash and depreciation are not running through the computer program. So, you will need to post these to the general ledger via a journal entry. I like to write any journal entries I need to make on a piece of scratch paper, before heading for the computer.

        When entering a new customer or vendor into the computer bookkeeping program, you will need to come up with an identification number. The best system I've found, over the years, is to use the first four letters of the company followed by two numbers - example: FEDE01 for Federal Express. The next "Federal" company would be "FEDE02".

    BACKING UP DATA
        I hope you know the importance of backing-up your work each and every day. Imagine, if you only backed-up once a month, and one day your hard-drive decided to quit on you. Not only would you need to try to recreate all of those transactions, and spend how much time doing it, but you'd need to explain *that* to your boss.

        The general consensus is to back-up once per day, at the end of the day. That way you'll never have any more than a day's work to reenter. Both QuickBooks and Sage 50 have built in back-up features, for this purpose. Your best bet will be to use a "flash" or jump drive that plugs directly into a USB port. Not only can you store large amounts of data on these, but they are quite tiny - like the size of a pinky finger.

> Defined: a *flash/travel/USB drive (aka: jump drive or thumb drive)* is a device used to back-up data. It is about the size of a finger and plugs directly into a USB port. They can hold a Giga byte or more of memory, are extremely fast to work with and very portable, as well.

        It would be advisable to store a back-up of the company's data off premises (like at home), and to update it once per week. This is in the event there is a fire, flood, break-in or other such catastrophe, at your workplace. That way you would have all but a week's worth of the company's records.

    PAYROLL TAX TABLE UPDATES
        You will, most likely, need to update your payroll tax tables - in your computer bookkeeping program each year, to be sure you're deducting the correct amounts. The companies who put out QuickBooks and Sage 50 make available tax table updates. Don't be surprised if the newer versions of these programs actually *require* the updates – in order to continue to operate the program into the new year. In all honesty, it's not that the tax rates/deduction amounts change that much, but a way for these companies to build in return business. As mentioned in Tasks > Year-End Items, they often mail an order form for it around November - for next year's updates. If you don't receive anything by early December, just call their customer service department.

Other Computer-Related Areas
        There are a couple of other areas I'd like to touch on, besides bookkeeping via a computer. You should be aware of the use of "office software" (defined below) and a computer consultant.

    OFFICE SOFTWARE
> Defined: *office software* typically refers to a word processing program and a spreadsheet program, and perhaps some others - to be used in an office setting.

Chapter 6 - Computers (continued)

Other Computer-Related Areas (cont.)

OFFICE SOFTWARE (cont.)

Besides the computer bookkeeping program, bookkeepers will need a spreadsheet program for help with Federal Unemployment Taxes - Form 940, and commissions, for instance. You will probably also need a word processing program, for any letters that need to be sent, as well as creating any forms you may need. Nearly all computers do come preloaded with some kind of office software like Microsoft Works.

If you do need to purchase office software, Microsoft Office is your best bet. There are several versions out there. The Home & Student version contains Microsoft Word - a word processing program, Microsoft Excel - a spreadsheet program, and PowerPoint - for presentations. This version costs approximately $150 and will be sufficient for most small businesses. Everything from the "Standard Version" to the "Small Business Version", and the "Full or Professional Version" add things like Microsoft Access - a database program, and Microsoft Outlook – an email program. These versions are at least double the price, and are typically more than any small business will need. Reference: http://www.microsoftstore.com/.

As far as compatibility with bookkeeping software, fear not. There really is little or no need for bookkeeping software and office software to integrate. I've not actually had to do anything like that myself. And the most I've heard of is exporting financial statements into a spreadsheet program in order to perform calculations with the data (for example: estimating Cost of Goods Sold as a percentage of sales; ref: Appendix D - Accounting Basics > Inventory & Cost of Goods Sold). Both Sage 50 & QuickBooks Pro should have these capabilities.

COMPUTER CONSULTANT

There will probably be times when you / your company will need to employ an outside computer person. Instances include any web-site development, and networking of your company's computers. Don't let management "pigeon-hole" you into taking on other 'administrative' areas, like the computers. Not only is full-charge bookkeeping enough for one person to take on, but you may neither have the skill, expertise, time or interest in taking on anything else. Note: it will pay to shop for a good consultant, as skills and fees vary.

Chapter 7 - **Insurance**

There are several different types of insurance, you, as the bookkeeper, may have to deal with. They include health insurance, "corporate liability insurance", and "worker's compensation insurance" (defined within the sections below).

Health Insurance

Since the inception of the Affordable Care Act (aka: "Obama-care"), probably the biggest question on bookkeeper's minds (particularly if they have to answer questions from employees) is, "Is our company required to offer health insurance?" And the answer is "no" - for companies with less than 50 full-time (or equivalent) employees. And your company is also NOT subject to the "Employer Shared Responsibility Payment" either. Reference: https://www.healthcare.gov/small-businesses/what-is-the-employer-shared-responsibility-payment/.

But, if the company you work for decides to offer a "group insurance plan" there are a few things bookkeepers should know about health insurance. First of all, bookkeepers should know that health insurance is subject to insurance company requirements, as well as federal and state laws. Bookkeepers should also have some knowledge about "COBRA", and the Health Insurance Portability and Accountability Act - HIPAA (all defined below).

Note: for companies with more than 50 full-time employees, *"The Employer Shared Responsibility Payment applies to some businesses with 50 or more full-time employees who don't offer insurance, or whose coverage doesn't meet certain minimum standards."* Reference: https://www.healthcare.gov/small-businesses/what-is-the-employer-shared-responsibility-payment/; downloaded April 22, 2015. The IRS also offers detailed Q&A at: http://www.irs.gov/Affordable-Care-Act/Employers/Questions-and-Answers-on-Employer-Shared-Responsibility-Provisions-Under-the-Affordable-Care-Act.

> Defined: a *group insurance plan* is one that is offered to your entire company, often with a minimum number of employees participating needed.

SUBJECT TO REQUIREMENTS

For example, in New Mexico, if an employer decided to offer health insurance the employer was required to pay at least fifty percent of the premiums. To illustrate, say there are ten employees at your company, and each individual's monthly premium is $100 per month. The total monthly premiums would be $1000 (10 x $100). In this example, your company would be required to pay $500 per month, and each employee would pay the other $50 per month to make up the difference.

Realize that there may be other laws or requirements applicable as well. I've heard of instances where employees are required to work so many hours per week - in order to be eligible for health insurance. The insurance company representative will probably be able to inform you of applicable state, federal and insurance company requirements.

"COBRA"

You will probably hear the term COBRA - in relation to health insurance.

> Defined: *COBRA* is a federal law that basically allows a terminated employee and family to continue health insurance coverage for up to 18 months - under certain circumstances. [It stands for "Consolidated Omnibus Budget Reconciliation Act".]

COBRA circumstances include job loss (voluntary or involuntary) and divorce. Do be aware that the cost to continue coverage can be as much as normal premiums. And know that COBRA only applies to companies with 20 or more employees in the prior year. [Some states have "mini-COBRA" - for employers of less than 20 employees (check with your state's insurance commissioner's office).] The bookkeeper will need to check with their insurance company to see what they will need for notification of terminated employees. For more information, visit http://www.dol.gov/ > A to Z Index > "C" > COBRA.

"HIPAA"

> Defined: *HIPAA* stands for "Health Insurance Portability and Accountability Act". This federal act enforces a lot of things including the protection of privacy.

Chapter 7 - Insurance (continued)

In relation to bookkeepers HIPAA requires that terminated employees, who had health insurance while employed, receive a letter or certificate of prior health coverage. [This certificate can aid these individuals with future health coverage - particularly if there are any pre-existing conditions.] In all likelihood, your insurance company will mail the certificate/letter themselves. But, you will need to call them to be sure! Since, as mentioned above, small companies do not have many administrative personnel working for them, you will be acting as, what the insurance companies call the "plan administrator" (defined below). For more information, visit http://www.dol.gov/ > A to Z Index > "H" > Health Insurance Portability & Accountability Act (HIPAA).

> Defined: a *plan administrator* is that person, in the company you work for, who works with the health insurance. In smaller companies this is often the bookkeeper.

Corporate Liability Insurance
> Defined: *corporate liability insurance* is a more general coverage for things like fire or property damage.

Corporate liability insurance is not specifically required by law, but for obvious reasons, very strongly suggested. This is something the company owner has probably taken care of some time ago. But, you need to be aware it exists, and particularly if the bills come your way. If, however, you find the company you work for does not have such insurance, you may do well to suggest it - to the company owner.

Workers' Compensation Insurance
> Defined: *worker's compensation insurance* is insurance in case an employee is injured on the job.

Worker's compensation insurance laws vary by state, but insurance is *widely* required to be carried. To check out the laws in your state go to www.workerscompensationinsurance.com. This site is not deemed an employ*er* website, but has links to all 50 states, including state laws and regulations. The owner of the company you work for has, most likely, set up workers' compensation insurance some time ago. But, you need to be aware of it for a number of reasons. First, as the bookkeeper, you will probably see the bills for this. You may want to ask your boss who carries the company's worker's compensation insurance and when to expect the bill, so you can be on the look-out for it. Sometimes it's billed monthly.

The second thing you should be aware of is that the insurance rates are often based on an annual "audit" performed by the insurance company. If they do audit, they usually take a look at things like the number of employees in the company, and the types of work each employee does. For instance, office employees are less likely to get injured on the job than those doing heavy lifting all day. So office employees' rates are typically lower. The insurance company will look to the administration department (or bookkeeper) to provide them this information.

> Defined: an *audit* is an examination of some aspect of the company you work for.

Note: *self-audit* - if your company has a 'good' record, some insurance companies will allow you to "self-audit", meaning you provide the information without them being present, per their form.

Finally, you need to know that if you have an independent contractor working for your company, as discussed in Chapter 2 - Tasks > Payroll > Independent Contractors, you will need to obtain a certificate of worker's compensation insurance from his or her insurance company, and keep it on file. Without your independent contractor's certificate of insurance, *your* insurance company will require you to list him/her on your bill, dramatically raising your insurance cost.

Chapter 8 - Industries

I'd like to mention a few of the industries out there, and some of what to expect when bookkeeping in those industries.

Note: *every industry* - it is not my intention to cover every industry, nor everything regarding each industry.

Bookkeeping is essentially bookkeeping - no matter what the industry. If you've studied full-charge bookkeeping and are diligent about your work, you should feel confident that you can show up to any bookkeeping job, in any industry, and perform admirably. Having said that, I would still like to expose you to some of the different types of industries out there, and some of the particularities to those industries - in order to raise your awareness level. The industries I'd like to touch on, in alphabetical order, are construction, food and beverage, manufacturing, retail, and the service industry. I will also say a few words about the non-profit sector.

Construction Industry

The construction industry includes everything from "site development" (eg. laying pipes for utilities) to the collection of the garbage from the construction sites. And, of all the industries out there, the construction industry is one of the most involved ones for a bookkeeper. There are a number of things you may run into in the construction field including job costing, progress billings, receiving payment for work performed, workers' compensation insurance certificates from independent contractors (aka: sub-contractors), specialized payroll reports for government jobs, and materialsmen liens.

    JOB COSTING

        Defined: *job costing* is a way of determining what each construction job is costing your company, in terms of materials, labor and any allocated 'overhead'.

        Defined: *overhead* refers to costs that are incurred whether any product is produced or not (eg. rent).

        One simple way of doing this is to set up a separate clipboard for each job. Then, when you get and/or pay a bill, put a copy of each bill on the clipboard. For payroll, you could either print a report, or create a form, for the amount of payroll spent on each job, attaching that to the clipboard as well. Allocating overhead to each job is a little trickier. Some might add say 15 or 20% on top of the materials and labor, as overhead. Others might try to be more precise in terms of the actual overhead hours spent, while your company is on that job, times an overhead rate. Be sure to check with the owner, to see if and how s/he has handled it in the past. It may also vary by client/job.

    PROGRESS BILLINGS

        Defined: *progress billings* means that your company can bill the customer for progress made to date, and not have to wait until the entire project is complete, to receive income.

        The construction contracts are typically set-up this way, with payments either monthly or in thirds: 1/3 billed after 1/3 completed, the second 1/3 billed after 2/3 completed, and the final third billed upon completion.

    RECEIVING PAYMENT FOR WORK PERFORMED

        Along the lines of progress billings, you will want to be paid for work performed. Do read carefully the contract that your company signed with your customer, particularly the paragraph about receiving payment for work performed. Each contract may be different regarding what documents your customer requires in order to pay you. Documents may include a "release of lien", payroll reports and your customer's own forms, typically notarized.

        Defined: a *release of lien* is a document showing that there is no lien attached to any of the material/s.

    WORKERS' COMPENSATION INSURANCE CERTIFICATES *FROM* INDEPENDENT CONTRACTORS

        In the construction industry independent contractors are known as "sub-contractors". And as previously discussed, if you have any sub-contractors working for your company, you, as bookkeeper, need to obtain a certificate of insurance, from your sub's insurance company, to keep on file. Without it, your insurance company will require you to list your sub (not your employee) on *your* bill, dramatically raising your insurance cost.

Chapter 8 - Industries (continued)

Construction Industry (cont.)
SPECIALIZED PAYROLL & REPORTS FOR GOVERNMENT JOBS
Any government construction jobs are subject to the Davis Bacon Act (setting minimum wages for classes of workers under contract). Reference: http://www.dol.gov/ > A to Z Index > D > Davis Bacon. If your company has a government contract don't be surprised if you are required to file special payroll reports, on a weekly basis, listing names, pay rates and amounts paid to workers on particular government jobs. Davis-Bacon also empowers the Secretary of Labor to determine "local prevailing wage rates" or how much particular workers in each locale are to be paid - on an hourly basis (for federally funded jobs). Reference: http://www.dol.gov/ > A to Z Index > D > Davis Bacon. And the workers may be asked at random, on the job site, how much they are making (to verify against what they were supposed to be making).

MATERIALSMEN LIENS
Defined: *liens* are a legal right to property, but represent ways of getting paid if you're having trouble collecting on construction work. And, *materialsmen* are people who work with material - such as construction material.

Lien laws are state or city specific. So, do research your local laws regarding materialsmen liens. I've found the internet is most useful in finding local statutes - search: "[your state's or city's] laws". Unfortunately, some construction companies are bad about paying, or won't pay unless a lien is filed upon them. To complicate matters, in some states, including New Mexico and Florida, you must file the lien before a certain amount of time has passed, or you lose the option to file! Some construction bills can be hefty. So, after determining the lien laws where you live, always leave yourself the option to file or you may lose out on being able to collect from that customer. Note: the bookkeeper or company owner may be able to accomplish some of this (eg. filling out a complaint). Or, you may prefer to contact an attorney, from the start. For other ways to collect, see Chapter 2 - Tasks > Collections.

BOTTOM LINE FOR THE CONSTRUCTION FIELD
The above items may not be the only particularities you run into in the construction field. Your best approach will be to (1) research any and all laws in your area (state/county/city); (2) read and study all the job contracts and guidelines that your company bids for and gets. And finally, not only should you read and study, but lay-out on your calendar and adhere to all fine print for the jobs you get - because *mistakes will be costly*.

Food and Beverage Industry
Defined: the *food and beverage industry* includes bars, restaurants, waiters and waitresses.

The most important particularity to the food and beverage industry is the minimum wage for wait staff. The federal minimum wage is set at $2.13/hour for wait staff - to take into account the tips they receive. In other words this $2.13 / hour minimum is good only as long as their tips make up the difference, to get to the per hour federal minimum wage rate or your local - state/city minimum wage rate if higher than the federal. The employer, not employee, must make up any wage difference. Source: U.S. Dept. of Labor @ http://www.dol.gov/ >A to Z Index >T >Tips, or http://www.dol.gov/dol/topic/wages/wagestips.htm.

However, it is the waiters' and waitresses' responsibility to: (1) *keep track of tips* - keep a good, day to day record of tips received, for every month, and (2) *report tips* - report the amount of tips received to their employer within 10 days, following the end of the month. The IRS has a form on which employees can track their daily tips, and a separate form on which they should report to their employer/you tips received each month. These forms are available in IRS Publication 1244, "Employee's Daily Record of Tips and Report to Employer".

The employee's monthly tip report/statement to the employer/you needs to contain: employee's name, address, social security number, employer's name and address, the month/period of the report, the total dollar tips received (both cash and credit card) and the report must be signed by the employee. Once the waiters and waitresses report their tips, it is the bookkeeper's responsibility to add the tips to their base wages ($2.13/hour), and use the total to determine the amount of federal income, social security and Medicare tax to withhold. In other words bookkeepers need to calculate taxes on the total of base wages plus tips! Reference: IRS Publication 15 > "Tips" chapter.

Chapter 8 - Industries (continued)

Manufacturing Industry
>Defined: the *manufacturing industry* typically involves buying raw materials, mass-producing items and then selling them "wholesale" to retail outlets.

>Defined: where *wholesale* means to sell, not directly to the public, but to retail outlets or go-between companies.

The things I'd like to point out are the importance of a physical inventory, tax-free wholesales, and an advanced bookkeeping concept entitled, "costing" in a manufacturing environment (defined below).

PHYSICAL INVENTORY
>You will find, in the manufacturing field, that keeping good track of inventory levels is important for more than one reason. Clearly, the manufacturing process can't happen without an inventory of raw materials. And, from the bookkeeper's standpoint, accurate beginning and ending inventory levels enable you to calculate the "Cost of Goods Sold" - required to produce an Income Statement. Please reference: Appendix D - Accounting Basics > Inventory & Cost of Goods Sold, and Appendix C - Financial Statements > Income Statement.

>Defined: *Cost of Goods Sold* is referring to the goods or products that your company sold to customers - what did they cost your company?

Note: *end of the year* - a physical inventory count is typically taken at the end of each year, and reconciled to the count on the books, adjusted by "shrinkage".

>Defined: *shrinkage* is loss of inventory, typically, due to theft.

TAX-FREE WHOLESALES
>Defined: *tax-free wholesales* means that in some states (New Mexico is one) if your company is a manufacturer or wholesaler and *not* selling to the public, but to a company who will resell your product (like a retailer), your company, the manufacturer, may *not* be required to charge sales tax.

The logic here is to avoid double taxation, since the retailer will be charging the sales tax. Typically, the retailer buying from you, the manufacturer, will give you a 'non-tax certificate' that you keep on file, to show authorities why you didn't charge that customer sales tax. There may also be different categories of non-tax, like non-profit organizations may be exempt from paying sales tax, as well. This is a state specific item. So, you will need to contact your state's department of taxation to determine if such a thing exists - in your state, and if so to request information.

AN ADVANCED BOOKKEEPING CONCEPT: "COSTING IN A MANUFACTURING ENVIRONMENT"
>Defined: *costing in a manufacturing environment* means to consider the cost of "direct material", "direct labor" and any "allocated overhead" to the cost of the product (see glossary for definitions).

Direct materials, direct labor, and allocated overhead are the three components to manufacture any product. And, if you become exposed to any cost analysis, in a manufacturing company, it will, in all likelihood, involve these components. In brief, direct materials means any and all raw material used to manufacture a product. Direct labor is referring to assembly workers, and their direct supervisors. Overhead refers to costs that are incurred just because the doors of the business are open - regardless of whether any product is produced or not. Examples include office workers wages, rent, most utilities. The idea is to allocate a portion of the overhead costs, to each unit of goods manufactured.

As mentioned in the Construction Industry section above, allocating overhead is a little trickier than materials and labor. Some might try to be precise in terms of the actual overhead hours spent - while product is being made, times an overhead rate. Others might just add, say, 15 or 20% on top of the direct materials and direct labor, as their "guesstimate" regarding overhead.

Chapter 8 - Industries (continued)

Retail Industry

Defined: the *retail industry* is any store that sells directly to the public.

I'd like to impress upon you the importance of inventory, related "shrinkage", and discuss one method of estimating "Cost of Goods Sold" (COGS) in the retail industry.

Defined: *shrinkage* is loss of inventory due to theft, or other cause.

Note: since we mentioned COGS in the Manufacturing section above, it is important to distinguish the difference between COGS in the manufacturing industry versus COGS in the retail industry.

MANUFACTURING INDUSTRY VERSUS RETAIL INDUSTRY - REGARDING 'COGS' :
Calculating COGS in a manufacturing environment will be vastly different (involving direct materials, direct labor, and some portion of overhead) versus a Retail Industry environment - where no such manufacturing is involved - simply wholesale purchases of inventory to sell.

ESTIMATING OR CALCULATING 'COST OF GOODS SOLD'
One method of estimating Cost of Goods Sold is by way of purchases of wholesale inventory. The idea here is, if you always keep a certain amount of each item on the shelves, then when an item is sold you will be restocking it; so purchases approximate (or equal) Cost of Goods Sold. [Direct calculation of COGS is: Beginning Inventory + Purchases = Goods Available for Sale, - Ending Inventory = COGS.]

INVENTORY & SHRINKAGE
Since Cost of Goods Sold is required to produce an Income Statement (reference: Appendix D - Accounting Basics > Inventory & Cost of Goods Sold, and Appendix C - Financial Statements > Income Statement.), accurate beginning and ending inventory levels will enable you to precisely calculate COGS. But, shrinkage can be a large problem in the retail industry. So, physical inventory counts are that much more important - in order to have a proper valuation of inventory, by determining how much shrinkage has occurred.

Service Industry

Defined: the *service industry* is one that does not involve a material product. Health care, child care, legal, accounting, engineering and architectural services are examples.

Obviously, inventory will not be a major thing in the service industry. Although it may involve some inventory - for example medicine in the health care industry. The biggest difference appears on the income statement. The Cost of Goods Sold account is substituted by the "Cost of Sales" account. Instead of product being sold, services are sold. So "direct salary expense" of those servicing the client - like a lawyer's salary, is the most major component of Cost of Sales. Any administrative and selling expenses still get listed under Operating Expenses Reference: Appendix C - Financial Statements > Income Statement.

The Non-Profit Sector

Bookkeeping for a non-profit organization can be quite a different animal. There will be major similarities and major differences. Things like payroll and payroll taxes should be very much the same. As far as differences, even the financial statements have different names. Learning on the job would be difficult at best. For more detailed coverage of bookkeeping for non-profits, I suggest another book such as "Bookkeeping for non-profits: a step-by-step guide to nonprofit accounting", or "Bookkeeping basics: what every non-profit bookkeeper needs to know."

Industry Audit Guides

As a final note, the IRS has available "Audit Technique Guides" for approximately 40 different industries, including retail and construction. These are the actual guides IRS auditors use for their audits, so they can be useful to see what might be important. They are available to view on-line @ http://www.irs.gov/Businesses/Small-Businesses-&-Self-Employed/Audit-Techniques-Guides-ATGs.//

Chapter 9 – **Dealing(s) with the CPA**

As the bookkeeper, there is a good chance that you will have one or two things to do with a CPA - if you are there for any length of time. Typically, you will need to contact the CPA in order to complete the corporate tax return(s) - federal and possibly state, for the CPA to review any other reports, and in order to make quarterly estimated tax payments.

Corporate Tax Return(s)

As mentioned in Chapter 2 - Tasks > Corporate Taxes, you will need to contact the CPA in early February (after you complete year-end items), in order to get the corporate tax return/s completed. Ask the CPA what documents s/he will need in order to produce the corporate tax return/s (federal is due March 15th). As stated previously, below are the typical and additional items for the CPA, a word about state corporate taxes, and other reports to go to the CPA, as well as a word about reviewing reports before sending them.

Typical Corporate Tax Items
*Financial Statements: Income Statement & Balance Sheet
*Check register(s)
*Summary Agings of Payables & Receivables
*General Ledger - Summary Transaction Listing

Note: a *summary GL listing* - might suffice as long as you provide detailed listings for the "Additional Items" listed below.

Additional Corporate Tax Items (May Include)
*"Fixed Asset" accounts - there maybe more than one (defined below).
*Computer Equipment Asset or Expense Account
*"Draws" Taken by the Owner Account (defined below).
*Charitable Contributions/Gifts Account

Defined: *fixed assets* is another name for "Property, Plant & Equipment" (PP&E). Where fixed assets are listed on the Chart of Accounts, PP&E are listed on the Balance Sheet. Examples include: land, buildings, vehicles, furniture, fixtures and equipment.

Defined: a *draw* taken by the owner is a removal of cash from the business, beyond the owner's salary (aka: a dividend).

State Corporate Taxes?
Realize that some states have a corporate income tax (New Mexico is one). But, your CPA should be aware of this and produce that return as well. It will behoove you though, to know your state's requirements, for your benefit and the benefit of your company. Search on-line, at "[your state's] corporate income tax". These returns should be copied by the CPA directly to your company owner. You, as the bookkeeper, may or may not end up with copies of these returns.

Review Reports
Before presenting your reports to the CPA, you will need to review them to be sure they look accurate. For instance, the Typical and Additional Items listed above - you will want to scan down the amounts to see if they appear reasonable (no gross errors) given your strong knowledge of the company. Scan the general ledger summary transaction listing - to be sure the amounts posted to your company's accounts appear reasonable.

Other Year-End Reports to the CPA?

Along with documents to produce the corporate tax return, your company's owner may want you to send the CPA the following: copies of payroll tax reports - both federal and state, and an employee payroll report, listing amounts paid to each employee for the year. You should have started a folder, entitled "Reports for CPA" from your year-end work (reference: Chapter 2 - Tasks > Year-End Items). Go ahead and add the corporate tax documents you've collected above - to this folder. Before presenting it to the CPA, you will need to 1) review the reports for accuracy - see below, and 2) let your company's owner know you have this file prepared for the CPA.

Chapter 9 - Dealings with the CPA (continued)

Quarterly Estimated Tax Payments
Defined: *quarterly estimated tax payments* are installments of corporate income tax due.

Do realize that as the bookkeeper you will be making the quarterly estimated tax payments. But the CPA will determine any payment amount. Note that the IRS now requires electronic deposit of these tax payments. The following are the deposit due dates and contact dates:

Tax Due Dates	Contact CPA Dates
April 15th	April 1st
June 15th	June 1st
September 15th	September 1st
December 15th	December 1st

"Evolving Relationship"
It is also possible that the extent of your dealings with the CPA may depend upon several things:
1. *Need to use* - how much your company's business owner feels the need to use the CPA.
2. *Your ability* - to complete bookkeeping tasks, which will probably evolve.
3. *Your relationship* - as bookkeeper, with the business owner.

For instance, some business owners may feel the need to use a CPA to produce all payroll tax reports, and monthly financial statements - in addition to the corporate tax return. This may be something that the owner decided long before hiring you - perhaps from a previous bad experience. But, you should keep in mind that no matter how competent you are, you may not be able to change the owner's mind about his or her need to use a CPA for certain items.

Regarding your ability to complete the bookkeeping tasks, as your knowledge and experience level increase, your confidence in your own abilities will go up as well. This will come across when interviewing, and more positively affect your relationship with the owner. Do keep in mind that the extent of your company's dealings with the CPA may be evolving, based on your presence. For instance, the owner may have been using a CPA for everything, but finally decided that was too expensive. So, the owner decides to hire a bookkeeper, but starts the bookkeeper out slowly, perhaps even with data entry. Then as the owner's confidence level increases, s/he may trust you with more. And, as you pick-up more tasks, the CPA is needed less.

Note: *handling more* - you might have to say to the owner, at some point, "I can handle XYZ", and then s/he may decide to trust you with that item.

Whatever the level your company engages the CPA, you must be sure s/he has all required documents to produce what the CPA is asked to produce, in a timely manner.

Chapter 10 - **Bookkeeper as Management?**

Q: Should a full-charge bookkeeper think of him or herself as management, or akin to management?
A: Yes, for two reasons:
    1. *Money = managerial importance* - whenever you're dealing with money, it takes on managerial importance.
    2. *"Full-charge"* - that you are a full-charge bookkeeper means that the company owner is relying on you to handle the books without much, if any, supervision.

Q: Should the bookkeeper tread lightly in this area?
A: Yes, definitely. Again, that you're dealing with money brings more significance to what you're doing. But, no matter how much the owner entrusts the books to you, you wouldn't want to be telling the owner how to run his or her business.

Q: So, where should you "draw the line"?
A: If it might/probably come back to "bite" you, as in the owner says, "Why didn't you mention *that*."

There are several topics regarding management-type activities for a full-charge bookkeeper. This chapter will touch on the following areas: having a watchful eye - over the books, supervisory situations bookkeepers may be subject to, being careful not to take on too much, if you must field phone calls regarding previous employees, and whether you should sign checks or not.

A Watchful Eye - Over The Books
This section discusses some of the higher functions of a good full-charge bookkeeper. That's why it comes near the end of the book. So, you may not want to consider taking on this function - until gaining significant experience with the rest of full-charge bookkeeping. Having said that, keeping a watchful eye over the books is an aspect of the job, and something you should be aware of. So, at least read this section - if you do nothing else with it.
EXAMPLES
Here are some examples of when you should at least think about intervening - as a manager of the business, and bring it (a concern) to the owner's attention.

<u>Shrinkage</u>
If you become aware of an unusually high amount of shrinkage, particularly in a certain area or of certain items, it would be your duty to report that fact to the business owner. After giving it some thought, you may be able to identify possible causes or a possible solution to the situation. First, bring it to the attention of the owner, and if you have come up with plausible cause(s)/solution(s) that you feel your owner may not be seeing, you might want to mention those as well. Again, tread lightly, but make sure the owner is at least aware of the situation.

<u>Change in Cash Flow</u>
For example, if you notice a sharp decrease in the cash flow of the business from one quarter (3-month period) to the next, and you know your sales have not dropped, it may behoove you to investigate. Pull an income statement from the previous period, and one for the current period - to compare expense categories. Find the category that has risen dramatically, or spiked. Then, you can speak to the owner. If there are no differences on the income statements, pull comparative balance sheets. Perhaps Inventory has risen dramatically, and that's where the money has gone. Be sure to present both financial statements, with the major difference(s) highlighted. If you're uncomfortable, say something like, "I didn't know if you would like me to bring these types of things, to your attention." The owner *should* appreciate your attempt at "looking-after-it", and value you that much more as an employee.

<u>Loose Ends</u>
As a final example of the management characteristics of a good bookkeeper, let's take a look at loose ends. By loose ends I mean situations that continue to go unaccounted for. For instance, I heard of one situation where tokens to video game machines were freely distributed to managers. No one was keeping track of the amounts, until someone thought it might be out of hand. It turned out it was out of hand, and had been for some time, but no one was looking at it. Again, tread lightly, but it might be worth investigating.

Chapter 10 - Bookkeeper as Management? (continued)

So, no matter how long it's "always been that way," if there is an unaccounted for situation, it is probably worth looking at - to see just how much money the business may be losing. Even if you just present the facts, and let the owner decide if that situation is worth changing, then you have done your part! Note: you may need to ask the owner if it's OK for you to look at, or monitor, a particular situation in order to determine exactly how much is being given out - again, treading lightly.

<u>Conclusion</u>

Remember that the finances of a small business are particularly important, and no matter how closely the owner may seem to go over the books, the possibility exists that s/he may not notice, or be paying attention to something relevant to success. About the toughest thing you should have to face as a full-charge bookkeeper is saying and doing what's best for the business - not necessarily what the owner may want to hear at the present time (while treading lightly). That would truly distinguish you as management.

Supervisory Situations

Two possibilities exist: (1) that you may have to supervise one or two employees (probably OK), and (2) that the full-charge bookkeeper position will report to someone other than the business owner (may not be OK).

First, the possibility exists that the full-charge bookkeeper position, at certain companies, will supervise one or two employees - like payroll or billing clerks. I recommend that you start slowly and work your way up to supervising. In other words, first take a full-charge position without any supervisory duties, and stay in that position for awhile. Two years is a good benchmark. Then, only take on one employee to supervise, and get used to that before taking on two employees. This way you won't be biting off more than you can chew, at any one point in time. If you have to supervise more than two employees, your title should probably be greater than just full-charge bookkeeper.

You may find in the job market a full-charge position that reports to a higher level position in accounting, like the Vice President of Finance, for instance. While reporting to a V.P. of Finance may seem like an opportunity to learn, I'd be remiss if I didn't point out the following. It's been my experience and observation that too many management layers in a bookkeeping department creates both waste (why have so many layers?), and resentment (from those doing the bulk of the work - typically the bookkeeper).

Don't Take On Too Much

In order to help you manage your relationship with your business owner, I include this section about not taking on too much. Even though there maybe additional tasks - like fielding phone calls about previous employees, or the possibility of supervising one or two employees, do not make the mistake of allowing the owner to greatly broaden your duties, in the name of 'administration'.

On A Personal Note:

For instance, one owner I worked for saw that I was looking after, or paying some attention to the human resource files - to be sure the proper documents (W-4 & I-9) made it in there, when we hired somebody. Well, the owner decided to deem me his HR Manager, at that point. I thought and said, "Whatever", at first - still intending only to keep up with the HR files' required documents.

But, when the owner ran into some other problem with an employee, he tried to tell me that I needed to handle it - because I was the HR Manager. Not needing that on my plate too, I promptly let him know I didn't know how to handle his situation, resigned as his HR Manager, and quietly returned to my office. Full-charge bookkeepers have enough to do, without being "pigeon-holed" into more.

If You Have to Field Phone Calls Regarding Previous Employees

As mentioned earlier, administrative personnel in smaller companies are few to none. So, the possibility exists that the bookkeeper may be the one to field phone calls regarding previous employees. It will behoove you to prepare for such calls by doing two things. First, research any state laws concerning "privacy of information" or "employment information". For instance, you may only be allowed to confirm employment dates, and a job title. Secondly, you should touch base with the owner to find out what information s/he is comfortable releasing (again - not exceeding any laws).

Chapter 10 - Bookkeeper as Management? (continued)

In the absence of laws and the owner's directions, I've found the safest way to handle such calls is to just "verify" information the callers have in front of them. Typical information that is safe to verify is job title, the dates of employment, and to perhaps confirm or deny the salary or wage, if the person calling can offer it. Remember that it is probably best to err on the conservative side of this task - providing *less* information. Your response to a caller, after verifying minimal information, can be phrased along the lines of, "state law prohibits..." (if it does), or "I'm not at liberty to release that (or any more) information."

Does The Owner Want You To Sign Checks?

The possibility exists that your company's owner may want you to be a signer on the checking account/s or may want to give you a "signature stamp".

> Defined: a *signature stamp* is a rubber stamp possessing the signature of a signer on a bank account. A signature stamp can be used to sign checks.

Possessing a signature stamp may be ok with the right framework (discussed below), but as mentioned in Tasks > Accounts Payable, I recommend against the bookkeeper being a straight-out signer for several reasons: (1) you have enough to do on a day-to-day basis, (2) it will keep you out of trouble with the owner as far as approving payments on your own, and (3) it will help maintain "segregation of duties" for security purposes. If you do, for some reason, wind up being a signer on an account, for security purposes someone other than yourself should be reconciling that bank account. That would be segregation of duties, under the broad umbrella of "internal controls".

> Defined: *segregation of duties* means to separate those tasks that, if not separated, could lead to undetected theft.

> Defined: *internal controls* means to have policies and procedures in place to ensure safe-guarding of assets, and accurate & timely reporting of financial information.

Possession of a signature stamp could, with the right precautions, be useful. For instance, if the owner were to leave town for a week or so, s/he may want you to have the ability to pay a bill or two. Precautions should include the owner maintaining possession of the signature stamp until s/he goes out of town, and the stamp be used only with another manager's initials (on the check). Having another manager initial the check will help the owner know that only necessary expenditures will be paid.

When I was given a signature stamp, I could use it only with three different managers' initials on the check. Of course, I was a "bookkeeping assistant" at the time. A final security measure might be to keep all the blank checks separate from the signature stamp when the owner's out of town, with one manager in possession of the checks, while the bookkeeper or other manager possesses the signature stamp. If you've not already guessed why, these are precautionary measures to provide some checks and balances (via, yes, segregation of duties).

Chapter 11 - A Word about Professionalism & Ethics

One would like to think that being a bookkeeper automatically causes one to conduct him or herself in a professional manner. But, imagine a bookkeeper who was always late to work. So, I thought a word about professionalism was in order. And, ethics are a two-way street. Not only is it important for a bookkeeper to be ethical, but for the bookkeeper's employ*er* to be ethical as well. So, I'm including a section on ethics.

Professionalism

There are, at least, a few aspects to professionalism, including timeliness, "due diligence" (defined below) and keeping organized, accurate records. When I think about being professional, the first thing that comes to mind is being timely in showing up for work, and in the completion of tasks. Be ten minutes early to work each day, and don't leave things half done, or undone, as a rule. Stay if you have to, to be sure all work that needs to be done is done. The owners will appreciate your diligence. And do be diligent in your work. If your bank reconciliation is $35 out of balance, make sure you take the time to find it. This is where the terms "due diligence", and what is "material" (or relevant) come into play.

> Defined: *due diligence* is putting forth the appropriate amount of effort for a particular situation.

> Example: while being $45 out of balance warrants an investigation, being one cent out of balance is not 'material' enough to spend gobs of time looking.

On the one hand, bookkeepers need to be diligent in balancing the books. But, one penny out of balance is not material enough to spend four days looking. Bookkeepers and business owners, usually, work out what is material, and how to handle a situation as it arises. Obviously, it behooves bookkeepers to balance reconciliations and the like. Finally, keeping organized and accurate records reflects on your professionalism, and competence as a bookkeeper. Doing these few things, although not necessarily simple in nature, goes a long way to proving a bookkeeper's character and worth.

Ethics

> Defined: to be *ethical* is to do what is legal, and to do what is the right thing to do.

The main reason I'm writing this section is to warn honest bookkeepers, of the potential hazards of the job. Just because you intend to do things properly, don't assume that everyone out there has the same intentions as yourself. This can be particularly sticky if the company owner, you work for, wants to try to get away with things, and put you in the middle. The term for this is to operate "below board".

> Defined: *below board* essentially means operating outside the law.

> Example: if the business owner does not want to pay time-and-a-half for overtime.

In the above example, not only is that trying to operate outside of federal law, but *that* puts you the bookkeeper in a bad position. If the owner has already decided to do that, do you think it would be hard for him or her to say to authorities, that you were told to pay overtime, but just weren't doing it - setting you up as the law-breaker? So, you can see how dicey it can get pretty quickly with an owner operating, or looking to operate, below board.

On A Personal Note:

Without naming any names, I do have personal experience in dealing with an owner like this. I took a hard-nosed approach from the start, and it paid off. I told him, if you can't operate within the law, then I can't work for you. At one point when I ran into illegalities in another area of the business, I told myself "the four walls of my office" - which meant as long as I was comfortable with the legalities in my own department, I was OK for the moment. When that was compromised (in my view) I left my keys and resignation letter on my desk, without notice, and did not return.

My advice to you would be as follows: if you know the company owner intends to operate below board, do not go to work for that person, in the first place. If you are unaware when hired, as I was, take steps to protect yourself. Do not sign reports - like payroll tax reports, particularly if you're not completely comfortable with the information. And consider finding other employment, to protect your integrity.

Chapter 12 - **A Word about 'Audits'**

Q: What is an "audit"?
A: An *audit* is an examination of some aspect of the company you work for. Audits typically examine the accounting / bookkeeping records, but can include other aspects of a company's operations.

Examples include: an audit of the books by the IRS or a CPA firm, and an audit of your company's operations by a state environmental department.

Reasons for An Audit

One cannot be in the bookkeeping world for too long, without at least hearing of audits. And, a bookkeeper should be aware audits exist, in order to be prepared - should one come along. It's been my experience that audits can come for several reasons. The first reason you might see an audit is for nonpayment or slow payment of taxes. For instance, the IRS audited one company I worked for because the company owner was behind in paying payroll taxes. I also heard of the IRS closing another business for nonpayment of payroll taxes. You don't want to mess with the IRS!

Another reason you might see an audit is if the business you work for has any bank loans. Then the loan covenants might require an audit by a CPA firm. Another company I worked for transported and stored hazardous materials as part of their waste management operation. At one point in time, New Mexico's state environmental department audited the company - regarding that aspect (hazardous waste transport and storage). This is called an "operational audit" (defined below). Finally, the only audit I've observed that might come regularly, as opposed to being prompted by something is an insurance audit. They might audit annually in order to be sure the rates they're charging your company for something like workers' compensation insurance are appropriate.

Sources and Types of Audits
SOURCES
An audit can come from a variety of places.
1. *At the federal level:*
    a. From the IRS - of the books.
    b. Other federal department - if a *non*-bookkeeping issue (aka: operational issue).
2. *At the state level:*
    a. From your state's Department of Taxation and Revenue or equivalent (typically for not making timely payment of taxes due).
    b. From another department - if an "operational audit" (defined below).
3. *Other:*
    a. An insurance audit - by your worker's compensation insurance company, sometimes annually, to adjust your rates. Reference: Chapter 7 - Insurance > Worker's Compensation Insurance.
    b. If your company's owner feels the need to have a CPA audit the books.

TYPES
There are basically three different types of audits you'll need to be prepared for. Below, we'll discuss them in a little more detail, and what your role in each would be. We'll start with the "easiest" and work our way up. The three types are:
1. *An insurance audit.*
2. *An operational audit.*
3. *An audit of the books.*

Insurance Audit

About the only audit you might otherwise be able to prepare for is an insurance audit. The insurance company will either call and schedule it, or ask you to "self-audit" (defined below) per their form. In either case, you will have time to prepare what information they need. Typically, in order to adjust worker's compensation insurance rates, they will look at things like the number of employees in the company, and the types of work each employee does.

Defined: a *self-audit*, in this case, is the insurance company allowing you to provide them the information they need by filling out their form, in lieu of them coming and auditing your paperwork.

Chapter 12 - A Word about Audits (continued)

Operational Audit

Defined: an *operational audit* is, not of the books, but some other aspect of the company you work for.

Example: if the company you work for transports or stores hazardous waste, your company might get audited by your state's Environmental Department.

If an operational audit comes along, your responsibility will be to answer whatever questions come your way, as the bookkeeper, honestly and to the best of your ability. Since they are not looking at the books, the questions will probably be along the lines of what you know about this other aspect or department of the company. For instance, a company I worked for was audited regarding the moving and storage of hazardous materials. The questions I was asked were concerning manifests, which are the paperwork required when moving hazardous material.

An Audit of the Books

The same goes for an audit of the books, as for an operational audit, in terms of answering whatever questions honestly and to the best of your ability. It really doesn't matter from where an audit comes, or may come, as long as you do your best to keep the books clean, and comply with the audit. The best way to keep the books clean is to do things the way they're supposed to be done. For example, file payroll tax reports on time and have/save adequate records or a "paper trail", showing that things were done correctly (copies of payroll tax reports).

Defined: a *paper trail* is the records showing how things were done or that they were done correctly (example: copies of payroll tax reports).

If a CPA firm does audit your company's books, either for the company owner or a bank loan, the audit can be comprehensive. The typical goals of an audit are:
1. *Providing reasonable assurance* - that your financial statements are "presented fairly" (defined below).
2. *Regarding fraud* - observing if anything funny has been going on with the books (eg. any findings of fraud).

Defined: *presented fairly* refers to financial statements - saying that they are free from "material" error.

Defined: *material* is another way of saying "relevant". And what is relevant is what would change a decision-maker's mind - when looking at financial statements.

I wouldn't be overly concerned with the company owner calling for too many audits. They are quite expensive and therefore rarely used for private or smaller companies. It doesn't really matter from where an audit comes, as long as you do your best to keep the books clean, maintain an adequate paper trail and comply with the audit.

Being Prepared for Audits

As mentioned above, there are several things you can do to help your department be prepared for an audit. First, be sure to do things they way they're supposed to be done. Second, and of paramount importance, have an adequate paper trail to display/prove that it was done correctly - like copies of payroll tax reports, and receipt/s for the day you filed them. Realize that this also includes noting important phone calls on documents - listing the person you spoke with and the date, for instance.

Audit Guides

Finally, as mentioned in Chapter 8 - Industries, a potentially useful resource is available from the IRS - "Audit Technique Guides". These are the actual guides IRS auditors use for specific industries, like retail and construction. They are available at http://www.irs.gov/Businesses/Small-Businesses-&-Self-Employed/Audit-Techniques-Guides-ATGs. These may help you know what an IRS auditor might be looking for - in order to be more prepared.

Note: now that you have completed this book, consider taking it to the next level - Certification. See this book's Preface > Certification, or visit: http://www.full-chargebookkeeping.com/Certification.html.

Appendices - Introduction

For more than one reason, we have posted a printable "pdf" copy of the appendices listed below, on our website @: http://www.full-chargebookkeeping.com/ > Resources & Links page. The first reason is in case you purchased this book as an e-book. For obvious reasons - charts, forms, schedules and financial statements do not translate well on ebook readers. The second reason, particularly for the Forms - is in case you'd like to use them, without having to photocopy them from this book (a pdf copy will expedite that process)!

The following Appendices are posted on our websites:
- Appendix A - Master Schedule
- Appendix B - Chart of Accounts (Sample)
- Appendix C - Financial Statement (Samples): Income Statement and Balance Sheet
- Appendix E - Sample Forms

There should be no other issue with the other appendices. The other Appendices: D - Accounting 'Basics'; Appendix F - A Word About Career Advancement; G - Career Resource Binder Kept At Home & H - Resources & Bibliography are either written in paragraph format or a simple list.//

Appendix A - **Master Calendar (Schedule)**

Note: *the actual schedule* - is on the next page.

Introduction

Q: What is a Master Calendar (Schedule)?
A: A Master Calendar (Schedule) is a monthly listing of all the full-charge bookkeeping tasks that need to be completed by certain deadlines - like: payroll tax reports, and quarterly estimated tax payments.

Q: Why do I need it?
A: It will help ensure you don't miss a deadline or important task.

Q: How do I use it?
A: Use it by taking the following steps.

1. *Determine your state's specific tax requirements* - including deadlines for filing all reports. See Appendix H - Resources, for how to determine your state's requirements.
2. *Make a photocopy* - of this book's master schedule and fill in your state's requirements. I've left blank lines.
3. *Obtain a desk calendar* - with enough room to write tasks on it.
4. *At the beginning of each year or month* - pull your newly-created Master Schedule and fill in your tasks or deadlines for the year or month - onto your desk calendar.

You may notice, I put an underscore line before each numbered task. This provides a line on which to put a checkmark once the item is listed on your calendar or completed. You have explicit permission to photocopy and use the Master Schedule, below.

Appendix A - Master Calendar (Schedule) (continued)

How to Use   Fill in your state's requirements on the blank lines, below. Use this Master Schedule to fill in your desk calendar.

Jan. 1st:
- __ 1) Load new year's tax tables, before first payroll (eg. obtain from QuickBooks, Sage 50…).
- __ 2) Do Form 941* - Quarterly (Due Date: Postmarked by January 31st).
- __ 3) Calculate / Deposit Fourth Quarter Federal Unemployment Tax (FUTA) (Due Date: Jan. 31st).
- __ 4) Do Form 940 FUTA Annual Report (Due Date: Postmarked by January 31st).
- __ 5) Do Forms W-2's* & any 1099's (Due Date: Postmarked by January 31st).
- __ 6) Record Retention: start new files for the new year, and store last year's files.
- __ 7) Gather year-end reports for corporate taxes (you'll be contacting the CPA in early February).
- __ 8) Print and save IRS changes to corporate tax law (Reference: IRS Publication 15 > "What's New").

_____

*Note: *Form 941 & W-2's* - reconcile the 4 quarterly Form 941's to the W-2 totals before mailing.

Feb. 1st:
- __ 1) Contact the CPA to find out what s/he needs to do the corporate income tax return(s).
- __ 2) Mail Forms W-3 and 1096 - the Transmittal of the W-2's and 1099's (Due Date: February 28th).

Mar. 1st: _____

Apr. 1st:
- __ 1) Do Form 941 - Quarterly (Due Date: Postmarked by April 30th).
- __ 2) Calculate / Deposit Quarterly Federal Unemployment Tax (FUTA) (Due Date: April 30th).
- __ 3) Contact the CPA to make the Quarterly Estimated Income Tax Payment (Due Date: April 15th).

May 1st: _____

Jun. 1st:
- __ 1) Contact the CPA to make the Quarterly Estimated Income Tax Payment (Due Date: June 15th).

Jul. 1st:
- __ 1) Do Form 941 - Quarterly (Due Date: Postmarked by July 31st).
- __ 2) Calculate / Deposit Quarterly Federal Unemployment Tax (FUTA) (Due Date: July 31st).

Aug. 1st: _____

Sep. 1st:
- __ 1) Contact the CPA to make the Quarterly Estimated Tax Payment (Due Date: September 15th).

Oct. 1st:
- __ 1) Do Form 941 - Quarterly (Due Date: Postmarked by October 31st).
- __ 2) Calculate / Deposit Quarterly Federal Unemployment Tax (FUTA) (Due Date: October 31st).

Nov. 1st:
- __ 1) Order W-2 Forms, and Tax Tables for next year (eg. obtain from QuickBooks or Sage 50…).

Dec. 1st:
- __ 1) Contact the CPA to make the Quarterly Estimated Tax Payment (Due Date: December 15th).

_____

Every Month
- __ 1) *Pay-period ending date* - collect timecards & distribute new timecards.
- __ 2) *Payroll calculation day* - prepare paychecks.
- __ 3) *Pay day* - distribute paychecks.
   Note: all three payroll tasks may or may not happen on the same day/s.
- __ 4) *Payroll taxes* - calculate / deposit liabilities, which are typically due after payroll.
- __ 5) *Bank reconciliation/s* - do within 3 business days of arriving in the mail.
- __ 6) *Petty cash* - do previous month's petty cash (if any), within the first 3 business days of the month.
- __ 7) *Monthly reports* - finish entering data and print financial statements / monthly reports.

References

Task(s) Above	Refer to Chapter
Forms 940 & 941, Calculate / Deposit FUTA……………….	Chapter 2 - Tasks > Payroll Taxes
Forms W-2, 1099, W-3 & 1096, Record Retention………….	Chapter 2 - Tasks > Year-End Items
Contact CPA Regarding Estimated Tax Payments……..…...	Chapter 2 - Tasks > Corporate Taxes

Appendix B - **Chart of Accounts (Sample)**

Introduction
Q: What is a Chart of Accounts, and why do I need it?
A: The chart of accounts lists every account in the general ledger. Every debit and credit gets posted to an account, from the chart of accounts. So, whenever you need to post a journal entry into the computer, you will pull out the chart of accounts, to determine which account(s) to debit and which account(s) to credit.

Below is a sample chart of accounts. Feel free to use this chart, or alter it depending upon your needs. Both Sage 50 Accounting and QuickBooks Pro allow for accounts to be added or altered. For example, if your company decides to add a Point-of-Sale system, you *should* add an account to the chart, to keep track of how much is spent!

1000 - ASSETS
1001 CURRENT ASSETS
1010 Cash in Bank Account XYZ
1030 Petty Cash
1050 Accounts Receivable
1060 Due from Employee Advance
1100 Inventory - Raw Materials Item #1   Reference: Glossary - for definitions.
1110 Inventory - Raw Materials Item #2
1120 Inventory - Work in Process Item #1
1130 Inventory - Work in Process Item #2
1140 Inventory - Finished Goods / Merchandise Item #1
1150 Inventory - Finished Goods / Merchandise Item #2
1160 Inventory - Finished Goods / Merchandise Item #3

1500 FIXED ASSETS
1510 Land
1520 Building
1530 Accumulated Depreciation - Building
1540 Vehicle #1
1550 Accumulated Depreciation - Vehicle #1
1560 Office Furniture
1570 Equipment

2000 - LIABILITIES
2001 CURRENT LIABILITIES
2010 Accounts Payable
2020 Line of Credit
2030 Federal Income Tax Withheld Payable
2040 FICA Payable - Employee
2050 FICA Payable - Employer
2060 FUTA Payable
2070 State Income Tax Withheld Payable
2080 SUTA Payable
2090 State Sales Taxes Payable
2100 Corporate Taxes Payable - Federal
2110 Corporate Taxes Payable - State
2120 Property Taxes Payable

2500 LONG-TERM LIABILITIES
2510 Note Payable

3000 - OWNER'S EQUITY
3010 Capital Stock

Appendix B - Chart of Accounts (continued)

3020 Additional Paid-In Capital
3030 Retained Earnings
3040 Draw - Owner (Dividends Paid)   Reference: Appendix D - Accounting Basics > "Draws" Taken by the Owner.

4000 - REVENUE
4010 Sales – Product/Service #1
4020 Sales – Product/Service #2
4100 Sales Returns
4110 Sales Discounts
4120 Other Income / Gains

5000 - EXPENSES
5010 Cost of Goods Sold
5030 Accounting Expense
5040 Advertising Expense
5050 Automobile Expense
5060 Bad Debt Expense
5070 Bank Service Charge
5080 Charitable Contributions   See Glossary (Differs From "Gifts Expense").
5090 Commissions
5100 Computer Expense
5110 Contract Labor
5120 Depreciation Expense
5130 Dues & Subscriptions
5140 Freight Expense
5150 Gifts Expense   See Glossary (Differs From "Charitable Contributions" Expense).
5160 Insurance - Health (Medical & Dental)
5170 Insurance - Corporate Liability
5180 Insurance - Worker's Compensation
5190 Interest Expense
5200 Legal Expense
5210 Maintenance & Repairs Expense
5220 Meals & Entertainment Expense
5230 Office Supplies Expense
5240 Postage
5250 Rent Expense
5260 Salaries & Wage Expense
5270 Shipping Supplies Expense
5280 Tax Expense, Corporate - Federal
5290 Tax Expense, Corporate - State
5300 Tax Expense, FICA
5310 Tax Expense, FUTA
5320 Tax Expense, SUTA
5330 Tax Expense, Property
5340 Tax Expense, Sales
5350 Travel Expense
5360 Utility Expense - Electric
5370 Utility Expense - Garbage Collection
5380 Utility Expense - Gas
5390 Utility Expense - Sewer
5400 Utility Expense - Telephone (Cell)
5410 Utility Expense - Telephone (Regular)
5420 Utility Expense - Water
5430 Other Expenses / Losses

Appendix C - **Financial Statement (Samples)**

Note: the *actual* financial statements are on the next two pages.

Introduction

The most common financial statements are the Income Statement (aka: Profit & Loss), and the Balance Sheet. The company owner will probably be more interested in the income statement, because it will tell him or her whether the company is operating profitably or not.

> Defined: an *Income Statement* subtracts expenses from revenues to give how much income you had for the period (month or year). It is one of the two main financial statements - the other is the Balance Sheet.

> Defined: a *Balance Sheet* lists assets, liabilities, and owner's equity, as of the last day in the period. It is one of two main financial statements - the other is the Income Statement.

Fear not, sample financial statements are provided here to give you the basic formats. And any good bookkeeping program, including Sage 50 & QuickBooks, not only has standard financial statements to printout, but will allow you to tailor your financial statements to suit your company's needs. For instance, your company may not use all of the particular "Operating Expense" categories listed in the sample Income Statement. Rather than have it print a zero amount each time, just eliminate that line item from your financial statement, by deactivating that account via maintaining the chart of accounts. Finally, you will need to be sure all relevant information is entered, before printing financial statements. Reference: Chapter 2 - Tasks > Financial Statements.

> Defined: *Operating Expenses* are found on the Income Statement, just below "Gross Profit". Examples of Operating Expenses include: "Advertising" and "Utilities" Expenses.

> Defined: *Gross Profit* is equal to Net Sales (Sales – Returns – Discounts) minus Cost of Goods Sold (ref: Appendix D - Accounting Basics > Inventory & Cost of Goods Sold).

Appendix C - Financial Statements (continued)

ABC Corporation
Income Statement (a.k.a. Profit & Loss)
For the year ending December 31, 20xx

Gross Sales..		$$
Less: Sales Returns..........................	<$$>	
Less: Sales Discounts......................	<$$>	
Net Sales..		$$
Cost of Goods Sold............................		<$$> Ref: Appendix D - Accounting Basics > Inventory & Cost of
Gross Profit...		$$ Goods Sold
Operating Expenses		
Accounting Expense..........	$$	
Advertising Expense..........	$$	
Automobile Expense..........	$$	
Bad Debt Expense..............	$$	
Commissions......................	$$	
Computer Expense.............	$$	
Depreciation Expense........	$$	
Dues & Subscriptions.........	$$	
Freight Expense..................	$$	
Insurance Expense..............	$$	
Interest Expense................	$$	
Legal Expense....................	$$	
Maintenance & Repairs......	$$	
Meals & Entertainment......	$$	
Payroll Tax Expense..........	$$	
Postage...............................	$$	
Rent Expense.....................	$$	
Salaries / Wage Expense...	$$	
Shipping Expense..............	$$	
Travel Expense..................	$$	
Utilities Expense...............	$$	
Total Operating Expenses.............................		<$$>
Operating Income..		$$
Other Income / Gains		
Gain on [list item(s)].......................		$$
Other Expenses / Losses		
Loss on [list item(s)]......................		<$$>
Income before Taxes.....................................		$$
Income Tax...		<$$>
Net Income..		**$$**

Notes: 1. *Two columns* - it is a normal convention on financial statements to have two columns, like above. The outside column for totals, and the inside column for amounts that make up the totals.
           2. *Chart of Accounts vs. Income Statement* - all of the Utility Expenses listed in the Chart of Accounts can be aggregated to arrive at one Utilities Expense for the Income Statement. Reference: Appendix D - Accounting Basics > Relationship Between Financial Statements and the Chart of Accounts.

Appendix C - Financial Statements (continued)

ABC Corporation
Balance Sheet
As of December 31, 20xx

Assets
    Current Assets   See Note #4 below for definition of "current"

	Cash..	$$	
	Accounts Receivable.....................	$$	
	Inventory......................................	<u>$$</u>	
Total Current Assets..		$$	
Property, Plant & Equipment			Note: specific items need *not* be listed - just totals for each category.
	Land..	$$	
	Buildings.......................................	$$	
	Vehicles...	$$	
	Office Equipment..........................	$$	
	Less Accumulated Depreciation.....	<u><$$></u>	Ref: Appendix D - Accounting Basics > Depreciating Assets.
Net Property, Plant & Equipment.......................		<u>$$</u>	
Total Assets...		**<u>$A</u>**	

Liabilities
    Current Liabilities   See Note #4 below for definition of "current"

	Accounts Payable...........................	$$	
	Payroll Taxes Payable....................	<u>$$</u>	
Total Current Liabilities......................................		$$	
Non-Current Liabilities			
	Note payable..................................	<u>$$</u>	
Total Non-Current Liabilities..............................		<u>$$</u>	
Total Liabilities..		$$	

Owner's Equity   See Glossary for definitions.

	Capital Stock.................................	$$	
	Additional Paid-in Capital.............	$$	
	Retained Earnings..........................	<u>$$</u>	
Total Owner's Equity...................................		<u>$$</u>	
Total Liabilities & Owner's Equity.............................		**<u>$A</u>**	

Notes:
1. *Two columns* - it is a normal convention on financial statements to have two columns, like above. The outside column for totals, and the inside column for amounts that make up the totals.
2. *Totals* - notice that the **<u>$A</u>** total for "Assets" above is equal to the **<u>$A</u>** total for "Liabilities & Owner's Equity", which follows the basic accounting equation Assets = Liabilities + Owner's Equity. Reference: Appendix D - Accounting Basics > Accounting Equations.
3. *Chart of Accounts* - the "Cash" account listed above is the total of all your bank accounts, as of the balance sheet date. Reference: Appendix D - Accounting Basics > Relationship Between Financial Statements and the Chart of Accounts.
4. *"Current" (Assets & Liabilities)* - is referring to cash or anything that can be generally converted to cash in less than one year. Therefore non-current or "long term" is greater than one year.

Appendix D - **Accounting 'Basics'**

Introduction

This appendix is not meant to be a substitute for a beginning course in accounting, but does cover these topics in a fair amount of depth. For those interested in studying these and other topics in greater detail, I suggest either taking an accounting course or studying an accounting textbook. I know this appendix can be a bit "heavy", so don't be too concerned if you have trouble taking it all in at one time. I suggest studying one topic at a time and reviewing that topic.

Here is the list of basics I discuss below:
1. Accounting Equations
2. Accounting Methods
3. Closing A Year
4. "Depreciating" Assets
5. "Draws" Taken by the Owner
6. Inventory and "Cost of Goods Sold"
7. Office Supplies (Expense?)
8. Relationship Between Financial Statements and the Chart of Accounts
9. "Retained Earnings"
10. "Writing-Off" A Receivable

Note: *new terminology* - above is defined below, in their respective sections.

Basics
1. ACCOUNTING EQUATIONS
   a. Assets - Liabilities = Equity (of the Owner) *or*
      Assets = Liabilities + Owner's Equity (aka: the "Basic Accounting Equation").
   b. Revenues - Expenses = Net Income

2. ACCOUNTING METHODS
   There are only two accounting methods - cash method, and accrual method.

   Defined: *cash method accounting* is when revenues and expenses are only recognized when cash is received or paid. Unpaid bills and unpaid sales are not recognized, until paid.

   Defined: *accrual method accounting* is when revenues and expenses are posted when bills are sent or received (incurred) regardless of when they are actually paid. Most companies use this method.

3. CLOSING A YEAR
   While your computer bookkeeping program is performing the necessary functions in order to properly close out a year, I think you should be aware of what takes place behind the scenes.

   Balance Sheet
   A balance sheet is simple. If you look at the title block at the top of the Balance Sheet in Appendix C, you'll see "As Of December 31, 20xx". The balance sheet is like a "snap shot" in time of the balances in those accounts. On this last day of the calendar year, these accounts had these balances. And, by the way, the January 1st - next year's beginning balance is by definition equal to the ending balance from the day before 12/31.

   Income Statement
   If you look at the title block of the Income Statement in Appendix C, you'll see the words "For the Year Ending December 31, 20xx". So, where a Balance Sheet is a snap shot of accounts on one particular day, the Income Statement reflects what's happened over a period of time (in the case of Appendix C, a year – income for the year, and expenses for the year).

Appendix D - Accounting Basics (continued)

3. CLOSING A YEAR (cont.)

"Zeroing Out"

Since the Income Statement reflects accounts for a certain period of time, it stands to reason that you would have to start from zero, at the beginning of the period - in order to have an accurate count for that period for those accounts. Therefore, while Balance Sheet accounts just keep going, Income Statement accounts get zeroed-out at the end of a period. In computer bookkeeping programs, this will happen behind the scenes.

Tie-In Between Income Statement And Balance Sheet

Finally, you should be aware that the Net Income for a period gets transferred over to the Balance Sheet's "Retained Earnings" account. Remember how all the Income Statement accounts get "zeroed out" - in order to start with zero for the next period? Well, Net Income is no exception, but we want to keep a running total of Net Income via the Balance Sheet. So, Net Income gets closed or zeroed out to the Retained Earnings account under "Equity" on the Balance Sheet.

4. "DEPRECIATING" ASSETS

Defined: to *depreciate* something is to treat it as an asset, being "used up" over time.

A bookkeeper's involvement with depreciation should be limited to two things. First, as mentioned in Tasks > Fixed Asset Purchases, you need to keep a list of fixed assets that are purchased each year in a "Fixed Assets" file folder. Attach to each year's list, a copy of each asset's receipt - showing the cost and date of purchase. At year-end you'll be giving a copy of your list to the company's CPA. In return, the CPA will be providing you with that year's journal entry for depreciation. The second thing you'll need to do is enter that journal entry into your computer bookkeeping program as of 12/31/xx – for the year you introduced those assets into service. In addition, I'd like you to have a basic understanding of depreciation, so I outline it below.

Note: *debits and credits* - recording depreciation expense involves debits and credits, so be sure to study Chapter 5 - Debits and Credits, before proceeding here.

Defined: *depreciation expense* is the expense associated with using-up an asset, during its "useful life".

Defined: *useful life* is how long an asset can be expected to produce, or be able to be used.

Note: *useful lives* - are determined by the IRS for different types of assets (like vehicles, or office equipment). Your company's CPA will, generally, be sorting out the different types and determining the assets' useful lives. [You can also reference IRS Instructions to Form 4562, "Depreciation", >"Classification of Property".]

Defined: a*ccumulated depreciation* is the 'offset' to Depreciation Expense, in all depreciation journal entries. Accumulated Depreciation is a Balance Sheet account - representing all of the depreciation expense taken against the asset, over all of its years. Accumulated Depreciation is what's called a "contra-asset" account.

Defined: *offset* is either the debit or the credit that makes the journal entry balance.

Defined: a *contra-asset (account)* is actually on the Balance Sheet but subtracts from (hence 'contra') the assets. It has a normal credit balance - instead of the normal debit balance for assets. Accumulated Depreciation is an example of a contra-asset account. See journal entry below.

Example: you purchase a vehicle for $10,000. It has a useful life of 10 years. Each year you depreciate it $1000 (10,000 / 10). After three years, Accumulated Depreciation = $3000 ($1000/yr. x 3 years).

Journal Entry (Each Year)

[Debit]	Depreciation Expense	$1000		=>*Increasing* an *expense*
[Credit]	Accumulated Depreciation - Vehicle		$1000	=>*Increasing* an *contra-asset*

Appendix D - Accounting Basics (continued)

4. DEPRECIATING ASSETS (cont.)
After 3 years, Accumulated Depreciation = $3000 and the "Book Value" = $7000 ($10,000 - $3000).

Defined: *book value* equals the original cost of an asset minus accumulated depreciation.

Book Value of An Asset
Asset (original cost of asset)	$10,000
<Accumulated Depreciation>	<$ 3,000>
Book Value of Asset (at that point in time)	$ 7,000

Notes: 1. *Convention* - on the balance sheet, the asset is *always* listed at its *original cost*. In the example above, $10,000 - no matter what year you are reporting (until it's removed from the books).
2. *Accumulated Depreciation* - is always listed below the asset's original cost (book value is not listed on the balance sheet).
3. *"Fully written-off"* - Accumulated Depreciation will increase until it eventually equals the original cost. At that point, the "book value" of the asset will equal zero and the asset is officially removed from the books (this is known as fully written-off).

Finally, Depreciation Expense (on the Income Statement) is not broken down per each asset, but listed as a total amount for the year. The CPA should give you the amount to record as Depreciation Expense, for each year, and how that breaks down for each asset's Accumulated Depreciation.

5. "DRAWS" TAKEN BY THE OWNER
Defined: a *draw* is a removal of cash from the business, beyond the owner's salary (aka: a dividend).

Note: *debits and credits* - recording "Draws Taken By The Owner" involves debits and credits, so be sure to study Chapter 5 - Debits and Credits, before proceeding here.

Example: say the owner gets paid $750 per week, from which you deduct the normal payroll taxes. One week, the owner decides to take an additional $500 out of the business. That $500 is considered a draw from the "equity" (defined below) left in the business. You will write a check to the owner for $500. Note: no taxes are taken out at this point and the journal entry for that is:

[Debit]	Draw - Owner	$500		=>*Increasing* a *contra-equity account*
[Credit]	Cash		$500	=>*Decreasing* an *asset*

Defined: a *contra-equity (account)* is a Balance Sheet account that subtracts from the Equity section. It has a normal debit balance (instead of the normal credit balance for Owner's Equity). "Draw - Owner" is an example of a contra-equity account.

Defined: *equity (aka: "owner's equity")* equals assets minus liabilities. Equity is found on the Balance Sheet, and is a measure of any "extra" an owner has in the business.

At the end of the year, you will print out all of the draws the owner has taken, for the year, in order for the owner to include it in his or her personal income taxes.

6. INVENTORY AND "COST OF GOODS SOLD"
Defined: *inventory* is the stock of "finished goods" on hand, to sell to customers. In a manufacturing company inventory can also include: "raw materials" and "work in process".

Defined: *Cost of Goods Sold* (COGS) is referring to the goods that your company sold customers. What did they cost your company (to either make or buy)?

Appendix D - Accounting Basics (continued)

6. INVENTORY AND COST OF GOODS SOLD (cont.)

Note: *debits and credits* - recording inventory and COGS involves debits and credits, so be sure to study Chapter 5 - Debits and Credits, before proceeding here.

Note: as mentioned in the Industries chapter, calculating COGS will involve direct materials, direct labor and some portion of overhead. It is much more likely a FCB will be working in more of a retail environment (versus a manufacturing one doing costing analysis). So, we will focus on calculating COGS relating to the retail industry.

Typically, retail companies count their inventory once per year. But, for expensive items like automobiles you will see companies counting these items every month, and use what's called "specific identification" (defined below) to keep track of that inventory.

Defined: *specific identification* means that each inventory item (like an automobile at a car dealership) is identified with a unique number (eg. Vehicle Identification Number).

Q: Why do we care about Cost of Goods Sold?
A: If you look closely at an Income Statement, you will notice that right after Sales is Cost of Goods Sold. This is a way to differentiate between the *cost* of product sold versus the other operating expenses. And, from the second Journal Entry below, you can see that COGS is the 'offset' (see Glossary) to inventory - when it's sold.

Since companies you will be working for are relatively small in size, I will be showing you what's known as a "perpetual inventory system" (defined below).

Defined: a *perpetual inventory system* is a way of keeping track of inventory levels by updating the Inventory account after every sale.

Journal Entry When Buying Inventory
[Debit]	Inventory	$$		=>*Increasing* an *asset*
[Credit]	Cash or A/P		$$	=>*Decreasing* an *asset*

Journal Entries When Selling Product (Inventory)
[Debit]	Cash or A/R	$10		=>*Increasing* an *asset*
[Credit]	Sales		$10	=>*Increasing* a *revenue*
[Debit]	Cost of Goods Sold	$5		=>*Increasing* an *expense*
[Credit]	Inventory		$5	=>*Decreasing* an *asset*

Notes: 1. *Journal Entries for Selling* - when selling product, the first journal entry above (Cash or AR / Sales) will be using the Sales price (less any sales tax payable). On the contrary, the second entry (COGS / Inventory) will be made for the Cost of the Inventory (not the sales price). It may seem weird, but if you think about it, it's how you end up with Net Income (when Revenue > Expenses).
2. *Manufacturing Company* - the above Journal Entries are for a Merchandising / Retail store. The journal entries for a Manufacturing Company are quite a bit more involved and beyond the scope of this text. Please refer to a Basic or Intermediate Accounting text for those entries. Reference: Appendix H - Resources & Bibliography.

At Year End

Typically, companies take a physical inventory count only at year-end. Theoretically, the inventory on the books (what you've been adjusting with each sale and purchase) should equal the *physical inventory count* and *extended cost* (defined below).

Appendix D - Accounting Basics (continued)

6. INVENTORY AND COST OF GOODS SOLD (cont.)

Defined: a *physical inventory count* is what product you actually find and count on the shelves of the store.

Defined: the *extended cost* equals the actual number of units counted on the shelves multiplied by the *cost* of each unit.

Note: the *cost of each unit* can vary depending on price increases, etc. For the purposes of this text we will assume a uniform cost. There are several methods of handling varying costs for the same product. Please refer to a Basic or Intermediate Accounting text for that.

When Actual And Book Inventory Values Differ
As mentioned above, in theory your inventory dollars on the books should match what inventory there is on the shelves. In practice, these two values rarely match exactly. Things get miscounted, misplaced or worse - stolen. There are several things a bookkeeper can do here, namely: be sure the books are set-up properly, have independent recounts, and finally write-down (or in rare instances, up) the inventory.

Be Sure Your Books Are Set-Up Properly
You, as the bookkeeper, should be sure the Inventory accounts (how many different ones you maintain) are in order. In other words, you will want to have not too few and not too many - for the product that your store sells. First, you should be sure to track all the major categories of Inventory in separate accounts, within the Chart of Accounts. Beyond that, the way to measure if you have too many is by the cost of tracking versus the benefit of tracking each individual account.

Independent Recount
Second, if amounts are significantly different between the books and actual for one or more items, be sure to recount those item/s. And, you should endeavor to use different personnel for the second count - than were used for the first count. If the second and first counts match, that is what your book inventory value should be adjusted to. If your first and second counts don't match, you will need a third count - probably taken by supervisor or management level personnel.

Adjust Books to Match Actual
Finally, after you've obtained counts that you're comfortable with, you will need to adjust the books to match the actual. This will involve writing up or most likely writing down those Inventory account(s) with an offset to a Loss or Gain account.

[Debit]	Other Expense / Loss	$$		=>*Increasing* an *expense*
[Credit]	Inventory		$$	=>*Decreasing* an *asset*
[Debit]	Inventory	$$		=>*Increasing* an *asset*
[Credit]	Other Income/Gain		$$	=>*Increasing* an *revenue*

Note: *inventory losses* - for any "Loss" that is greater than acceptable, you will want to consider, with the company owner, what safeguards that should be taken! Reference: Chapter 10 - Bookkeeper As Management?

If You Can't Maintain Inventory Levels Throughout A Month
If, for some reason, it's not cost effective for you to update the Inventory accounts after every sale, you will need to know how to estimate COGS - in order to produce monthly Financial Statements. Fear not, there are two ways to estimate cost of goods sold: (1) via purchases of inventory, and (2) as a percentage of sales, outlined below.

(1) Estimating Cost of Goods Sold as a Percentage of Sales:
The idea here is that, over the years, Cost of Goods Sold has proven to be a certain *percentage* of sales. Therefore, COGS could be estimated, using the same percentage, multiplied by sales - for the current month.

Example: say, during the first ten years of business, COGS was calculated to be 45% of Sales.
If sales, in the current month, were $100,000 then COGS could be reasonably estimated at: 45% x $100,000, or 0.45 x 100,000 = $45,000.

Appendix D - Accounting Basics (continued)

6. INVENTORY AND COST OF GOODS SOLD (cont.)

If you use this percentage of sales method, be sure to tweak your percentage each year, after you take a physical inventory and determine the exact percentage. Tweak it annually by calculating the *actual* COGS percent of sales for the current year, and then averaging your COGS percentage over all years.

(2) *Estimating Cost of Goods Sold Via Purchases*:

I worked for a retail company that used this concept. The idea here is, to figure that Beginning and Ending Inventory levels are maintained to be the same, throughout a month. This is a reasonable assumption - if the product is kept on the same shelf and replenished on a timely basis. Then using the formula below, COGS is approximated by purchases of Inventory.

	Example (Note: this is the "Cost of Goods Sold Formula")		For Instance
	Beginning Inventory	$120,000	January 1, 2001
+	**Purchases of Inventory**	+ 70,000	During January
=	Goods Available for Sale	$190,000	During January
-	Ending Inventory	- 120,000	January 31, 2001
=	**Cost of Goods Sold**	= $ 70,000	During January

Since purchases of inventory throughout the month can be easily tracked, you can see how this approach works. Note: "Beginning Inventory" is really simple. It's simply equal to Ending Inventory of the previous period. For example, Beginning Inventory for January 1, *2001* is equal to Ending Inventory for December 31st, *2000*.

A Mixed Approach

A popular method of dealing with inventory & Cost of Goods Sold is what I'll call a mixed approach. Depending on your company's products, you could count just the largest items every *month* (eg. sewing machines) and use a formula to calculate or estimate the cost of goods sold for the rest of the inventory (needles & thread). This will enable you to generate more accurate monthly financial statements, with minimal effort regarding inventory.

Note: *service industries* - the above "Cost of Goods Sold" obviously applies to the sale of product not the sale of services. In a service industry, they track not COGS, but what's called "Cost of Sales" (COS). For example, an architect's salary or work related paid hours would be an Architect firm's COS.

7. OFFICE SUPPLIES (EXPENSE?)

Q: Are you saying we treat office supplies like an expense? They seem like an asset.
A: Yes, we should treat office supplies as an expense, not an asset, and the example below will tell why.

Example: you buy a waste paper basket. It seems like an asset, but assets are normally depreciated over their useful lives. Well, it would *not* be cost effective or efficient to "capitalize", and then depreciate a $20 waste paper basket. So we expense it in the current period (or year).

Defined: to *capitalize* is to treat as an asset and then depreciate it, as opposed to treating it as an expense.

Only large ticket items - furniture, fixtures, heavy equipment, vehicles, buildings, do we capitalize or treat as an asset and then depreciate. All else (office supplies, shipping supplies) expense in the current period - month or year.

8. RELATIONSHIP BETWEEN FINANCIAL STATEMENTS AND THE CHART OF ACCOUNTS

You may or may not have noticed the following relationship between the Chart of Accounts and Financial Statements. The chart of accounts either transfers directly, line item for line item, or aggregates into the line items of the financial statements. For instance, an expense such as advertising would transfer directly from the chart to a line item on the income statement. But all the utility expenses, in the chart (gas, electric, water..) may be summed into *one* utilities expense on the Income Statement.

Appendix D - Accounting Basics (continued)

8. RELATIONSHIP BETWEEN FINANCIAL STATEMENTS AND THE CHART OF ACCOUNTS (cont.)

Other accounts that typically aggregate include cash and insurance. All the separate bank accounts in the chart aggregate, or sum, to give one line item, cash, on the balance sheet. There may be other accounts, and this can be a gray area that you and your boss work out as you see fit. Where the broad categories on the Financial Statements, such as Assets, Property, Plant and Equipment, and Cost of Goods Sold should not be played with, there is some room or gray within the Operating Expenses category. Reference: Appendix B - Chart of Accounts, and Appendix C - Financial Statements.

9. "RETAINED EARNINGS"
Defined: *retained earnings* are earnings, or net income, that have been retained in the company and not distributed to the owners.

There is an equation to describe how Retained Earnings (RE) work:
  Beginning Retained Earnings (RE at the beginning of the year)
  + Net Income (calculated via the Income Statement)
  - Dividends (aka: Draws taken by the owner)
  = Ending Retained Earnings (RE at the end of the year).

Notes: 1. *The first year you're in business* - you will have no beginning retained earnings.
2. *Ending RE* - by definition, your Ending RE of one year becomes your Beginning RE of the next year.

10. "WRITING OFF" A RECEIVABLE
Defined: *writing* it *off* means taking a receivable off the books.

Note: *debits and credits* - writing of a receivable involves debits and credits, so be sure to study Chapter 5 - Debits and Credits, before proceeding here.

When an accounts receivable (A/R) becomes uncollectible (for example, your customer goes out of business) then you will need to 'write-off' the receivable. This is done with a journal entry, as in the example below.

Example: say Joe Default Company owes your company $150, but files for bankruptcy, and notifies you that they won't be able to pay your company the money they owe. After any and all (legal) proceedings, you are unable to collect. So, you must remove Joe Default Company from your Accounts Receivable, as follows:

[Debit]   Bad Debt Expense $150   =>*Increasing* an *expense*
[Credit]   A/R - Joe Default Company $150   =>*Decreasing* an *asset*

If you subsequently collect from Joe Default Company, you must first reverse the above journal entry, reinstating the receivable:

[Debit]   A/R - Joe Default Company $100   =>*Increasing* an *asset*
[Credit]   Bad Debt Expense $100   =>*Decreasing* an *expense*

Then show the collection of it:
[Debit]   Cash $100   =>*Increasing* an *asset*
[Credit]   A/R - Joe Default Company $100   =>*Decreasing* an *asset*

Appendix E - **Sample Forms**

Introduction

      For two reasons, we have posted a printable "pdf" version of these Sample Forms on our website @: http://www.full-chargebookkeeping.com/ > Resources & Links page. The first reason is in case you purchased this book as an e-book. For obvious reasons, forms do not translate well on ebook readers. The second reason is in case you'd like to use them without having to photocopy them from this book (a pdf copy will expedite that process)!

      Bookkeepers will often find that forms make their life easier. I've included in this section the typical forms that bookkeepers use. I created these forms using either a spreadsheet program or word processing program. Feel free to use them, or create your own - to suit your / your company's needs. I did debate about including Human Resource (HR) forms here, particularly the "Employee Warning Notice".

      There are two reasons I've included HR forms here. First, in a small company, some of the human resource function may fall to the full-charge bookkeeper, and these forms will help you stay organized. And second, a bookkeeper needs to know that State Unemployment Tax (SUTA) rates are often based on unemployment claims - from your company's previous employees. And, documented reasons for dismissal (ie. HR - Employee Warning Notice) can help keep SUTA rates lower.

Note: *"Collection Form" versus "Past Due Notice"* - the Collection Form (below) would be used to place a phone call to any company that has past due amounts, while the Past Due Notice (also below) would be used for the same reason, but placed in the mail instead.

      Here is a way to organize your own forms.
1. *File folder* - keep them in a file folder entitled "Forms".
2. *Original* - put your original in a sheet-protector. You could trim off the 3-hole punch strip, or put a post-it note on it labeling it "Original".
3. *Copies* - paper clip copies in front of the original.
4. *Out of copies* - when you've used up all of your copies you will reach the original, and know it's time to make more copies.
5. *Alphabetical* - file your forms, alphabetically, by form title.

You have permission, at your own "risk", to photocopy and use all Appendix E - Sample Forms.

Collection Form

    Customer Name _____ Phone # _____
    Contact Person _____ Fax # _____
    Invoice #(s), Date(s) & Amount(s) _____

Date	Action Taken	Response	Follow-up Action	Follow-up Date
____	_____	_____	_____	_____
____	_____	_____	_____	_____
____	_____	_____	_____	_____
____	_____	_____	_____	_____
____	_____	_____	_____	_____

[Possible Actions: 1. Phone Call(s); 2. Past Due Notice; 3. Suspension of Service; 4. Legal Action]

- -

Collection Form

    Customer Name _____ Phone # _____
    Contact Person _____ Fax # _____
    Invoice #(s), Date(s) & Amount(s) _____

Date	Action Taken	Response	Follow-up Action	Follow-up Date
____	_____	_____	_____	_____
____	_____	_____	_____	_____
____	_____	_____	_____	_____
____	_____	_____	_____	_____
____	_____	_____	_____	_____

[Possible Actions: 1. Phone Call(s); 2. Past Due Notice; 3. Suspension of Service; 4. Legal Action]

- -

Collection Form

    Customer Name _____ Phone # _____
    Contact Person _____ Fax # _____
    Invoice #(s), Date(s) & Amount(s) _____

Date	Action Taken	Response	Follow-up Action	Follow-up Date
____	_____	_____	_____	_____
____	_____	_____	_____	_____
____	_____	_____	_____	_____
____	_____	_____	_____	_____
____	_____	_____	_____	_____

[Possible Actions: 1. Phone Call(s); 2. Past Due Notice; 3. Suspension of Service; 4. Legal Action]

Commission Spreadsheet Form

_____   Pay Period: ___/___/___ - ___/___/___
Employee Name (printed)   Beg. Date   End Date

Invoice #	Date	Sales $'s	x	Commission %	=	Commission $'s	Customer Name / Reference
_____	_____	_____	x	_____	=	_____	_____
_____	_____	_____	x	_____	=	_____	_____
_____	_____	_____	x	_____	=	_____	_____
_____	_____	_____	x	_____	=	_____	_____
_____	_____	_____	x	_____	=	_____	_____
_____	_____	_____	x	_____	=	_____	_____
_____	_____	_____	x	_____	=	_____	_____
_____	_____	_____	x	_____	=	_____	_____
_____	_____	_____	x	_____	=	_____	_____
_____	_____	_____	x	_____	=	_____	_____
_____	_____	_____	x	_____	=	_____	_____
_____	_____	_____	x	_____	=	_____	_____
_____	_____	_____	x	_____	=	_____	_____
_____	_____	_____	x	_____	=	_____	_____
_____	_____	_____	x	_____	=	_____	_____
_____	_____	_____	x	_____	=	_____	_____
_____	_____	_____	x	_____	=	_____	_____
_____	_____	_____	x	_____	=	_____	_____
_____	_____	_____	x	_____	=	_____	_____
_____	_____	_____	x	_____	=	_____	_____
_____	_____	_____	x	_____	=	_____	_____
_____	_____	_____	x	_____	=	_____	_____
_____	_____	_____	x	_____	=	_____	_____
_____	_____	_____	x	_____	=	_____	_____
_____	_____	_____	x	_____	=	_____	_____

Page Totals: _____ x _____ = _____
           Sales $'s   Commission %   **Commission $'s**
                        (if the same %)

_____   Paid: _____   _____
Preparer's Signature   Check #   Date

Fax Cover Sheet

(# of pages including cover sheet _____)
Date:_____

To:_____ **From:** _____

Company:_____ **Phone #:** (_____) _____-_____

Dept.:_____ **Fax #:** (_____) _____-_____

Fax #: (_____) _____-_____ **Email:** _____

Message:_____

_____

_____

_____

_____

_____

_____

_____

_____

_____

FUTA - SUTA Spreadsheet Design

Q: What is a FUTA - SUTA Spreadsheet, and why do I need it?
A: Every company, with paid employees, needs to file Federal Unemployment Taxes (FUTA). And, every state has its own unemployment compensation program, including State Unemployment Taxes (SUTA). So, a FUTA-SUTA spreadsheet is a way to calculate the amount of federal, and state unemployment taxes owed.

Introduction

I am not able to impart a working spreadsheet to you through the pages of this book, because a spreadsheet, by its very nature, contains formulas that do calculations. But, below is the type of spreadsheet - headings that you should create, in order to calculate unemployment taxes. Use a spreadsheet program such as Microsoft Excel. As mentioned in Chapter 2 - Tasks > Payroll Taxes, there is no Federal Unemployment Tax *report* to file each quarter, just payment of the tax. But, you will need to calculate how much tax you owe, and you may have a *state* report due each quarter (like in New Mexico).

Note: *State Unemployment Tax Agencies* - the U.S. Department of Labor maintains a list of State Unemployment Tax agencies here: http://www.workforcesecurity.doleta.gov/unemploy/agencies.asp.

How to Proceed

BE SURE TO DO ANY *STATE* UNEMPLOYMENT TAXES FIRST - BECAUSE *FEDERAL* UNEMPLOYMENT TAXES ARE REDUCED BASED ON THE AMOUNT OF STATE TAXES PAID.

The best way to proceed is with two spreadsheets - one for state and one for federal. First calculate and complete your state unemployment taxes using their instructions and your spreadsheet. Then calculate the quarterly Federal Unemployment Tax payment due, using IRS instructions and your federal spreadsheet. Reference: IRS Publication 15, > "Federal Unemployment (FUTA) Tax". Finally, if it's at year-end, fill out Form 940, "Employer's Annual Federal Unemployment (FUTA) Tax Return". Reference: IRS "Instructions for Form 940".

Spreadsheet Design

ABC Corporation
FUTA or SUTA
xx Quarter Reporting

SSN	Employee Name	1st Q' Wages	2nd Q' Wages	3rd Q' Wages	4th Q' Wages	* YTD Wages	* Taxable Wages	* Excess Wages	Tax

Where: SSN= Social Security Number   *For "YTD, Taxable and Excess Wages" see Note below.
Q'= Quarter
YTD= Year-to-Date

Notes: 1. *YTD Wages* - will be the sum of the 1st Quarter - 4th Quarter wages. Obviously, if you're in the 1st Quarter, quarters 2 - 4 will have zero wages.
2. *Taxable Wages* - will be all wages up to the "wage base" (for example: up to $7000).
3. *Wage Base* - is the maximum amount of wages for a year, upon which tax is applied (eg. up to $7000).
3. *Excess Wages* - will be those earned beyond taxable wages / the wage base. For instance, if an employee earned $9000 in wages and only $7000 is taxable, Excess Wages = $2000.
4. *SUTA Wage Base* - your state's wage base will probably be different than the federal wage base. That's another reason to create a separate spreadsheet for the state.

Obviously, with this many headings - above, the spreadsheet would fit better in "landscape format" rather than "portrait format".

Defined: *landscape format* is a sideways orientation of the page - with the height 8.5" and the width 11".

Defined: *portrait format* is a normal orientation of the page - with the height 11" and the width 8.5".

HR - Employee Update Information Form

_____   _____
       Employee's Name   Date

Change (eg. address): _____
_____

_____   _____
      Authorized Signature   Entered
    (eg. employee or bookkeeper)

[Once completed, return to employee's personnel file.]

HR - Employee Update Information Form

_____   _____
       Employee's Name   Date

Change (eg. address): _____
_____

_____   _____
      Authorized Signature   Entered
    (eg. employee or bookkeeper)

[Once completed, return to employee's personnel file.]

HR - Employee Update Information Form

_____   _____
       Employee's Name   Date

Change (eg. address): _____
_____

_____   _____
      Authorized Signature   Entered
    (eg. employee or bookkeeper)

[Once completed, return to employee's personnel file.]

HR - Employee Request for Time Off Form

I _____ Request _____ .
     Employee Name (printed)   Above Time

_____
Purpose / Reason

_____   _____
Employee's Signature   Today's Date

_____   _____
Owner Approved   Date

[Once completed, return to employee's personnel file.]

HR - Employee Request for Time Off Form

I _____ Request _____ .
     Employee Name (printed)   Above Time

_____
Purpose / Reason

_____   _____
Employee's Signature   Today's Date

_____   _____
Owner Approved   Date

[Once completed, return to employee's personnel file.]

HR - Employee Warning Notice

_____   _____
Employee's Name   Date

Explanation of problem _____
_____
_____
_____
_____
_____
_____

Action taken (if any) _____
_____
_____

_____   _____
Manager's Signature   Date

Employee's Response (if any) _____
_____
_____
_____

_____   _____
Employee's Signature   Date

_____
Owner's Initials

[Once completed, return to employee's personnel file.]

Past Due Notice

Company_____   Date_____

To Whom It May Concern,

This note is intended to bring to your attention that the following amount(s) are past due.

        $_____ 30 Days Past Due

        $_____ 60 Days Past Due

Please remit to: _____

                             _____

                             _____

If payment has been made, please disregard this note.

Thank you.

PETTY CASH - RECEIPT		PETTY CASH - RECEIPT
_____ $_____ Date Amount _____ _____ **Initialed** For What [Staple to vendor receipt.]	I I I I I	_____ $_____ Date Amount _____ _____ **Initialed** For What [Staple to vendor receipt.]

- -

PETTY CASH - RECEIPT		PETTY CASH - RECEIPT
_____ $_____ Date Amount _____ _____ **Initialed** For What [Staple to vendor receipt.]	I I I I I	_____ $_____ Date Amount _____ _____ **Initialed** For What [Staple to vendor receipt.]

- -

PETTY CASH - RECEIPT		PETTY CASH - RECEIPT
_____ $_____ Date Amount _____ _____ **Initialed** For What [Staple to vendor receipt.]	I I I I I	_____ $_____ Date Amount _____ _____ **Initialed** For What [Staple to vendor receipt.]

Petty Cash - Change Order		Petty Cash - Change Order
$20's _____ $10's _____ $5's _____ $1's _____ Quarters _____ [$10 per roll] Dimes _____ [$5 per roll] Nickels _____ [$2 per roll] Pennies _____ [50 cents/roll] TOTAL $ _____ _____ Initials	I I I I	$20's _____ $10's _____ $5's _____ $1's _____ Quarters _____ [$10 per roll] Dimes _____ [$5 per roll] Nickels _____ [$2 per roll] Pennies _____ [50 cents/roll] TOTAL $ _____ _____ Initials

- -

Petty Cash - Change Order		Petty Cash - Change Order
$20's _____ $10's _____ $5's _____ $1's _____ Quarters _____ [$10 per roll] Dimes _____ [$5 per roll] Nickels _____ [$2 per roll] Pennies _____ [50 cents/roll] TOTAL $ _____ _____ Initials	I I I I	$20's _____ $10's _____ $5's _____ $1's _____ Quarters _____ [$10 per roll] Dimes _____ [$5 per roll] Nickels _____ [$2 per roll] Pennies _____ [50 cents/roll] TOTAL $ _____ _____ Initials

- -

Petty Cash - Change Order		Petty Cash - Change Order
$20's _____ $10's _____ $5's _____ $1's _____ Quarters _____ [$10 per roll] Dimes _____ [$5 per roll] Nickels _____ [$2 per roll] Pennies _____ [50 cents/roll] TOTAL $ _____ _____ Initials	I I I I	$20's _____ $10's _____ $5's _____ $1's _____ Quarters _____ [$10 per roll] Dimes _____ [$5 per roll] Nickels _____ [$2 per roll] Pennies _____ [50 cents/roll] TOTAL $ _____ _____ Initials

Record Retention Form

Note: *a convenient way to label the box # is* - the year followed by dash one, then dash two: eg. 20xx-1, 20xx-2...

Box # (20xx-1	Major Contents Accounts Payable	Additional Contents / Description Also contains Accounts Receivable "A-C"	Today's Date 1/15/xx	Disposal Date 1/15/xx)

TIME SHEET FOR EMPLOYEES

_____ Pay Period: ___/___/___ - ___/___/___
Employee Name (printed)   Beg. Date   End Date

Date	Time In	Time Out	Subtotal	Time In	Time Out	Subtotal	Day's Total
____	_____	_____	_____	_____	_____	_____	_____
____	_____	_____	_____	_____	_____	_____	_____
____	_____	_____	_____	_____	_____	_____	_____
____	_____	_____	_____	_____	_____	_____	_____
____	_____	_____	_____	_____	_____	_____	_____
____	_____	_____	_____	_____	_____	_____	_____
____	_____	_____	_____	_____	_____	_____	_____

FOR OFFICE   Commission: _____   Total Hours (for the week): _____   Pay Rate(s) $'s
USE: Vacation: _____   Regular Hours (max. 40.0): _____   x _____ = _____
Week's Totals: Sick: _____   Overtime (any > 40.0):   _____   x _____ = _____
                                                              Week's Gross Wages ($'s) = _____

Date	Time In	Time Out	Subtotal	Time In	Time Out	Subtotal	Day's Total
____	_____	_____	_____	_____	_____	_____	_____
____	_____	_____	_____	_____	_____	_____	_____
____	_____	_____	_____	_____	_____	_____	_____
____	_____	_____	_____	_____	_____	_____	_____
____	_____	_____	_____	_____	_____	_____	_____
____	_____	_____	_____	_____	_____	_____	_____
____	_____	_____	_____	_____	_____	_____	_____

FOR OFFICE   Commission: _____   Total Hours (for the week): _____   Pay Rate(s) $'s
USE: Vacation: _____   Regular Hours (max. 40.0): _____   x _____ = _____
Week's Totals: Sick: _____   Overtime (any > 40.0):   _____   x _____ = _____
                                                              Week's Gross Wages ($'s) = _____

Date	Time In	Time Out	Subtotal	Time In	Time Out	Subtotal	Day's Total
____	_____	_____	_____	_____	_____	_____	_____
____	_____	_____	_____	_____	_____	_____	_____

FOR OFFICE   Commission: _____   Total Hours (for two days): _____   Pay Rate(s) $'s
USE: Vacation: _____   Regular Hours (max. 40.0): _____   x _____ = _____
2-Day Totals: Sick: _____   Overtime (any > 40.0):   _____   x _____ = _____
(See Note below)   **Two-Day Gross Wages ($'s)** = _____

```
                          ┌─────────────────────────┐
                          |    For Office Use Only   |    Total Gross Wages ($'s) = _____
                          | Gross Wages _____    |
                          | (Less) Deductions:       |    Commission Total: _____
X_____      | FICA (7.65%) (_____)   |    Vacation  Total:  _____
   Employee's Signature   | Federal W/H  (_____)   |    Sick Total:       _____
                          | State W/H (if)(_____)  |
X_____      | Other _____ (_____)   |
   Supervisor's Signature | Net Wages $ _____    |    Bookkeeper's Initials: _____
                          └─────────────────────────┘
```

Note: *uses for this timesheet* - this timesheet can be used for Weekly, Biweekly (every two weeks), and Semi-Monthly (twice per month) payrolls. For semi-monthly payrolls, the first pay-period of the month would be the 1st through the 15th, and the second pay-period of the month would be the 16th through the 31st. That's where the Two-Day totals get added to the previous two weeks to make up a 15 or 16 day semi-monthly payroll.

TRAVEL MILEAGE FORM

Employee Name (printed)   Time Period

Date	Odom. In	To Where / Reference	Odom. Out	Mileage

X _____   _____   _____
Employee's Signature   Date   Total Mileage

X _____   _____   x   _____
Manager's Signature   Date $'s / mile

Paid: _____   _____   _____   =   _____
Check #   Date   Bookkeeper's Initials   **Total $'s**

Appendix F - **A Word about Career Advancement**

There are two areas I'd like to cover, concerning career advancement. The first is, "How to Work Your Way Up", and the second area is "Supervisory Situations". First of all, don't misunderstand. Some individuals may be perfectly content at whatever positions they have attained. And, there is nothing wrong with that. In fact some might say, I'd rather be content where I'm at, job wise, than constantly try to find something better. If you are happy in the job you have, don't be concerned about having to advance. No one says you have to. And one is not 'better' than the other - just whatever is right for each individual.

How to Work Your Way Up
Having worked my way up from an assistant bookkeeper to bookkeeping supervisor, I learned a thing or two about advancing. If you are interested in advancing, my advice would be as follows. Take responsibility for your own career development, and a large part of this is not only your experience base, but knowledge base as well.

EXPERIENCE BASE
As far as your experience base, the single most important thing you can do to help this is to do a good job in whatever position you have, at the time, no matter how small the job may seem. And one key to success here is attention to detail. You will be building a personal reputation, whether you realize it or not. That may seem elementary, but to continue to focus on your present job may not be as easy, all the time. A good rule of thumb is to plan on being in one position for at least two years, before looking to broaden horizons. Anything less than that and you will probably be considered a job jumper.

KNOWLEDGE BASE
As far as your knowledge base, learn all you can in and around your present job, and avail yourself of continuing education opportunities. If a state taxing authority or your insurance company is putting on a seminar, be sure to attend. You'd be surprised what that does for you. Keep your eyes and ears open. Don't be afraid to take on an extra task, every now and then. And study a book like this one - to learn the ins and outs of the business.

I would also suggest starting a "Career Resource Binder" you keep at home. This is a binder used to accumulate things valuable to your career. For instance, collect your state's specific tax requirements, your own copies of federal forms, instructions, publications, and job search information - materials you would want to have if you change jobs. See Appendix G - "Career Resource Binder" Kept at Home.

SEEKING A JOB
If or when seeking a new job, don't be afraid to use the job advertisements (classifieds) in the newspaper to aid your search. Below is a brief list of job titles, and what you might expect in those jobs.

<u>Job Titles and Brief Descriptions</u>
1. *Accounting Clerk / Bookkeeping Assistant* - performs one task, such as Accounts Payable.
2. *Intermediate Bookkeeper* - more than assistant, not ready for full-charge, putting 2-3 tasks together (see below).
3. *Full-Charge Bookkeeper* - performs all tasks, except corporate taxes (may supervise one or two).
4. *Accounting Manager* - also accomplishing all tasks, except corporate taxes, but supervises one or two individuals.
5. *Controller* - same as accounting manager, but supervises probably three or more individuals.

<u>Intermediate Bookkeeper</u>
The only exception to the job titles and descriptions above is what I have called an "intermediate bookkeeper". I created this title myself. You, typically, will not find it in the job ads, but it is an important step. In the job ads, you will find assistant positions and full-charge positions with little or nothing in between.

On A Personal Note:
After three years as an assistant bookkeeper, I was ready to broaden my horizons, but not near ready for a full-charge position. That's when I realized I needed to put two to three tasks together, in one job, as my next position (eg. payables, receivables & payroll). Such a position was not in the job ads, so I negotiated for it.
(continued next page)

Appendix F - A Word about Career Advancement (continued)

In one of the assistant position interviews, I said, "I'll take the job if...you will allow me to take on two to three tasks..." After briefly explaining why, I was able to persuade the accounting manager, who was flexible and willing to help. Besides, this would lighten his load. This paid off well. I focused on one or two tasks at first, then when time presented itself, I saw how I could fit in another task. Thinking a little more about it, I could see how I would be able to move from one task to the next. When it was time for my next position, I was ready for full-charge.

Supervisory   **Situations**

Two possibilities exist: (1) that you may supervise one or two employees (probably OK), and (2) that the full-charge bookkeeper position will report to someone other than the business owner (may not be OK).

First, the possibility exists that the full-charge bookkeeper position, at certain companies, will supervise one or two employees - like a payroll or billing clerk. I recommend that you start slowly and work your way up to supervising. In other words, first take a full-charge position without any supervisory duties, and stay in that position for awhile. Two years is a good benchmark. Then, only take on one employee to supervise and get used to that, before taking on two employees. This way you won't be biting off more than you can chew, at any one point in time. If you have to supervise more than two employees, your title should probably be greater than just full-charge bookkeeper.

You may find in the job market a "full-charge" position that reports to a higher level position in accounting, like the Vice President of Finance, for instance. While reporting to a V.P. of Finance may seem like an opportunity to learn, I'd be remiss if I didn't point out the following. It's been my experience and observation that too many management layers in a bookkeeping department creates both waste (why have so many layers) and resentment (from those doing the bulk of the work - typically the bookkeeper).

Appendix G - "**Career Resource Binder**" Kept at Home

Introduction
Q: What, on earth, is a "career resource binder"?
A: A place, or binder, you keep at home to store information you have collected for your career.

Q: Why do I need one?
A: It can be particularly important for a full-charge bookkeeper. Once you discover your state's specific tax requirements, you will want to keep a copy of that information for yourself. This way, if you leave a job, you will have that *valuable* information, for your next bookkeeping job.

I recommend starting with a three-ring binder and four tabs: (1) Federal Information, (2) State Information (3) Job Search Information, and (4) Changes to Tax Information.

Federal Information
Here is a short list of the federal information I recommend. IRS items are available at www.irs.gov.
*IRS, Publication 15 (Circular E), "Employer's Tax Guide".
*IRS, Form 940, "Employer's Annual Federal Unemployment (FUTA) Tax Return".
  Recall: there are no *quarterly* Form 940 reports to file.
*IRS, Form 941, "Employer's Quarterly Federal Tax Return". Note: there is no *annual* Form 941.
*IRS, Form W-4, "Employee's Withholding Allowance Certificate"
*IRS, "Instructions for Form 940"
*IRS, "Instructions for Form 1099-MISC"
*Form I-9, "Employment Eligibility Verification", available at www.uscis.gov > FORMS > Form Number > I-9.

There are several ways of obtaining the federal forms and instructions, but a trip to your local IRS office may be the most efficient, since the list is fairly long. If your local IRS office is inconvenient, you may call the 1-800-829-3676 (1-800-TAX-FORM) to order forms / instructions. You'd be surprised at the secure feeling - from having your own copies, whether you actually print them out with "Property of (your name)" or just store them electronically!

State Information
As mentioned earlier, your state's specific tax requirements and authorities can be obtained by various means. But, probably the best approach is to call your state's authorities directly. Tell them you are a bookkeeper, and see if they will mail you a copy of the forms / information. I have had luck with this approach.

Job Search Information
Over the years I've run into articles on résumés and interviewing. A home career resource binder is a good place to store them. Newspaper clippings are easily cut and taped to lined paper. Then, they can be placed directly into the binder.

Changes to Tax Information
Finally, I suggest keeping track of IRS changes to these forms. Instead of obtaining new instructions or forms every year, the IRS has simplified changes by listing them, each year, on the first page of publications and instructions. So, what you would do, come January, is get on-line at www.irs.gov, pull up the new year's IRS Publication 15, for instance and print the first page - listing of "What's New". For completeness, print the following.

<u>Print "What's New"</u>
*IRS, Publications 15 & 15-B, "Employer's Tax Guide" and " Employer's Tax Guide to Fringe Benefits".
*IRS, Publication 535, "Business Expenses".
*IRS, "Instructions for Forms 940 & 941"
  Note: *duplication* - there will probably be some duplication in "What's New", particularly with Forms 940 & 941.

A good way to store these is by writing at the top the year followed by "Tax Changes" (example: "20xx Tax Changes") and collecting them in your home career resource binder or a separate file folder.

Appendix H - **Resources & Bibliography**

Federal Forms, Instructions and Publications
    INTERNAL REVENUE SERVICE (IRS)
*IRS Form 940, "Employer's Annual Federal Unemployment (FUTA) Tax Return"
*IRS Form 941, "Employer's Quarterly Federal Tax Return". Note: there is no *annual* Form 941.
*IRS Form 941 - Schedule B, "Employer's Record of Federal Tax Liability" (For Semi-Weekly Depositors).
*IRS Form 1096, "Annual Summary and Transmittal of U.S. Information Returns" - used to transmit 1099's.
*IRS Form 1099-MISC, "Miscellaneous Income"
*IRS Form SS-4, "Application for Employer Identification Number" - for companies.
*IRS Form SS-8, "Determination of Worker Status for Purposes of Federal Employment Taxes and Income Tax Withholding" (ref: Chapter 2 - Tasks > Payroll > Independent Contractors).
*IRS Form W-2, "Wage and Tax Statement"
*IRS Form W-3, "Transmittal of Wage and Tax Statements" - used when sending W-2's.
*IRS Form W-4, "Employee's Withholding Allowance Certificate"
*IRS Form W-9, "Request for Taxpayer Identification Number and Certification" - for individuals.
*IRS "Instructions for Form 940"
*IRS "Instructions for Form 941"
*IRS "Instructions for Form 1099-MISC"
*IRS Publication 15, Circular E, "Employer's Tax Guide"
*IRS Publication 15-A, "Employer's Supplemental Tax Guide"
*IRS Publication 15-B, "Employer's Tax Guide to Fringe Benefits"
*IRS Publication 463, "Travel, Entertainment, Gift, and Car Expenses"
*IRS Publication 535, "Business Expenses"
*IRS Publication 966, "Electronic Choices to Pay All Your Federal Taxes".
*IRS Publication 1244, "Employee's Daily Record of Tips and Report to Employer" (Food & Beverage Industry).

    IRS FORMS & INSTRUCTIONS MAY BE OBTAINED
1. *On-line* - at www.irs.gov.
2. *From your local IRS office.*
3. *Over the phone* - by calling 1-800-TAX-FORM (1-800-829-3676).

    IRS "AUDIT TECHNIQUE GUIDES"
    The guides IRS auditors use are available for approximately 40 different industries - including retail and construction. Since these are the actual guides IRS auditors use, they might be useful to see what is important, and help you prepare should an audit come. They are available at http://www.irs.gov/Businesses/Small-Businesses-&-Self-Employed/Audit-Techniques-Guides-ATGs.

Determining State Specific Requirements
    Here is how you may determine your state's specific (tax) requirements / authorities:
1. *SUTA Agencies* - http://www.workforcesecurity.doleta.gov/unemploy/agencies.asp lists all 50 States' Unemployment Tax Authorities for SUTA.
2. *Search* - the previous bookkeeper's files for prior tax reports.
3. *Search* - on-line, requesting:
    "(your state's) government"
    "(your state's) Taxation Department", "Treasury Department" or "Department of Labor"
    "(your state's) payroll tax requirements"
4. *Look in* - the government pages of your phone book (and make some calls).

Appendix H - Resources & Bibliography (continued)

Computer Bookkeeping Programs
*QuickBooks (Intuit Company): visit: http://quickbooks.intuit.com/ or call 1-877-683-3280.
*Sage 50 Accounting: visit: http://na.sage.com/us/sage-50-accounting or call 1-877-495-9904.

The 50 States' Information
*MINIMUM WAGE RATES: all 50 states' minimum wage rates are listed @
   http://www.dol.gov/whd/minwage/america.htm .
*STATE UNEMPLOYMENT TAX (SUTA) AGENCIES: all state agencies are listed by the U.S. Dept. of Labor:
   http://www.workforcesecurity.doleta.gov/unemploy/agencies.asp.
*WORKERS' COMPENSATION INSURANCE: links to all 50 states workers' compensation laws can be found @
   www.workerscompensationinsurance.com .

Resources By Chapter
   HUMAN RESOURCE
*IRS Form W-4, "Employee's Withholding Allowance Certificate" available @ www.irs.gov.
*Form I-9, "Employment Eligibility Verification" Note: this is *not* an IRS form, but can be obtained online @
   http://www.uscis.gov/ > FORMS > Form Number > I-9.

   PAYROLL
*Federal Minimum Wage: http://www.dol.gov/dol/topic/wages/minimumwage.htm, or call 1-866-4-USWAGE.
*State Minimum Wage: http://www.dol.gov/whd/minwage/america.htm .
*Overtime: http://www.dol.gov/dol/topic/wages/overtimepay.htm .
*Recordkeeping: http://www.dol.gov/dol/topic/wages/wagesrecordkeeping.htm .
*Poster Requirements: www.dol.gov > A to Z > P > Posters.

   PAYROLL TAXES
*IRS Publication 15, "Employer's Tax Guide" available @ www.irs.gov.
*IRS Publication 966, "Electronic Choices to Pay All Your Federal Taxes".
*State Unemployment Tax Agencies: http://www.workforcesecurity.doleta.gov/unemploy/agencies.asp.

   CORPORATE TAXES
*Quarterly Estimated Tax Payments: IRS Form 1120-W available @ www.irs.gov.
*Depositing Electronically: IRS Instructions to Form 1120-W > Method of Payment.
*Registering For Electronic Deposit: enroll @ https://www.eftps.gov/eftps/ or by calling 1-800-555-4477.

   INSURANCE
*COBRA: http://www.dol.gov/ > A to Z [Index] > "C" > Consolidated Omnibus..(COBRA).
*HIPAA: http://www.dol.gov/ > A to Z [Index] > "H" > Health Insurance Portability & Accountability Act.
*Workers' Compensation Insurance is widely required: www.workerscompensationinsurance.com has links to all 50
   states, including state laws.
*The Affordable Care Act (aka: "Obama-care"): https://www.healthcare.gov/small-businesses/

   OTHER AUTHORITIES
*To Track Any Workplace Injuries: http://www.osha.gov/ > A to Z Index > R > Recordkeeping.
*Compliance With American Disabilities Act: http://www.ada.gov/ .

Accounting Textbooks
   Meigs, Walter B., and Robert F. Meigs. Accounting: The Basis For Business Decisions.
      Fifth Edition. New York: McGraw-Hill, 1981.

   Dyckman, Thomas R., Roland E. Dukes, and Charles J. Davis. Intermediate Accounting.
      Revised Edition. Homewood, IL: Richard D. Irwin, Inc., 1992.

   Nikolai, Loren A., and John D. Bazley. Intermediate Accounting. Seventh Edition.
      Cincinnati, Ohio: Southwestern College Publishing, 1997.

Glossary

1099's: see "Form 1099" (below).

2/10, Net 30: an accounts receivable term meaning 2 % can be taken off the invoice amount, if the invoice is paid within 10 days of the invoice date. Otherwise the balance is due within 30 days, from the invoice date.

a.k.a.: abbreviation for "also known as".

A/P: abbreviation for "accounts payable" (see below).

A/R: abbreviation for "accounts receivable" (see below).

Access: see "Microsoft Access" (below).

accounting clerk / bookkeeping assistant: one of the first positions in corporate bookkeeping – often performing just one task, such as "accounts payable".

accounting manager: a position in corporate accounting, that accomplishes all tasks except corporate taxes, but also supervises one individual.

accounting methods: the only two accounting methods are "accrual method", and "cash basis" method.

accounting period: see "period" (below).

accounts payable: are the bills that your company owes - to other companies.

accounts payable aging: a listing or chart of the bills your company owes, at any point in time. It can be either a summary aging - just showing a total for each vendor, or a detailed aging - printing every invoice, date and amount, along with totals. Reference: Chapter 2 - Tasks > Accounts Payable > Aging Example.

accounts receivable: what customers owe your company.

accounts receivable aging: a listing of what customers owe your company. These can be either a summary aging - showing a total for each customer, or a detailed aging, printing every invoice, date and amount, along with totals.

accrual method (accounting): is when revenues and expenses are posted when bills are sent or received (incurred) regardless of when they are actually paid. Most companies use this method.

accumulated depreciation: is the "offset" to Depreciation Expense, in all depreciation journal entries. Accumulated Depreciation is a Balance Sheet account, representing all of the depreciation expense taken against an asset, over all of its years. Reference: Appendix D - Accounting Basics > "Depreciating" Assets.

additional paid-in capital: any moneys added to the business as equity, after the business is started-up.

advance: see "employee advance" (below).

advanced bookkeeper: has been doing full-charge bookkeeping for several years.

aging: see "accounts payable aging", and "accounts receivable aging" (above).

allocated overhead: to assign a portion of the overhead costs, to each unit of goods manufactured.

assets: a category found on the "Balance Sheet". Examples of assets include: Cash, Inventory & A/R.

Glossary (continued)

audit: is an examination of some aspect of the company you work for. Audits typically examine the accounting / bookkeeping records, but can include other aspects of a company's operations. Examples include: an audit of the books by the IRS or a CPA firm, and an audit of your company's operations by a state environmental department.

audit guides: these are the actual guides IRS auditors use for specific industries, like retail and construction. They are available for about 40 different industries at: http://www.irs.gov/Businesses/Small-Businesses-&-Self-Employed/Audit-Techniques-Guides-ATGs.

authorities: include those government departments, at both the federal and state levels, responsible for collecting taxes or administering laws. An example of an authority is the IRS.

bad debt expense: the expense of having an accounts receivable become uncollectible - for example if your customer went out of business. Reference: example in Appendix D - Accounting Basics > "Writing-Off" a Receivable.

balance: has two meanings -
1. An amount. Example: the *balance* or amount, in the account, is $35.
2. That one amount equals another amount. Example: in the case of a journal entry, it is in *balance* when all debits equal all credits.

Balance Sheet: lists assets, liabilities, and owner's equity, as of the last day in the period (month or year). It is one of the two main financial statements - the other one is the income statement.

balancing the general ledger: means that all debits equal all credits posted for the month.

basic accounting equation: Assets = Liabilities + Owner's Equity. This is derived from: Assets - Liabilities = Owner's Equity.

beginner / beginning bookkeeper: knows little or nothing about bookkeeping, so would perform no more than one task, such as accounts payable.

below board: operating outside the law.

biweekly (payroll): every two weeks, as opposed to "semi-monthly" (twice per month).

black: see "operating in the black" (below).

bonus: is extra money given to an employee usually for a particular reason - like a Christmas bonus.

book value (of an asset): is equal to the original cost of the asset minus "accumulated depreciation". Reference: Appendix D - Accounting Basics > "Depreciating" Assets.

bookkeeping assistant / accounting clerk: one of the first positions in corporate bookkeeping - performing one task, such as accounts payable.

business license fee: buys a right to operate a business within the city or county lines.

"business-owner style" bookkeeping: manual bookkeeping without debits and credits and without a computer.

calendar year: January - December (as opposed to "fiscal year").

capital stock: what money is initially put into the business - to get it started.

Glossary (continued)

capitalize: to treat or record an item as an asset and then "depreciate" it, as opposed to treating it as an expense.

career resource binder: a binder you keep at home, to accumulate things valuable to your career - for instance your state's specific tax requirements, your own copies of federal forms, instructions, publications, and job search information. Reference: Appendix G - Career Resource Binder Kept at Home.

cash basis: see "cash method" (below).

cash method (accounting): is when revenues and expenses are only recognized when cash is received or paid. Unpaid bills and unpaid sales are not recognized, until paid.

cd-rewrite drive/disk: another way of storing data - via a compact disk.

"Charitable Contributions" Expense: an account listed on the Chart of Accounts. Charitable Contributions are gifts given to "charitable organizations" (as opposed to "Gift Expense", see below). References: IRS Publication 526, "Charitable Contributions" and IRS Publication 535, "Business Expenses" > Index > "Charitable Contributions".

chart of accounts: lists every account in the general ledger. See Appendix B - Chart of Accounts.

Circular E: see "Publication 15" (below).

close / closing - an accounting period: involves bringing income statement accounts (revenues & expenses) to zero balances in order to start counting from zero - in the next accounting period. Otherwise, your next period's (month or year's) sales would include the previous period's sales.

COBRA: is a federal law which allows a terminated employee or covered family member - under certain circumstances to continue health insurance coverage for up to 18 months. Stands for "Consolidated Omnibus Budget Reconciliation Act".

code: see "coding - petty cash slips" below.

coding - petty cash slips: indicating which account, from the "Chart of Accounts", a particular expenditure belongs to. It simply means putting the chart-of-accounts account number at the top of the petty cash slip.

COGS: abbreviation for "Cost of Goods Sold" (see below).

collection letter: see "Past Due Notice" (below).

collections: means collecting accounts receivable from customers who are not paying timely enough.

columnar paper (a.k.a. ledger paper): pale green-lined paper, with two or more columns on the right hand side, specifically used for posting debits and credits in a paper-based system.

commissions: are pay earned, by a sales person, on sales made.

complaint (legal): see "legal complaint".

computer accounting program: a computer program such as QuickBooks or Sage 50 Accounting, through which you do bookkeeping.

computer bookkeeping program: see "computer accounting program".

computer consultant: an expert in a computer field, to help with things like web-site development and networking.

Glossary (continued)

cont.: abbreviation for "continued".

contra-asset (account): is a Balance Sheet account that *subtracts* from an asset account. It has a normal credit balance (instead of the normal debit balance for assets). Accumulated depreciation is an example of a contra-asset account. Reference: Appendix D - Accounting Basics > "Depreciating" Assets.

contra-equity (account): is a Balance Sheet account that *subtracts* from the Equity section. It has a normal debit balance (instead of the normal credit balance for Owner's Equity). "Draw - Owner" is an example of a contra-equity account. Reference: Appendix D - Accounting Basics > "Draws" Taken by the Owner.

contract labor: these are people who are doing work for your company, but are self-employed - not employees of your company. They pay their own taxes. So, you pay them straight wages, without any taxes deducted (aka: independent contractors).

controller: a position in corporate accounting that accomplishes all tasks except corporate taxes, and supervises two or more individuals.

corporate accounting: another name for the field, describing all of the bookkeeping tasks that businesses need to accomplish.

corporate bookkeeping: see "corporate accounting" above.

corporate liability insurance: also known as "liability insurance", is a more general coverage for things like fire or property damage.

corporate taxes: tax on the income of a business for a year (either calendar year, or fiscal year).

Cost of Goods Sold (COGS): is referring to the goods that your company sold customers. What did they cost your company? Reference: Appendix D - Accounting Basics > Inventory and "Cost of Goods Sold".

cost of goods sold formula: COGS is equal to Beginning Inventory plus Purchases minus Ending Inventory. Reference: Appendix D - Accounting Basics > Inventory and "Cost of Goods Sold".

Cost of Sales (COS): in a service industry, Cost of Goods Sold is referred to as Cost of Sales.

CPA: abbreviation for "Certified Public Accountant".

CR: abbreviation for "Credit" in an example of a journal entry (see also "DB" abbreviation for "Debit").

crashed (hard-drive): no longer continues to operate or work.

credit: has three meanings -
    1. To be able to buy something, without presenting payment at the time of the purchase.
    2. The meaning *non*-accounting people know is to increase (or *credit*) an account.
    3. The "debit and credit" meaning is, the right side of a ledger or entry in a "double-entry system".

credit application: a form sent from one company to another, typically requesting credit references before extending credit.

current liability: due in less than one year from now.

DB: abbreviation for "Debit" in an example of a journal entry (see also "CR" abbreviation for "Credit").

debit: simply means the "left" side of a ledger or entry in a "dual-entry system".

Glossary (continued)

deductions: what is subtracted from gross wages to arrive at net wages (includes: federal income tax withheld, FICA, and any state income taxes withheld).

deposits in transit: deposits you've posted to the books but have not yet posted at the bank.

depreciable assets: see "fixed assets" or "Property, Plant & Equipment".

depreciable life: see "useful life" below.

depreciate: to treat as an asset, being "used up" over time.

depreciation expense: is the expense associated with using-up an asset, during its "useful life". Reference: Appendix D - Accounting Basics > "Depreciating" Assets.

direct labor: assembly workers' wages, and their direct supervisor's salaries, needed to manufacture product.

direct materials: any and all "raw materials" used to manufacture a product.

dividend: a removal of "equity" from the business.

draws - taken by the owner: a draw is a removal of cash from the business, beyond the owner's salary. It is equivalent to a dividend. Reference: Appendix D - Accounting Basics > "Draws" Taken by the Owner.

double-entry system: see "dual-entry system" below.

dual-entry system: means that every transaction affects two accounts. For example, when you pay a bill, your cash account will decrease, but your accounts payable account will decrease as well.

due diligence: putting forth an appropriate amount of time and effort for a particular situation.

DVD-writer: another way of storing data; can store much more data than CD-rewrite disks.

earnings: net income.

EFTPS: abbreviation for "Electronic Federal Tax Payment System" (see below).

EIN: abbreviation for "Employer Identification Number" (see below).

Electronic Federal Tax Payment System (EFTPS): the electronic means by which the IRS collects taxes.

employee advance: for instance, if the company loaned an employee one hundred dollars, in order to make it to payday.

Employer Identification Number (EIN): a nine-digit number assigned by the IRS to identify business taxpayers.

equity: see "owner's equity".

estimated taxes: is a means of paying taxes throughout the year. This is required of many corporations, and some individuals. Check with the CPA.

ethical: is to do what is legal, and to do what is the right thing to do.

exempt employees: also known as "salaried" employees, because they are not paid for overtime.

Glossary (continued)

factoring (of accounts receivable): selling receivables to another company, for say 80 cents on the dollar. The other company then owns and collects those receivables.

federal payroll tax deposits: federal payroll tax deposits are made after payrolls to pay taxes withheld from pay checks, plus taxes due from the employer. These are called #941 payments.

federal quarterly payroll tax reports: are (1) Form 941 entitled "Employer's Quarterly Federal Tax Return", and (2) *payment* of Federal Unemployment Taxes (FUTA). Reference: Chapter 2 - Tasks > Payroll Taxes.

Federal Unemployment Tax (FUTA): one of the payroll taxes, paid quarterly to the IRS, but filed annually with Form 940. Reference: Chapter 2 - Tasks > Payroll Taxes.

FICA tax (Federal Insurance Corporation Act): the means by which the federal government collects social security and Medicare for the elderly, by imposing payroll taxes on businesses. The current FICA rate is 7.65% of gross wages, imposed on both the employee *and* employer.

finished goods (inventory): goods or product that is ready to be sold to the customer - no longer being manufactured, as opposed to "raw materials" inventory or "work-in-process" inventory.

fiscal year: the twelve month period in which your business operates, which may or may not coincide with the January 1 - December 31, calendar year (example: July 1 - June 30).

fixed assets: is another name for "Property, Plant & Equipment" (PP&E). Where fixed assets are listed on the Chart of Accounts, PP&E are listed on the Balance Sheet. Examples include: land, buildings, vehicles, furniture, fixtures and equipment.

flash / travel / USB drive (aka: jump drive, memory stick or thumb drive): is a device used to back-up data. It is about the size of a finger and plugs directly into a USB port. They hold up to a Giga byte or more of memory, are extremely fast to work with and very portable, as well.

floppy (disk/drive): a way people used to back-up information in the computer. At any rate, flash/jump drives can store much more data.

Form 940: IRS form entitled, "Employer's Annual Federal Unemployment (FUTA) Tax Return".

Form 941: IRS form entitled, "Employer's Quarterly Federal Tax Return".

Form 1096: IRS form entitled, "Annual Summary and Transmittal of U.S. Information Returns". This form is used to transmit all of the year-end 1099-MISC forms that a bookkeeper may need to submit.

Form 1099: see "Form 1099-Misc".

Form 1099-Misc: IRS form entitled, "Miscellaneous Income". It's used by the bookkeeper to indicate amounts paid to "contract labor" - in excess of $600 per contract labor person, per year. Less than $600 and you need not file Form 1099.

Form I-9: is a form entitled, "Employment Eligibility Verification". It is not an IRS form, but U.S. Citizenship & Immigration Services - available at http://www.uscis.gov/i-9-central. It is required of all employees, and if \ filled out correctly, indicates that the person is legal to work in the United States.

Form SS-4: IRS form entitled, "Application for Employer Identification Number", to obtain a federal ID number for a new business.

Glossary (continued)

Form SS-8: IRS form entitled, "Determination of Worker Status for Purposes of Federal Employment Taxes and Income Tax Withholding". It is used to ask the IRS to make a determination if a worker should be treated as an employee or treated as "contract labor".

Form W-2: IRS form entitled, "Wage and Tax Statement". They are mailed by bookkeepers at the end of the year, indicating each employee's wages and taxes paid for that calendar year.

Form W-3: IRS form entitled, "Transmittal of Wage and Tax Statements", used to transmit the totals for all W-2's.

Form W-4: IRS form entitled, "Employee's Withholding Allowance Certificate". It is required of all employees to be filled out when hired, and contains the employee's name, address, social security number and personal or withholding allowances.

Form W-9: IRS form entitled, "Request for Taxpayer Identification Number and Certification". This form is used to obtain a taxpayer ID number for "contract labor".

formula for calculating "Cost of Goods Sold": COGS is equal to Beginning Inventory plus Purchases minus Ending Inventory. Reference: Appendix D - Accounting Basics > Inventory and "Cost of Goods Sold".

full-charge bookkeeper: a bookkeeper who performs all of the bookkeeping tasks of a small business, including payroll taxes and monthly financial statements, with little or no supervision. About the only task needed to be "outsourced" is the corporate taxes.

FUTA: abbreviation for "Federal Unemployment Tax Act" (see above).

garnishment: a legal order or judgment to deduct wages from a person, and send those wages to a government agency or third party. Examples include: collecting for child support, alimony and back taxes due.

general journal: is that place in a manual bookkeeping system where all transactions (debits and credits) are posted by date. See also "general ledger" below.

general journal entry: see "journal entry".

general ledger: is the place where *all* transactions (or debits and credits) get posted.

"Gifts" Expense: an account listed on the Chart of Accounts. Gifts differ from "Charitable Contributions" (above) in that gifts are those *not* given to "charitable organizations" (a gift to a friend for example). The IRS generally allows a $25 gift deduction per recipient per year. Reference: IRS Publication 463, "Travel, Entertainment, Gift and Car Expenses" > Gifts.

GL: abbreviation for "general ledger" (see above).

gross profit: is found on the "Income Statement", and is equal to "Net Sales" minus "Cost of Goods Sold".

gross receipts tax: is a tax levied by states, typically on products *and* services sold. See also "state sales tax".

gross wages: are equal to hours worked multiplied by the hourly wage (does not include deductions).

group insurance plan: is one that is offered to your entire company, often with a minimum number (eg. 10) of employees needed to participate.

HIPAA: stands for "Health Insurance Portability and Accountability Act". Reference: Chapter 7 - Insurance.

Glossary (continued)

historical cost (of an asset): how much you paid the day you bought it. This is also known as the "original cost" or "purchase value" of an asset.

HR: abbreviation for "human resource (administration)". See below.

human resource administration: a task often aided by the full-charge bookkeeper, in a small business.

I-9: see "Form I-9" (above).

immaterial: mean not material or irrelevant.

"in the black": see "operating in the black" (below).

"in the red": see "operating in the red" (below).

in-house: completed by an employee of *your* company. Example: all bookkeeping is done in-house, by our full-charge bookkeeper (as opposed to "outsourced").

Income Statement (a.k.a. a Profit and Loss Statement): subtracts expenses from revenues to give how much income you had for the period (month or year). It is one of the two main financial statements - the other is the Balance Sheet.

independent contractor: see "contract labor" (above).

intangible property tax: is a tax on a business asset like Accounts Receivable, but is found in very few states. Reference: Chapter 2 - Tasks > Other Taxes.

intermediate bookkeeper: a bookkeeper who is ready to put 2-3 tasks together, more than an assistant position but not quite ready for full-charge.

internal audit: an audit performed by someone from within your company. It doesn't happen too often in a smaller company.

internal controls: means to have policies and procedures in place to ensure safe-guarding of assets, and accurate & timely reporting of financial information.

Internal Revenue Service: the Federal agency responsible for collecting taxes from individuals and businesses.

inventory: a stock of "finished goods" available for sale to customers. Note: in a manufacturing environment inventory can also include "raw materials" and "work-in-process". For more information, reference Appendix D - Accounting Basics > Inventory and "Cost of Goods Sold".

invoice: another name for a company bill - usually created from within a company. It can be either a bill you owe another company, or one that your customer owes you.

invoice date: the date an invoice is created.

IRS: abbreviation for "Internal Revenue Service" (see above).

job costing: a way of determining what each construction job is costing your company.

journal: a binder or notebook in which you keep track of transactions.

Glossary (continued)

journal entry: debits and credits, in balance, describing a transaction. Example:
    [Debit]   Petty Cash $$ =>*Increasing* an *asset*
    [Credit]   Cash $$ =>*Decreasing* an *asset*

jump drive: see "flash drive" above.

landscape format: is a sideways orientation of the page - with the height 8.5" and the width 11" (as opposed to "portrait format").

ledger: (1) a listing or breakdown of an account, and (2) abbreviation for "ledger paper" (defined below).

ledger paper (a.k.a. columnar paper): pale green paper, lined, with two or more columns on the right hand side, specifically used for posting debits and credits.

legal complaint: a document you file in your local courthouse to pursue a legal remedy, e.g. against an un-paying customer.

liability: what is owed. Liabilities are found on the "Balance Sheet" (see above). Examples of liabilities include accounts payable and notes payable.

liability insurance: is more general coverage for things like fire or property business damage.

lien: is a legal right to property, but represents a way of getting paid, if you're having trouble collecting on construction work (a.k.a. "materialsmen lien").

long-term liabilities: see "non-current liabilities".

manual bookkeeping system: to use only paper to record all bookkeeping transactions (ie. to not use a computer).

manufacturing industry: typically involves buying raw materials, mass producing items, and then selling them "wholesale" to retail outlets.

master schedule: is a listing of all the full-charge tasks that need to be completed, by certain deadlines. Reference: Appendix A - Master Schedule.

material: is another way of saying "relevant". And what is relevant is what would change a decision maker's mind - when looking at financial statements (reference: "presented fairly" below).

materialsmen: is one who works with materials, such as construction materials.

materialsmen lien: is a legal means of getting paid, if you are a materialsmen.

Medicare (tax): a component of the FICA tax - equal to 1.45% of gross wages.

memory stick: see "flash drive" above.

Microsoft Access: a database program published by Microsoft (MS) and found in MS Office, Professional version.

Microsoft Excel: a spreadsheet program published by Microsoft (MS) and found in MS Office, Home & Student version.

Microsoft OneNote: a program for taking or writing notes, published by Microsoft (MS) and found in MS Office, Home & Student version.

Glossary (continued)

Microsoft Outlook: the professional email program, published by Microsoft (MS) and found in MS Office, Professional version.

Microsoft Outlook Express: the non-professional version of the email program, published by Microsoft.

Microsoft PowerPoint: a program for presentation published by Microsoft (MS) and found in MS Office, Home & Student version.

Microsoft Word: a word processing program published by Microsoft (MS) and found in MS Office, Home & Student version.

module (computer): is a section or feature of a computer bookkeeping program (eg: tracking inventory).

net income: equal to revenues minus expenses.

net sales: is found on the Income Statement and is equal to Sales minus Sales Returns minus Sales Discounts.

net wages: equal to gross wages minus deductions.

networked computers: hooked together, so data is updated and shared between them.

non-current liabilities: due in more than one year from now.

non-profit organization: any organization that is engaged in activities without pursuing profit (examples: a church, and any government).

non-profit sector: is the area of business/industry that encompasses all organizations who operate without the pursuit of profit (see also "non-profit organization" above).

office software: typically refers to a word processing program and a "spreadsheet" (see below) program - to be used in an office setting.

offset: either the debit or the credit that makes a journal entry balance.

OneNote: see "Microsoft OneNote" (above).

operating expenses: are found on the Income Statement, just below "Gross Profit". Examples of operating expenses include: Advertising and Utilities Expenses.

"operating in the black": means to be operating profitably as a business, or to have a positive amount of net income on the income statement (aka: "in the black", as opposed to "operating in the red").

"operating in the red": means to be taking losses on the business or to have a negative amount of net income on the income statement (aka: "in the red", as opposed to "operating in the black").

operational audit: one, not of the books, but of some other aspect of the company.

original cost (of an asset): how much you paid the day you bought it. This is also known as the "historical cost" or "purchase value" of an asset.

OT: abbreviation for "overtime" (see below).

outage: is an out of balance situation, or an amount that you're out of balance.

Glossary (continued)

Outlook: see "Microsoft Outlook" (above).

outsource: to hire another company or individual to perform a task. An example is hiring a CPA firm to do the payroll taxes (as opposed to "in-house").

outstanding checks: checks you've written that have not yet cleared the bank.

overhead: refers to costs that are incurred whether any product is produced or not. Examples include: rent, marketing, accounting, and office workers.

overtime: any hours worked over 40 in a 7 day period.

owner's equity: equals assets minus liabilities. It is a measure of any extra an owner has in the business, and is an account that's found on the "Balance Sheet".

packing slip: is a form shipped with product (not services). It represents receipt of the goods purchased by your company. Note: you may want to see a signature or initials of whoever received the product, on the packing slip.

paper trail: the records showing how things were done or that they were done correctly (example: copies of payroll tax reports).

past due notice: standardized form letter indicating payment is past due and intended to prompt payment of overdue Accounts Receivable. See Appendix E - Sample Forms > Past Due Notice.

payable: see "accounts payable" (above).

payroll tax deposits: see "federal payroll tax deposits" (above).

payroll taxes: are taxes that arise from, or are related to payroll. This includes: federal income tax withheld, Federal Unemployment Taxes, FICA (social security and Medicare), and all state related payroll taxes - State Unemployment Tax and any state income tax withheld.

period (aka: accounting period): either a month, quarter, or year. Example: what was our net income in the last period?

perpetual inventory system: a way of keeping track of inventory levels by updating the Inventory account after every sale. Reference: Appendix D - Accounting Basics > Inventory and "Cost of Goods Sold".

personal allowances: found on Form W-4, determines how much federal income tax will be withheld from each paycheck - based on the number of dependents claimed.

personal guarantee: a pledging of *personal* assets to cover debts. This often occurs when one company obtains credit with another company (for A/P or A/R). The company owner agrees to a personal guarantee to obtain credit.

petty cash: is a small amount of cash kept on hand, preferably in a locked box, for incidental items.

plan administrator: is that person, in the company you work for, who works with the health insurance. In smaller companies this is often the bookkeeper.

point of sale system: is a computer program, tied into the cash registers, that updates inventory levels after every sale (aka: "perpetual inventory system").

Glossary (continued)

portrait format: is a normal orientation of the page - with the height 11" and the width 8.5" (as opposed to "landscape format").

POS: abbreviation for "point of sale" system (see above).

post: to enter or record debits and credits. Example: be sure to post the transaction into the computer.

post manually: to manually enter debits and credits, into the computer, via a "journal entry" (as opposed to "posts automatically" - see below).

posts automatically: the computer accounting/bookkeeping program automatically records debits and credits, each time a transaction is entered (as opposed to "post manually" - see above).

PowerPoint: see "Microsoft PowerPoint" (above).

PP&E: abbreviation for "Property, Plant & Equipment" (see below).

presented fairly: refers to financial statements - saying that they are free from "material" error.

prior period: a month or year prior to the one you are currently working in.

process servers: are people who serve "legal complaints" for a small fee.

Professional Association (P.A.): see "Professional Corporation" (below).

Professional Corporation (P.C.): is a corporation formed by professionals such as lawyers, accountants, architects, engineers, and doctors. PC's are typically not subject to corporate estimated tax payments (a.k.a. Professional Association).

professionalism: to conduct oneself in a professional manner. This includes, but is not limited to, arriving at work on-time and completing all tasks in an efficient and timely manner.

Profit and Loss Statement: see "Income Statement" (above).

progress billings: in the construction industry, to bill the customer for progress made to date, and not have to wait until the entire project is complete - in order to receive any income (determined in the contract).

Property, Plant & Equipment: a category found under Assets on the "Balance Sheet" - listing all land, buildings and equipment owned by the company (aka: "depreciable" or "fixed assets").

property tax: tax levied, by local authorities, on land and/or buildings.

Publication 15: IRS publication entitled "Circular E, Employer's Tax Guide". It contains all the information needed for payroll taxes, as well as federal income tax withholding tables - used for doing payroll manually.

purchase order: is an order or approval to purchase something. Purchase orders contain the price(s) agreed on, and will be approved with a signature, by either the owner or person authorized to approve a purchase.

purchase value (of an asset): how much you paid the day you bought it (aka: "historical cost" or "original cost").

quarterly estimated tax payments: are installments of corporate income tax due. Generally, they are required of all corporations whose corporate income tax is greater than five-hundred dollars, annually. Source: IRS Form 1120-W. Contact your company's CPA for more information.

Glossary (continued)

QuickBooks: a computer bookkeeping program put out by Intuit Company. Visit: http://quickbooks.intuit.com/ or call 1-877-683-3280 (see also "Sage 50 Accounting").

raw materials (inventory): material that is purchased from vendors and used to manufacture a product.

receivable: see "accounts receivable" (above).

record retention: another term for the storing of bookkeeping records, often kept on a schedule.

record retention schedule: is a plan for how long to store which types of documents.

red: see "operating in the red" (above).

ref: abbreviation for "reference".

release of lien: is a document showing that there is no lien attached to any of the material(s).

retail industry: is any store that sells directly to the public.

retained earnings: are earnings or income that have been retained in the company, and not distributed to the owner.

revenues: sales.

S-Corporation: a corporation organized under U.S. Tax Code entitled, "Subchapter S". It is for small, closely owned companies, and typically not subject to corporate estimated tax payments. Check with the CPA or business owner to see if the company you work for is an S-Corporation.

Sage 50 Accounting: a computer bookkeeping program. Visit: http://na.sage.com/us/sage-50-accounting or call 1-877-495-9904 (see also "QuickBooks").

sales journal: a journal used in a manual bookkeeping system, to record only and all sales transactions.

Sales Returns and Discounts: are subtracted from the "Sales" account to arrive at "Net Sales" on the Income Statement.

sales tax: see "state sales tax" (below).

segregation of duties: means to separate those tasks that, if not separated, could lead to undetected theft.

self-audit: refers to an insurance company audit - when the insurance company allows you to provide them the information they need by filling out their form, in lieu of them coming and auditing your company.

semi-monthly (payroll): twice per month, as opposed to "biweekly" (every two weeks).

service industry: is one that does not involve a material product. Examples include the following industries: health care, child care, legal, accounting, engineering and architectural services.

serve: to officially give a "legal complaint" to the person or entity (company) being complained about. "Process servers" are often used for this.

shrinkage: loss of inventory due to theft (or other cause).

shut-off notice: is a written communication, usually from a utility company - that says the company you work for has an unpaid / overdue bill. It's telling you that your company is about to lose (utility) service.

Glossary (continued)

site development: developing a site for a construction project (example - laying pipes for utilities).

social security (tax): a component of "FICA tax" (see above) - equal to 6.2% of gross wages.

specific identification: means that each inventory item, like an automobile at a car dealership, is identified with a unique number (eg. Vehicle Identification Number).

spreadsheet: a computer worksheet, like Microsoft Excel, on which you can list figures and do calculations. This is useful for calculating things like commissions, and state / federal unemployment taxes.

state-specific tasks: tasks required by, or reported to the state in which you live.

state income tax: tax on income earned - paid to the state. It can be a tax on individuals or corporations (not all states have income tax).

state sales tax: is a tax generally levied by states on retail sales - of just products sold (see also "gross receipts tax").

State Unemployment Tax (SUTA): it is one of the payroll taxes, and specific to the state in which you live. Reference: Tasks > Payroll Taxes, and Sample Forms > FUTA - SUTA Spreadsheet Design.

statement (A/P or A/R): a detailed listing of all unpaid (outstanding) bills or invoices. It would be a "vendor statement" for Accounts Payable and a "customer" or "receivables statement" for A/R.

statements of account: are typically sent once per month listing all outstanding invoices.

sub-contractor: what "independent contractors" are known as in the construction industry.

SUTA: abbreviation for "State Unemployment Tax Act" (see above).

tangible property tax: is a tax on business personal property like office equipment, but is found in very few states.

tasks - bookkeeping: things to do as a bookkeeper - listed in the Table of Contents, Chapter 2. This includes things like Accounts Payable, Accounts Receivable, Payroll, and Payroll Taxes.

tax-free wholesales: in some states (New Mexico is one), if your company is a manufacturer and *not* selling directly to the public, but to a company that will resell your product, your company (the manufacturer or wholesaler) may *not* be required to charge state sales tax. This is to avoid double taxation.

Taxpayer Identification Number (TIN): the number used by the IRS to identify taxpayers. For individuals, this number is their social security number. For businesses this number is their Employer Identification Number (EIN).

thumb drive: see "flash drive" (above).

TIN: abbreviation for "Taxpayer Identification Number" (see above).

transaction: an event in bookkeeping that can be described by a debit(s) and a credit(s). Example: purchasing something or selling something are transactions.

transaction listing: lists all transactions (debits and credits) for selected accounts, over a specified period of time.

transmittals (for W-2's and 1099's): see "Form W-3" and "Form 1096" respectively.

Glossary (continued)

transposition error: is one where you reversed the order of two numbers - causing an out of balance situation. Example: $954.00 (the correct amount) was entered as $945.00 (reversing the order of the 5 and 4). Transposition errors always divide evenly by nine.

trial balance: a detailed listing of all debits and credits posted to the general ledger, hopefully with all debits equaling or balancing to all credits posted.

uncollectible: unable to collect (eg. an accounts receivable).

unemployment taxes: tax collected by the federal government and often by states, assessed on companies to help pay for unemployment compensation.

USB drive: see "flash drive" (above).

useful life: how long an asset can be expected to produce, or be able to be used. It is typically associated with depreciation. Reference: Appendix D - Accounting Basics > "Depreciating" Assets.

vendor: a company that sells a product or service to your company.

vendor statement: see "statement" (above).

W-2: see "Form W-2" (above).

W-3: see "Form W-3" (above).

W-4: see "Form W-4" (above).

W-9: see "Form W-9" (above).

wage base: see "wage limit" (below).

wage cap: see "wage limit" (below).

wage limit: the maximum amount of wages for a year, upon which tax (eg. social security) is applied. Reference: Chapter 2 - Tasks > Payroll Taxes (aka: "wage base" or "wage cap").

wholesale: to sell, not directly to the public, but to retail outlets or go-between companies.

withholding allowances: see "personal allowances" (above).

work-in-process (inventory): goods that are in the middle of being manufactured. They are neither raw materials, nor finished goods inventory, yet (aka: "work-in-progress" inventory).

worker's compensation insurance: is insurance in case an employee is injured on the job. Laws vary by state, but it is widely required to be carried. Visit http://www.workerscompensationinsurance.com/ to find your state's laws.

write-off (accounts receivable): to take an account that has become uncollectible, off the books. Reference: Appendix D - Accounting 'Basics' > Writing-Off a Receivable.

year-to-date (information): information from January 1 through today's date, whatever date today is. Examples include: sales year-to-date, and net income year-to-date.//

Full-Charge Bookkeeping

STUDY OUTLINE

by
Nick J. DeCandia, CPA

Copyright 2015
All Rights Reserved.

STUDY OUTLINE
Preface

You might think that covering a 110 page text in a semester is challenging. But, if you break it down via an outline, with approximately one bullet point per paragraph, the task becomes more manageable. In fact, most chapters or tasks I cover in a one-page outline. For chapters longer than the one-page outline, I leave two or more days to study. To proceed, you should first spend ~15-20 minutes reading the associated chapter/pages in the book. For instance, since I've divided the "Accounts Payable" chapter into two classes, you should read approximately half of that chapter. Next, spend ~10-15 minutes reviewing the bullet points (for that chapter / those pages) in the Study Outline. And, finally, spend another 10-15 minutes reviewing the associated Questions and Answers (Q & A) in the Test Bank, that follows the Study Outline. Spending three classes per week (35-50 minutes per class), you will finish 38 classes in less than 13 weeks.

Note: the material in the Appendices is subject to testing on the certification exam. So, I have outlined what you need to know, after Class 38. There are four outline pages, covering the Appendices - which should present less than a week of additional study material.

Table of Contents & Suggested Schedule

Class 1: Ch. 1 - Introduction, Ch. 2 - Tasks > Human Resource Administration	pg. 117
Class 2: Ch. 2 - Tasks > Accounts Payable	pg. 118
Class 3: Ch. 2 - Tasks > Accounts Payable	pg. 119
Class 4: Ch. 2 - Tasks > Accounts Receivable	pg. 120
Class 5: Ch. 2 - Tasks > Collections	pg. 121
Class 6: Ch. 2 - Tasks > Payroll	pg. 122
Class 7: Ch. 2 - Tasks > Payroll	pg. 123
Class 8: Ch. 2 - Tasks > Commissions & Bonuses	pg. 124
Class 9: Ch. 2 - Tasks > Payroll Taxes	pg. 125
Class 10: Ch. 2 - Tasks > Other Taxes	pg. 126
Class 11: Ch. 5* - Debits and Credits	pg. 127
Class 12: Ch. 5* - Debits and Credits	pg. 128
Class 13: Ch. 2 - Tasks > General Ledger	pg. 129
Class 14: Ch. 2 - Tasks > General Ledger, Fixed Assets	pg. 130
Class 15: Ch. 2 - Tasks > Bank Reconciliations	pg. 131
Class 16: Ch. 2 - Tasks > Petty Cash	pg. 132
Class 17: Ch. 2 - Tasks > State-Specific Tasks	pg. 133
Class 18: Ch. 2 - Tasks > Financial Statements or Monthly Reports	pg. 134
Class 19: Ch. 2 - Tasks > Financial Statements or Monthly Reports	pg. 135
Class 20: Ch. 2 - Tasks > Year-End Items	pg. 136
Class 21: Ch. 2 - Tasks > Year-End Items	pg. 137
Class 22: Ch. 2 - Tasks > Corporate Taxes	pg. 138
Class 23: Ch. 3 - Authorities	pg. 139
Class 24: Ch. 4 - Manual Bookkeeping	pg. 140
Class 25: Ch. 6* - Computers	pg. 141
Class 26: Ch. 6* - Computers	pg. 142
Class 27: Ch. 7 - Insurance	pg. 143
Class 28: Ch. 7 - Insurance	pg. 144
Class 29: Ch. 8 - Industries	pg. 145
Class 30: Ch. 8 - Industries	pg. 146
Class 31: Ch. 8 - Industries	pg. 147
Class 32: Ch. 8 - Industries	pg. 148
Class 33: Ch. 9 - Dealing(s) with the CPA	pg. 149
Class 34: Ch. 10 - Bookkeeper as Management?	pg. 150
Class 35: Ch. 10 - Bookkeeper as Management?	pg. 151
Class 36: Ch. 11 - A Word about Professionalism & Ethics	pg. 152
Class 37: Ch. 12 - A Word about 'Audits'	pg. 153
Class 38: Ch. 12 - A Word about 'Audits'	pg. 154
Study Outline for Appendices (Certification Exam Material)	pg. 155

* Note: *Chapter 5 - Debits and Credits* is purposefully out of sequence to provide that information when needed.

Chapter 1 - Introduction

- *What is a "Full-Charge" Bookkeeper?*
    - One who performs all of the bookkeeping tasks of any small business, including payroll taxes and monthly financial statements, with little or no supervision.
    - The only exception is corporate taxes - which are typically outsourced to a CPA.

- The scope of this course is to cover:
    - Profit-sector businesses (non-profit organizations are another subject).
    - All *federal* laws/taxes associated with bookkeeping.
    - The majority of the different state laws/taxes you'll run into.

- How to Get Started, When Hired:
    - Questions to Clarify / Defining the Position:
        - What exactly will I be responsible for (any tasks that will be outsourced)?
        - Are there any areas that need more urgent attention?
    - Getting Started:
        - Make a list of current employees - to be prepared for your first payroll.
        - Human resource files: contain Forms W-4 & I-9 (both required by law).
        - Get a handle on the company bills, and then the company receivables.
    - Damage Control?
        - Was the bookkeeper's position vacant for long - before you arrived?
        - If so, have all payroll tax reports been filed, any "shut-off notices"?

- After Getting Started (Above) Review the "New Job Checklist" at the end of Chapter 1.

- Filing System:
    - Are bookkeeper's file drawers organized well enough?
    - File drawer organization typically includes the following:
        - 1 or 2 drawers for Accounts Payable (Paid separate from Unpaid).
        - 1 or 2 drawers for Accounts Receivable (Paid separate from Unpaid).
        - A drawer for Payroll Timesheets, Payroll Tax Reports & Monthly Reports

---

Chapter 2 - Tasks > Human Resource Administration

- Why Human Resource Administration for the Bookkeeper?
    - Small companies have few or no other administrative personnel.
    - You will need information from Form W-4 for payroll.
    - Form I-9 tells you that person is legal to work in the United States.

- How should the Human Resource files be organized?
    - Terminated employees' files separated from active employees' files.
    - Both sections alphabetized by employees' last names.

Chapter 2 - Tasks > Accounts Payable

- What are Accounts Payable? Answer: the bills (or 'invoices') your company owes.

- Locate Two File Drawers:
    - Paid Bills
    - Unpaid Bills

- Incoming Mail: pay attention to who is receiving the bills.

- Packing Slips:
    - Defined: is a form shipped with product representing receipt of goods.
    - Store in folder entitled, "Packing Slips", alphabetized by company name.
    - Match to Invoice (when invoice arrives).

- Purchase Orders:
    - Defined: a *purchase order* is an approval to purchase something - includes prices.
    - Often used in companies with at least $5 million in sales.
    - Used to verify prices on incoming bills.

- Freight: glance at the shipping charge - to be sure it's not ridiculous.

- Enter into the (computer) system, check mark, and file invoice.

- Vendor Statements:
    - Defined: a *vendor* is a company that sells a product or service.
    - Defined: *vendor statements* list all outstanding or unpaid bills (aka: invoices), and are sent once per month.
    - Balance to monthly statements & make sure all invoices/payments are accounted for.
    - *Post* finance charges. Note: *paying* them is ~between your boss & the vendor.

- Summary:
    - *Incoming mail* - if you can't do them when they come in, file bills and statements in "Unentered Bills" folder you can keep in you In-Box.
    - *Match bills to packing slips* - verifying receipt of goods.
    - *Compare bills to purchase orders* - verifying prices charged, if PO's are used.
    - *List significant vendor communications* - like "Past Due" or any "Shut-Off Notices"
    - *Enter bills into the system* - glancing at the freight charge.
    - *Balance to vendor statements* - posting any finance charges.
    - *File bills & statements* - alphabetically in the "Unpaid" or "To Be Paid" Drawer

- Defined: a *shut-off notice* is a written communication, usually from a utility company, saying that your bills are past due and you are about to lose service.

(continued next page)

Chapter 2 - Tasks > Accounts Payable (cont.)

- Should Bookkeeper Be A Signer On The Checking Account?
  - The Author Recommends Against It For Several Reasons:
    - You Have Enough To Do
    - To Stay Out of Trouble With The Owner - As Far As Approving Payments On Your Own.
    - To Maintain "Segregation Of Duties" For Security Purposes.
    - Defined: *segregation of duties* means to separate those tasks that, if not separated, could lead to undetected theft.

- Aging of Accounts Payable:
  - Defined: an *aging* is a listing of companies, invoices, dates and dollar amounts.
  - See example in the book.

- Two Types of Companies Out There:
  - If Your Company Pays Bills Timely:
    - You should work to take the discounts offered in the fine print.
    - For example "2/10, Net 30" - means 2% discount can be taken if invoice is paid within 10 days, with the balance due in 30 days.
  - If Your Company Does *Not* Pay Timely:
    - You will need to keep up with, and pass along communications from vendors.
      - Use Telephone Message Pad For Payment Requests Via Phone
      - Read Statements & Letters Carefully
      - Write a List of Requests to Include: Dates, Amounts & Basic Message.
      - Photocopy & Give to Owner Regularly.
    - If threatened action is critical to your companies operation that day, like a shut-off notice, bring to owner's attention immediately.

- Producing a check: include account number and invoice/s paid - on memo line or check stub.

- Credit applications: it is typically the bookkeeper's responsibility to fill-out the applications, but the owner's responsibility to provide the information used.

- Factoring:
  - Defined: *factoring* means to sell accounts receivable to another company, for say 80 cents on the dollar.
  - Bookkeeper needs to be aware that some companies sell their receivables. The invoice should have a 'notice' stamped on it, indicating the same.

Chapter 2 - Tasks > Accounts Receivable

- What are Accounts Receivable? Answer: What customers owe your company.

- The key is keeping organized records:
    - Separate 'Paid' from 'Unpaid'.
    - File by company name, not month of sale.

- Aging of Accounts Receivable:
    - Defined: *accounts receivable aging* lists what customers owe you, including dates and dollar amounts.
    - See example in the book.

- Statements of Account:
    - Defined: a *statement of account* is a detailed listing of unpaid bills/invoices.
    - Typically statements are sent once per month in order to keep accounts straight and let the other party know if money is owed.
    - Do consult with your boss before starting any 'stringent' collection activity.

- Effective Credit Policy / Extending Credit:
    - Use a credit application:
        - Gets name of A/P contact person.
        - Gets signature agreeing to finance charges.
        - Gets physical address (in case you need to serve a legal complaint).
        - Get some idea of how this customer's been paying others.
    - Offer "2/10, Net 30" to encourage prompt payment.
    - 60-Day Cut-Off Policy: if bills reach 60 days old either they pay or you don't provide product / service.

- What is "factoring"?   Also mentioned in A/P, above.
    - Defined: *factoring* means selling A/R to another company, for say 80 cents on the dollar.
    - This arrangement can be useful because you receive your money upon shipment of your product - by wire the next business day.

Chapter 2 - Tasks > Collections

- What are "collections"?
    - Answer: collecting accounts receivable from customers who are not paying timely enough.

- "Statements of Account" are a good place to start collections - for several reasons:
    - Defined: *statements of account* are typically sent once per month listing all outstanding invoices.
    - They help keep balances straight between you and your customers.
    - They let them know you have attention on how much they owe you.
    - They provide a place on which to jot a note, like "When might we expect payment?".

- Beyond Statements:
    - Collections should start *only* with your boss' approval.
    - He or she may have made certain arrangements with certain customers.

- Start softly:
    - They may have never received or lost your invoice.
    - Just get in communication with them.

- The Next Approach:
    - Continue to pursue, by phone - *with steady determination.*
    - If you can't get through via the telephone (eg. getting the run-around), mailing a "Past Due Notice" (Appendix E) may be an option.
    - Document your actions. Reference: "Collection Form" - Appendix E.
    - If you're still not getting anywhere, go to your boss for the next approach.

- Delaying or suspending shipment of product / services may be needed.

- Document, communicate and follow-up is the best way to stay on top of collection activity.

- If they are no longer a customer, you may need to consider legal remedy.
    - Laws vary by state/locale.
    - But an attorney is not always necessary for this approach.

- A 60-Day cut-off policy may help with collections.
    - Apply the policy across the board - to all customers.
    - When your customers' bills reach 60 days out either they make payment or you don't ship product/services.
    - You can let them know it's not personal - just part and parcel to your survival.

Chapter 2 - Tasks > Payroll

- Start with a current list of employees, their pay rates and withholding allowances.

- What you need to know before doing any payroll:
    - *Minimum Wage*:
        - Last Federal minimum wage increase was July 24, 2009 to: $7.25/hour.
        - January 1, 2015: 20 states increased their minimum wage rate.
        - 29 states now have minimum wage rates higher than the federal.
        - IF A STATE'S MINIMUM WAGE IS HIGHER THAN THE FEDERAL, THE STATE RATE APPLIES!
        - Food & Beverage Industry: $2.13/hr. is the minimum, as long as tips get it to federal minimum wage. (Some states have a higher base wage.)
    - *Overtime*: federal law requires any hours worked over 40 in a seven-day period, be paid overtime - not less than time and a half.
    - *Record keeping*: federal law requires companies to keep the following records for hourly employees:
        - Identifying information (name, address, social security #).
        - Hours worked and wages earned.

- Doing Payroll via a Computer:
    - Set-up: payroll module running, employee information current.
    - Doing It: reference steps 1-14 in the book.

- Doing Payroll Manually:
    - Set-up - you will need the following:
        - List of current employees' names, and pay rates.
        - Tax Tables: can be found in IRS's Publication 15, "Employer's Tax Guide".
        - Employees' Exemptions: found on their completed Form W-4.
        - Adding machine or calculator.
    - Doing It: reference steps 1-14 in the book.

- Notes:
    - If your employee is reporting tips in the Food & Beverage Industry, you are required to collect tax on those tips.
    - If you need to reimburse an employee (example: for travel) do a separate check.
    - If your employee wants someone else to "pick-up" his/her pay check:
        - Get a note from your employee signed, naming the person.
        - When the person shows up, look at his/her ID.
        - File the note in your employee's HR file.
    - The check date always determines the tax quarter of a payroll not the pay-period ending date.

(continued next page)

Chapter 2 - Tasks > Payroll (cont.)

- Independent Contractors:
  - What is an independent contractor?
    - People who are doing work for your company.
    - They are self-employed.
    - They pay their own payroll taxes.
    - We pay them straight wages without taxes deducted.
  - Example: in the construction industry they are known as "sub-contractors", eg. the electrician.
  - Even though you aren't deducting taxes, they still owe the government taxes, and you must help report their income, via Form 1099 (at year-end).
  - IRS is "cracking down" in this area, in order to ensure receipt of all taxes due.
    - Publication 15-A, "Employer's Supplemental Tax Guide", chapter entitled "Employee or Independent Contractor?" lists all the requirements.
    - Penalties can be stiff, so it's better to 'err' on the side of employee rather than independent contractor.
    - The IRS can make a determination for you via IRS Form SS-8, "Determination of Worker Status...".
  - If you do have one working for your company:
    - Start a file-folder and obtain the following:
    - Form W-9 completed: this lists his or her Taxpayer ID Number.
    - A certificate of worker's compensation insurance: without this *your* company will be required to pay for his/her insurance.

Chapter 2 - Tasks > Commissions & Bonuses

- Defined: *commissions* are pay earned by a sales person on sales made, while a *bonus* is extra money given to an employee usually for a particular reason - eg. Christmas.

- If you have no commissioned employees or if the sales people are salaried, you will not pay any commissions.

- Be sure you know the exact percentage(s) agreed to between the owner & commissioned employee.

- Calculating Commissions:
    - If you have a single % commission situation (same rate for all sales), you can easily calculate commissions manually.
    - For multiple % commission situations (different rates depending on: how much or to whom it's sold) use of a computer spreadsheet program will help.
    - Reference: Appendix E > Commission Spreadsheet Form.

- Review examples in the book, for single percentage and multiple percentage commission situations.

- Commissions and bonuses are fully taxable:
    - Deduct federal withholding and FICA from commissions and bonuses.
    - Include them when calculating Federal Unemployment Tax.
    - And include them on your employee's W-2, at year-end.
    - Reference: IRS Publication 15, "Supplemental Wages" chapter.

- Store commissions in a separate binder for each commissioned employee to make it easy for the boss to locate.

Chapter 2 - Tasks > Payroll Taxes

- Defined: (simply put) *payroll taxes* are taxes that arise because of payroll, and consist of both federal and state specific taxes.

- Scope - as mentioned above, it's not within the scope of this course to detail:
  - The specifics of any one state nor the specifics of any one tax year.
  - Rather we will detail: all federal payroll taxes, the typical state ones, and how to find both your state's specifics and the specifics of any one tax year.

- Federal Taxes:
  - Federal payroll taxes consist of deposits, quarterly reports and annual reports.
  - Deposits: Reference: IRS Publication 15 (Circular E), "Depositing Taxes"
    - Defined: federal payroll tax deposits are made after payrolls to pay taxes withheld from each employee plus taxes due from the employer.
    - Amount =
      - Employ*ee*'s FICA (7.65%) +
      - Employ*er*'s 'Matching' FICA (7.65%) +
      - Federal Income Tax Withheld from Employee
      - = 15.3% Gross Wages + Federal Withholding
    - When to Deposit: your company will be under either the "monthly" or "semi-weekly" schedule.
    - How to Deposit: IRS requires electronic deposit, using EFTPS (Electronic Federal Tax Payment System). Reference: IRS Publication 15.
  - Quarterly Reports:
    - Defined: there are two *federal quarterly reports* - Form 941 and just payment of FUTA.
    - Form 941 - "Employer's Quarterly Federal Tax Return": if all payroll tax deposits were made, no payment will be needed - just Form 941 to mail.
    - Payment of FUTA (Federal Unemployment Tax):
      - There is no form to file, just payment each quarter - Form 940 is an annual form.
      - FUTA tax is generally reduced by the amount of State Unemployment Taxes (SUTA) paid.
      - Reference: IRS Circular E > "Federal Unemployment (FUTA) Tax".
  - Annual Report/s:
    - Form 940 "Employer's Annual Federal Unemployment (FUTA) Tax Return" is the only federal annual payroll tax return.
    - Form 941 is strictly a *quarterly* report.

- State Payroll Taxes:
  - The typical state payroll taxes are:
    - State Unemployment (SUTA) Tax
    - State income tax.
  - Each state is different. Reference: "Ways to Uncover Your State's Payroll Tax Requirements" in Ch. 2 - Tasks > Payroll Taxes > State Payroll Taxes. ///

Chapter 2 - Tasks > Other Taxes

- Defined: *other taxes* are the typical ones a bookkeeper might run into that aren't payroll or corporate taxes. They vary by state, but the typical other taxes are:
    - State sales tax
    - Property tax and
    - A business license fee.
    - Intangible Taxes are *not* very typical.

- State Sales Tax (aka "Gross Receipts Tax"):
    - Defined: *state sales tax* is generally levied on retail sales of just products, while *gross receipts tax* is typically levied on products and services sold.
    - Some transactions, within a state, may not be subject to sales tax.
        - Example: non-profit organizations are exempt from sales tax in New Mexico.
        - See book for ways to uncover your state's requirements.

- Property Tax:
    - Defined: *property tax* is generally levied on land & buildings - based on their assessed values.
    - The higher the assessed value the higher the tax.

- Business License Fee:
    - Defined: a *business license fee* buys a right, or permit, to operate a business within the city or county lines.
    - Example: the City of Albuquerque levies $35 per year in order to conduct business with the city limits.

Note: knowledge of debits and credits - is needed for General Ledger Journal Entries, so this chapter is taught before proceeding to Tasks > General Ledger.

Chapter 5 - Debits and Credits

- Q: Why do I need to know debits & credits?
- A: For starters, knowing debits and credits will allow you to make journal entries - for things like petty cash & depreciation.

- Defined: *debit* (in accounting usage) simply means "left" side of a ledger, and *credit* means, simply, the right side of a ledger.

- Debits and credits are used in a "dual entry" system.
  - Defined: *dual entry* means every transaction affects 2 accounts.
  - Example: you buy equipment - your cash account will decrease, but your equipment account will increase (ref: Chart of Accounts - Appendix B).

- In order to do debits and credits you really only need three facts:
  - Assets - Liabilities = Equity of the Owner *or*
    Assets = Liabilities + Owner's Equity ("Basic Accounting Equation")
  - All debits must equal all credits - in a journal entry (aka: the journal entry "balances").
  - To increase assets, debit them. Notice assets are on the left/debit side of the equation.
  - The rest of debit & credit usage can be derived from these three facts.

- Assets, Liabilities & Owner's Equity:
  - Derive, using opposites:
    - Since debiting increases Assets, crediting decreases them.
    - Liabilities and Owner's Equity are on the right side of the Basic Accounting Equation (opposite Assets) so to increase them, credit them.
    - Since crediting increases Liabilities & Owner's Equity, debiting decreases them.
  - Let's do some examples, and reference the "Brief Review" in the text.
    - See Example 1 in the book: buying equipment for cash.
    - See Example 2: you pay a bill.

- Notes on Conventions:
  - Not all journal entries consist of just one debit and one credit. You can have as many of either, just as long as the entry balances (all debits = all credits).
  - It is customary, however, to list all debit(s) first and then all credit(s).

(continued next page)

Chapter 5 - Debits and Credits (cont.)

- Revenues & Expenses:
    - We've just covered Assets, Liabilities & Owner's Equity. All that's left is Revenues & Expenses.
    - Revenues:
        - I like to think of a sales transaction.
        - You just made a sale so your cash increases or gets debited.
        - To balance it you need a credit. So to increase Revenues, credit them.
        - See Example 3, in the book ("You make a sale").
    - Expenses:
        - Here's how I remember expenses.
        - When you pay an expense you decrease cash, or credit cash.
        - To balance the transaction, you need a debit.
        - So, debit expenses to increase or record one.
    - Feel free to make up some more examples.

- Note: *debits and credits* - are not something you read once and say, "Oh, I get that now."
    - No, first you will need to practice them.
    - Then, it is something you will have to "put there" - in your mind, each time you have to journalize a transaction.
    - And to put it there I say to myself, "To increase assets, debit them."
    - Then I find things start to flow from there.

- Refer back to this chapter as needed.

Chapter 2 - Tasks > General Ledger

- Defined: the *general ledger* is that place - in the computer where all transactions (debits and credits) get posted.

- Note: if you have not studied debits and credits, you need to, before proceeding with the general ledger.

- Manual bookkeeping with debits and credits is pretty much a thing of the past, so we will focus on the general ledger in relation to computers, here.

- There are several things to do with the General Ledger:
    - Put journal entries in for some transactions
    - Print transaction listings and
    - Maintain the "chart of accounts".

- Journal Entries:
    - Defined: a *journal entry* is nothing more than debits and credits "in balance" describing a transaction (where: "in balance" here means all debits equal all credits.
    - Most transactions entered into the computer will automatically post to the General Ledger.
    - For example:
        - Issuing a payroll check through the Payroll module, or
        - Paying bills through the Accounts Payable module,
        - These transactions will automatically post to the General Ledger.
    - But, the bookkeeper needs to be on the look-out for transactions not automatically hitting the computer (for example: petty cash).
        - Defined: *petty cash* is a small amount of cash kept on hand for incidental items (example: buying pizza for lunch).
        - Using cash like that, will happen without going through the computer - at all. So, you will need to enter it manually into the computer (via a journal entry).
        - Similarly, depreciation (or the "using-up" of an asset) will come from the CPA and not otherwise be entered into your bookkeeping program. So, you will need to enter that manually (via a journal entry) as well.
    - Journal entries access the Chart of Accounts (example: Appendix B).

- Producing a Transaction Listing:
    - Defined: a *transaction listing* lists all of the transactions (debits and credits) for selected accounts, over a specified period of time.
    - At certain times, you may need to produce a transaction listing (example: if you wanted to research how much was spent on a "point-of-sale" system).
    - Fear not: generating a transaction listing is self-explanatory, within that area of the bookkeeping program.

(continued next page)

Chapter 2 - Tasks > General Ledger (cont.)

- Maintaining the "Chart of Accounts":
  - Defined: the *chart of accounts* lists every account in the general ledger. Reference: Appendix B - Chart of Accounts.
  - Most computer bookkeeping programs have preloaded charts, which you can tailor a bit to your needs.
  - Don't delete any accounts with transactions attached and be particular about what accounts you add.
  - For example: you might add an account if your store does purchase a "Point-of Sale" system - in order to track how much is spent on it.

- Balancing the General Ledger:
  - Defined: *balancing* in this instance means all debits equal all credits posted for the month.
  - Fortunately, most (if not all) computer bookkeeping programs today will not allow you to post a transaction that's not in balance - so, the G/L balances automatically.
  - If your (bookkeeping) program does not balance automatically you will need to:
    - Run a "trial balance".
    - Defined: a *trial balance* is a detailed listing of all debits and credits posted to the general ledger, for a certain period of time (usually one month).
    - If the trial balance does not balance, you will have to:
      - Hunt/find the out of balance transaction(s).
      - Correct it.
      - Reference: Tasks > Bank Reconciliations > Finding Outages.

Chapter 2 - Tasks > Fixed Assets

- Defined: *fixed assets* are another name for "Property, Plant & Equipment". Where fixed assets are listed on the Chart of Accounts, PP&E are listed on the Balance Sheet.

- Examples include: land, buildings, vehicles, furniture, fixtures and equipment.

- Your Responsibility:
  - Track fixed assets purchased during the year.
  - Post those assets to the General Ledger.
  - Communicate this information to the CPA at the end of the year.

- The best way to track fixed assets is keep a file-folder with a hand written list and copies of the invoices behind the list.

- Post assets to the GL as purchased and communicate to the CPA at year-end.

Chapter 2 - Tasks > Bank Reconciliations

- *No Difference* - a corporate bank reconciliation is no different than reconciling your own personal bank account - just longer.

- Do use a form, typically the one provided by the bank, to reconcile - so as to leave a proper and adequate "paper trail".

- Defined: a *paper trail* is records showing how things were done or that they were done correctly.

- Even if using a computer bookkeeping program to reconcile, do complete a *paper reconciliation* first, then enter the data. It will give you something to work off of.

- If credit cards are involved, photo copy the bank statement & highlight off the easiest figures first.

- Finding Outages:
  - Defined: an *outage* is an out of balance situation, or an amount that you're out of balance.
  - Use analytical powers:
    - Come up with one or two places to look.
    - Start in the place that either:
      - Most likely contains the outage (in your mind) *or*
      - Is the easiest to search through.
    - Leave no stone unturned (even if you think "that" is certainly not the place).
    - Don't spend 4 days looking for one penny.
  - Two tips:
    - Divide by 9 tip: if you have a transposition error (defined below), your outage will divide evenly by nine!
    - Defined: a *transposition error* is one where you reversed the order of two numbers - causing an out of balance situation. Example: $954.00 (the correct amount) was entered as $945.00 (reversing the order of the 5 and 4). Transposition errors always divide evenly by nine.
    - Divide by 2 tip: if you added rather than subtracted or vice versa your outage will be twice the transaction amount. Dividing by two will help you find it easier.
    - Note: the above tips really only work if you have just one reason you are out of balance.

Chapter 2 - Tasks > Petty Cash

- Defined: *petty cash* is a small amount of cash kept on hand for incidental items.
    - Preferably kept in a locked box
    - Example: buying pizza for the office for lunch.

- Note: dealing with petty cash involves debits & credits so be sure to study Chapter 5 - Debits and Credits before proceeding here.

- Usage Controls:
    - If you just started at the company, be sure the cash you inherit is correct (what the General Ledger says is there).
    - Petty cash should be kept in a locked box with, at most, the bookkeeper & company owner accessing (for control purposes).
    - Purchases from petty cash should involve:
        - Approval from the company owner (verbal approval is ok).
        - Signed petty cash receipt from those receiving cash.
        - Reference: Appendix E - Sample Forms > Petty Cash - Receipts
        - Store receipt(s) & change brought back.
        - Staple petty cash slip & store receipt together and store in the box.
    - To refund the petty cash box when empty cash a check at the bank. Reference: Appendix E - Sample Forms > Petty Cash - Change Order

- If your business uses a cash register:
    - You probably won't need a petty cash box, but you will still need:
        - A paper trail: slip of paper indicating cash was removed, by whom, and for what purpose - best left either in the cash register or with the bookkeeper.
        - Bookkeeper to make a journal entry, into the computer bookkeeping system.

- End of Month:
    - Balance petty cash: make sure that the beginning amount of cash in the box, less all petty cash slips/receipts, for the month, equals what cash is left.
    - Post to the General Ledger:
        - Note: if your petty cash expenses are less than say $100 for the year, you may be able to just put those expenses to "office supplies".
        - If not you'll need to "code" all petty cash slips:
        - Defined: *code* means to write the corresponding account numbers, from the Chart of Accounts, on each slip for each expense used.
        - Example: #5220 'Meals & Entertainment' for pizza.
        - You can have more than one account per petty cash slip.
        - Run an adding machine tape(s) to get totals for each account.
        - Enter it into the General Ledger through a journal entry. See example in book.
    - Store Receipts:
        - You can use a manila envelope (9 x 12").
        - Label: "Petty Cash - January 20xx". ///

Chapter 2 - Tasks > State Specific Tasks

- Defined: *state specific tasks* are tasks required by, or reported to the state in which you live, (not including state payroll taxes).

- While it's not within the scope of this text to list all states' requirements, there will probably not be too many state-specific tasks (other than payroll taxes).

- There is one common to all states - Personal Responsibility and Work Opportunity Reconciliation Act (PRWORA):
  - Enacted by Congress.
  - But reported to your state's directory.
  - Requires employers in all 50 states to report new hires & rehires to the directory
  - This helps facilitate child support payments for parents who change jobs frequently.
  - Uses state forms and your state's directory for reporting.
  - You can probably find your state's directory on-line @ "[your state's] new hire directory".

- The text lists ways to uncover state requirements.

- Remember, smaller companies do not have many administrative personnel working for them, so any state specific tasks will typically fall to the bookkeeper.

Chapter 2 - Tasks > Financial Statements or Monthly Reports

- Don't let the words "financial statements" scare you.
  - There are typically only 2 financial statements used in a small business:
    - "Income Statement" (aka: "Profit and Loss")
    - "Balance Sheet" (defined below)
    - Appendix C - Financial Statements: has samples of both.
    - Computer bookkeeping programs (including QuickBooks and Sage 50) have financial statements built in.

- Defined: an *Income Statement* subtracts expenses from revenues to give how much income you had for the period (month or year).

- Defined: a *Balance Sheet* lists assets, liabilities, and "owner's equity" as of the last day in the period.

- Defined: *owner's equity* equals assets minus liabilities. It is a measure of the 'equity' an owner has in the business.

- Note: owners will typically have other reports they want to see (listed below).

- Enter All Data - Before Printing Any Reports:
  - Enter all invoices for payable & receivables.
  - Typically, businesses allow the mail ~3-7 days after month-end, to be sure all of last month's invoices have been received.
  - If you hand write checks, be sure all of last month's checks are entered.
  - Do any journal entry for petty cash.
  - Balance last month's bank statement.
  - If you have a really old version of bookkeeping software you may need to balance the General Ledger. (See: Tasks > General Ledger > Balancing).

- Print Reports:
  - Print reports at the beginning of every month (for the previous month - after all data is entered).
  - Typical reports include:
    - Financial Statements:
      - Income Statement
      - Balance Sheet
    - Check Register(s)
    - Agings of:
      - Payables
      - Receivables
    - General Ledger Transaction Listing.
  - Income Statement may need to show "Year to Date" figures as well as the previous month's figures.
  - Copy reports to the business owner, as well as into a folder or binder.

Chapter 2 - Tasks > Financial Statements or Monthly Reports (cont.)

- Changing to the Next Accounting Period / Month:
    - "Closing" the month is typically not required anymore.
    - If need to "close", the program should prompt what you need to do.

- Prior Period Amount Missed:
    - Defined: a *prior period* is a month or year prior to the one you are currently in.
    - Scenario: you discover an $8 invoice that originally got lost in the mail (say it's 2 to 3 months old).
    - You might consider the cost vs. benefit of entering an $8 invoice in a prior period & having to reprint, copy, & distribute reports again.
    - Possible Solution:
        - Pencil in today's date (the date you received it) - on the invoice.
        - Enter it in the computer for this (today's) date.

Chapter 2 - Tasks > Year-End Items

- Year-end items include the following:
  - W-2's
  - 1099's
  - Record Retention
  - Gathering Year-End Reports for Corporate Taxes.

- Form W-2's:
  - Defined: *W-2's* are the forms mailed by companies at the end of the year, indicating each employee's wages and taxes paid, for the calendar year.
  - They need to be done in January, after all payroll checks are generated for December.
  - W-2's should include all of an employee's commissions & bonuses, for the year.
  - QuickBooks and Sage 50 have W-2 & 1099 generating capabilities.
  - Do your 4th quarter payroll taxes, and compare totals (payroll from all 4 quarters versus W-2 totals).
  - Use Form W-3 to "transmit" & mail all of your W-2's.
  - Since accounting for wages, print "Draws Taken by the Owner".
    - Defined: a *draw* is a removal of cash from the business, beyond the owner's salary.
    - Give one copy along with his/her W-2 to the owner & file a copy.

- Form 1099-Misc:
  - Defined: *Form 1099-MISC* is the IRS form entitled, "Miscellaneous Income".
    - Bookkeepers are required to file a 1099-Misc when amounts paid to any contract labor exceed $600 for a calendar year.
    - Ref: Tasks > Payroll > Independent Contractors.
  - Printing 1099's:
    - Most computer bookkeeping programs will print in the correct boxes once blank forms are loaded.
    - If not, blank forms from your local IRS office & a typewriter will do.
  - Use IRS Form 1096 to transmit and mail any/all 1099's.

- Blank Forms on Which to Print W-2's & 1099's:
  - Sources:
    - W-2's: office supply stores or QuickBooks / Sage 50 companies.
    - 1099's: the local IRS office is good if you just need a few.
  - Multi-copy Forms:
    - W-2's you need at least 4 copies: 3 for employee (Federal taxes, State taxes, and a copy for employee), and 1 copy for bookkeeper's file,
    - 1099's:
      - Are themselves a 3-copy form: IRS, State & recipient.
      - Be sure to make a copy for the bookkeeper's file.
  - Window envelopes: make mailing W-2's much easier - no need to address envelopes.

(continued next page)

Chapter 2 - Tasks > Year-End Items (cont.)

- ➢ Record Retention:
  - o Defined: *record retention* includes the storing of last year's files & the starting of new ones - for the upcoming year.
  - o Storing of last year's files:
    - Realize that it is important to save records for "audit" purposes.
    - Most save records according to a schedule:
      - Defined: a *record retention schedule* is a list showing how long to save which types of records
      - Example: retain Accounts Payable records 3-5 years
    - You work for them: so if they want to create their own schedule or store them indefinitely, that may be fine.
  - o Keep a list of your numbered boxes, contents and dates of stored files.
    - Reference: "Record Retention Form" - Appendix E.
    - Label the outside of boxes, with the box number and brief contents.
  - o Destroying:
    - Some companies just toss box(es) in dumpster.
    - Others shred, particularly the more sensitive documents - such as G/L reports, commissions & payroll records - showing $'s.
  - o Start new files: typing labels makes a more professional looking file system, and is easier on the eyes.

- ➢ Start Gathering Corporate Tax Items for the CPA:
  - o Corporate taxes are the only bookkeeping task to outsource.
  - o Come early February, call the CPA to see what s/he will need.
  - o Typical Corporate Tax Items Include:
    - Financial Statements: Income Statement & Balance Sheet.
    - A detailed list of fixed assets purchased during the year (including the date/s the item/s were placed in service).
    - Check register(s).
  - o Other Year-End Reports to CPA:
    - A detailed list of any charitable contributions made by your company.
    - Copies of payroll tax reports.
    - Employee payroll reports - showing summary amounts paid.
  - o Having the CPA review these reports will bolster confidence(s).
  - o Review your reports, for reasonableness, before presenting them to CPA.
  - o Hold these in a file-folder and reference Tasks > Corporate Taxes for a more complete list of things to do.

Chapter 2 - Tasks > Corporate Taxes

- Defined: *corporate taxes* are a tax on the income of a business for the year.

- Note: some companies use a "fiscal" rather than a calendar year.

- Defined: a *fiscal* year would be any 12 months other than the usual January 1 - December 31.
    - Example: July 1 - June 30.

- Bookkeeper's Responsibility:
    - Provide CPA needed information to produce the return/s.
    - Make "quarterly estimated tax payments".

- Defined: *quarterly estimated tax payments* are 'installments' of corporate income tax due.

- Providing the CPA the needed information to produce the return/s.
    - After doing "year-end items" in January, come February contact the CPA to see what s/he will need.
    - Typical corporate tax items may include:
        - Financial Statements
        - A detailed list any fixed assets added
        - Check register/s
        - Summary agings of payables & receivables
        - General Ledger - summary "transaction listing".
            - Defined: a *transaction listing* lists all of the transactions - debits and credits, for selected accounts over a specified period of time.
    - Additional items may include - "detailed transaction listings" for:
        - Computer Equipment Asset or Expense
        - Charitable Contributions/Gifts account
        - "Draws" by the Owner - account
            - Defined: a *draw* is a removal of cash from the business, beyond the owner's salary.
    - Note: some <u>states</u> have a corporate income tax return due.
    - The owner may also want you to send the CPA (mentioned previously):
        - Copies of the payroll tax reports and
        - An employee payroll report.

- Making quarterly estimated tax payments: contact the CPA two weeks prior for deposit amount, & method of payment.
    - Due dates and contact dates:

Tax Due Dates	Contact CPA Dates
April 15th	April 1
June 15th	June 1
September 15th	September 1
December 15th	December 1

    - Method of deposit/payment: IRS requires deposit electronically. //

Chapter 3 - Authorities

- Defined: *authorities* include those government agencies, at both the federal and state levels, responsible for either collecting taxes or administering laws (eg. the IRS).

- Authorities are very important to a full-charge bookkeeper, for things like payroll taxes.

- Authorities Frequently Used:
    - IRS:
        - Is about the only federal authority used frequently.
        - Has publications & forms to administer tasks like payroll & payroll taxes:
            - IRS Publication 15, "Employer's Tax Guide" is the first publication a bookkeeper should look at.
            - Forms 940 & 941 are the payroll tax forms at the federal level.
    - State-Specific Authorities:
        - Generally speaking, each state is different in what taxes it collects & how it collects them.
        - As mentioned previously, the typical state taxes are:
            - State Unemployment Tax (SUTA)
            - State sales tax, and
            - State income tax
        - It is also possible that your state will have more than one authority.
        - For example - in New Mexico:
            - The Tax & Revenue Dept. collects both state sales tax and state income tax.
            - And the N.M. Dept. of Workforce Solutions collects State Unemployment Tax.
        - Ways to Determine Your State's Tax Authorities:
            - Search the previous bookkeeper's files for prior tax reports.
            - Search on-line, requesting:
                1) "(your state's) Taxation Department", "Treasury Department" or "Department of Labor",
                2) "(your state's) payroll tax requirements"
                3) "(your state's) government"
            - Look in the government pages of your phone book, and make some calls.
- Other Authorities / Laws:
    - Most of these are covered in separate chapters.
    - Those not separately covered:
        - OSHA - Public Law 91-596: requires companies to track workplace injuries using pre-designed forms. Visit: www.osha.gov > A to Z > R > Recordkeeping.
        - Family Medical Leave Act: applies to companies with 50 or more employees.
        - American Disabilities Act: requires accommodation to handicapped.   ///

Chapter 4 - Manual Bookkeeping

- In order to learn to do bookkeeping well, or even correctly, one should learn it in this order: manual bookkeeping, debits & credits, followed by computer bookkeeping.

- Manual bookkeeping today would look something like - how a business owner/operator would run a business, without debits and credits or a computer.

- So, what can a business owner accomplish without debits / credits or a computer?
    - Maintain a checkbook, and therefore pay bills.
    - Do payroll, using tax tables provided by the IRS.
    - Calculate and pay payroll taxes (using IRS Publication #15, "Employer's Tax Guide").
    - Keep track of what customers owe you (on regular paper).
    - Calculate and pay any commissions.
    - Calculate and pay "other" taxes (like: state sales tax).
    - Reconcile the bank account/s.
    - Do any human resource administration (applications, I-9's & W-4's).

- What's left? Surprisingly little!
    - Financial Statements / Monthly Reports: which may *not* be a priority for a do-it-yourself business owner.
    - Corporate Taxes: are "outsourced" - regardless.

- The Next Steps:
    - Perhaps get a computer, not to do any debits and credits, but to help with spreadsheet-type tasks including:
        - Tracking what customers owe you,
        - Tracking any commissions,
        - Calculating any sales tax owed, and
        - Generating monthly totals.
    - Get an outside accountant to generate an Income (Profit/Loss) Statement, using the check register/s and monthly sales.
    - Finally, hire a full-charge bookkeeper:
        - If or when the business grows, and
        - If business owner tires of doing bookkeeping & can afford one.

Note: Chapter 5 - Debits and Credits is taught out of sequence. Since debits and credits are needed for the General Ledger it is taught just before that task in Chapter 2.

Chapter 6 - Computers

- If you haven't had a chance to learn about computers, it will help with:
  - Computer bookkeeping,
  - Finding employment (no matter what your field), and
  - Other tasks - whether at work or home.

- Bookkeeping Via A Computer:
  - Note: be sure to study debits & credits, because you will need it in order to put journal entries into the computer for things like petty cash & depreciation.
  - If there's a computer already in place, your job will be to make sure you know how to use the bookkeeping program - by going through the tutorial(s).
  - If you are to purchase a new computer bookkeeping program:
    - QuickBooks & Sage 50 Accounting are probably your best bets.
    - Sold in office supply stores and on-line.
    - Find the version that will best suit your company's needs. Read about what "modules" or features are included - with each version.
      - Defined: a *module* is a section of a computer bookkeeping program (for example: the Payroll module).
    - If your state has income tax, be sure those tax tables are loaded.
  - Remember most transactions will post automatically to the general ledger.
    - For example: when printing payroll checks through the payroll module.
    - So, you'll need to be on the look-out for transactions *not* automatically posting to the general ledger - like petty cash.
  - Then, you'll need to post those "manually" as a "journal entry".
    - I like to write-out my debits and credits on scratch paper before heading to the computer.
  - A good system for vendor ID numbers is the first four letters followed by two numbers. Example: FEDE01 for Federal Express.
  - Payroll Tax Table Updates:
    - You will, most likely, need to update the tax tables in your computer bookkeeping program once per year (for federal & state).
    - The newer versions of bookkeeping software often *require* updates or the programs won't deduct any taxes at all.
    - You will probably receive ads for the updates from the company who put out your bookkeeping software (around November).

(continued next page)

Chapter 6 - Computers (cont.)

- Bookkeeping Via A Computer (cont.):
  - Backing-up Your Data:
    - It's important to back-up your work each and every day!
    - Imagine backing-up once a month, having your hard drive quit, losing three weeks work and trying to explain that to your boss.
    - Your best bet will be to use a "flash" or "jump drive".
    - Defined: a *flash/travel/USB drive (aka: jump or thumb drive)* is a device used to back-up data.
      - It's about the size of a finger.
      - It plugs directly into a USB port.
      - They hold a Giga byte or more of memory.
      - They are very fast to work with and quite portable, as well.
    - It's also a good idea to keep a back-up copy "off premises" (home with you), and update it once per week (in case of a catastrophe at work, like fire / flood).

- What Else?
  - 'Office' Software:
    - Defined: *office software* typically refers to a word processing program and a spreadsheet program to be used in an office setting.
    - A word processing program for any letters that need to be sent, plus any forms you may want/need to create.
    - A spreadsheet program in order to calculate Federal Unemployment Taxes, for instance.
    - New computers typically come pre-loaded with some form of 'office' software like Microsoft Works.
    - If a purchase is in order, the author suggests:
      - A "Home / Student" version of Microsoft Office.
      - It comes with Word and spreadsheet capabilities - which is all a small business will need.
  - Computer Consultant - use for the following situations:
    - Web-site work
    - Network set-up.

Chapter 7 - Insurance

- We will be discussing:
  - Health Insurance,
  - "Corporate Liability Insurance" and
  - "Worker's Compensation Insurance" (defined within the sections below).

- Health Insurance:
  - Is not required for companies, with less than 50 full-time employees, to offer.
  - But is subject to state laws or insurance company requirements:
  - For example, in New Mexico most insurance companies required the employer to pay at least 50% of the premium(s).
  - The insurance company's "group plan" representative will know applicable laws/requirements.
  - Defined: a *group plan* is one that is offered to your entire company.
  - Bookkeepers need to have some knowledge of COBRA & HIPAA.
    - COBRA:
      - Defined: *COBRA* is a federal law that allows terminated employees and their families to continue health insurance coverage for up to 18 months (under certain circumstances).
      - Circumstances include job loss (voluntary or involuntary) & divorce.
      - Cost to continue coverage can be as much as normal premiums.
      - COBRA only applies to companies with 20 or more employees in the prior year.
      - Bookkeepers should check with the insurance company to see what they need for notification of terminated employees.
      - For more information, visit www.dol.gov >A to Z Index>C >COBRA.
    - HIPAA:
      - Defined: *HIPAA* stands for "Health Insurance Portability and Accountability Act". This federal act enforces a lot of things including the protection of privacy.
      - Re: bookkeepers, it requires "plan administrators" (may be the bookkeeper) to provide terminated employees, who had health insurance, a certificate of prior health coverage.
      - Defined: a *plan administrator* is that person, in the company you work for, who works with the health insurance. In smaller companies this is often the bookkeeper.
      - Typically, insurance companies will issue this certificate, but you'll need to check with them to be sure.
      - For more information, visit www.dol.gov >A to Z Index>H >HIPAA.

- Corporate Liability Insurance:
  - Defined: *corporate liability insurance* is more general coverage for things like fire or flood.
  - It's usually not required by law, but strongly suggested.
  - Bookkeepers need to be aware it exists, particularly if the bills come their way.

Chapter 7 - Insurance (cont.)

- Workers' Compensation Insurance:
  - Defined: *workers' compensation insurance* is insurance in case an employee is injured on the job.
  - Laws vary by state but it is *widely* required to be carried.
  - www.workerscompensationinsurance.com has links to all 50 states including state laws & regulations.
  - Your company's owner has probably set this up long ago, but you need to know about it and you'll probably see the bills.
  - Insurance rates are often based on an "audit".
    - Defined: an *audit* is an examination of some aspect of the company you work for.
    - They look at things like:
      - The number of employees in your company *and*
      - The type/s of work your employees do.
      - For instance, office workers will typically have lower insurance rates, than those doing heavy lifting all day.
    - The insurance company will look to the admin./bookkeeper to provide this information.
    - If you have a good record, they may allow you to "self-audit" (provide them the information yourself - per their form).
  - If you have an independent contractor working for your company:
    - Be sure to obtain a certificate of worker's compensation insurance from him/her.
    - Or *your* insurance company will require you to list him/her on your bill.

Chapter 8 - Industries

- Bookkeeping is essentially bookkeeping - no matter what the industry.

- But, let's look at some particularities to some of the industries out there.

- We'll look at:
    - Construction industry
    - Food and beverage industry
    - Manufacturing industry
    - Retail industry
    - Service industry
    - And we'll say a few words about the non-profit sector.

- Construction Industry:
    - Defined: the *construction industry* includes everything from site development (laying pipes for utilities) to garbage collection from the sites.
    - There are a number of things you may run into in the construction field including job costing and progress billings. We'll cover these and more.
    - Job Costing:
        - Defined: *job costing* is a way of calculating what each job cost your company.
        - One simple way is to set-up a clip board for each construction job & put a copy of each bill for that job to that clip board.
        - Allocating any 'overhead' may be trickier.
            - Defined: *overhead* refers to costs that are incurred whether any product is manufactured or not (eg. rent).
            - Ask your company owner if and how they've allocated any overhead in the past, or would like to do it now.
    - Progress Billings: means your company can bill the customer for work done to date & not wait until completion (reference: the construction contract).
    - Receiving Payment for Work Performed:
        - Read contract carefully & don't be surprised about what your customer may require in order to pay you.
        - Items can include: payroll reports & a "release of lien" (a document showing there is no lien attached to any of the materials).
    - Worker's Comp. Insurance Certificates for Independent (Sub) Contractors:
        - If you have any sub-contractors working for you.
        - Be sure to obtain a certificate of worker's compensation insurance from them.
        - Otherwise your insurance company will want you to list them on your bill.
    - Specialized Payroll & Reports for Government Jobs:
        - The Davis Bacon Act requires certain wages for classes of workers on government-funded jobs.
        - Also don't be surprised if your government jobs require you to file very particular payroll reports - to help verify correct wages are paid.
        - Reference: www.dol.gov > A to Z Index > "D" > Davis Bacon.
        - For state wage specifics visit: http://www.gpo.gov/davisbacon/allstates.html.

Chapter 8 - Industries (cont.)

- Construction Industry (cont.):
  - Materialsmen Liens:
    - Defined: *liens* are a legal right to property and represent a way to collect on work done (*materialsmen* are those who work with materials).
    - Lien laws are state or city specific, so you'll need to research your local laws regarding materialsmen liens.
    - I find the internet is most useful in finding local statutes.
    - Beware:
      - Some companies are bad about paying - without a "lien".
      - And some states require filing before a certain amount of time has passed, or you lose the option to file - the lien!
    - Note: much of this paperwork can typically be handled by the bookkeeper or company owner.
  - Bottom-line for construction work:
    - Research all the construction related laws (particularly in your area).
    - Read, study and adhere to your job contracts!

- Food & Beverage Industry:
  - Defined: the *food and beverage industry* includes bars, restaurants, waiters & waitresses.
  - The biggest particularity here is the minimum wage for wait staff.
    - The federal minimum wage for wait staff is $2.13/hour, but only to take into account tips received.
    - In other words, $2.13 is ok only as long as their tips get them to the legal minimum wage - the higher of the federal or state/local minimum.
    - It is the waiters & waitresses responsibility to:
      - Keep a good day to day record of tips received.
      - Report tips received to employer within 10 days of the end of the month.
    - Reference: IRS Publication 1244, "Employee's Daily Record of Tips and Report to Employer".
    - It is the bookkeeper's responsibility to add tips received to their base wage in order to calculate taxes.

- Manufacturing Industry:
  - Defined: the *manufacturing industry* typically involves buying raw materials, mass-producing items, and reselling them "wholesale" to retail outlets.
  - Particularities to the manufacturing industry include:
    - The importance of physical inventory.
    - Tax-free wholesales.
    - "Costing" in a manufacturing environment.

(continued next page)

Chapter 8 - Industries (cont.)

- Manufacturing Industry (cont.):
  - Physical Inventory:
    - Manufacturing can't happen without inventory of raw materials.
    - Accurate beginning & ending inventory levels enable you to calculate "Cost of Goods Sold" needed to produce an Income Statement.
    - Defined: *Cost of Goods Sold (COGS)* is referring to the goods that your company sold. What much did they cost your company?
    -
    - A physical inventory count is taken typically once per year, at year-end.
  - Tax-Free Wholesales:
    - Defined: *tax-free* wholesales means that in some states (New Mexico is one) if your company is a manufacturer or wholesaler, and not selling directly to the public, but to a company who "resells" your product, then the manufacturer/wholesaler may not be required to charge sales tax.
    - The logic here is to avoid 'double taxation'.
    - This is state specific, so you'll need to contact your state's department of taxation or equivalent.
    - You should also be aware that there may be different categories - like non-profit organizations may also be tax-exempt.
  - "Costing" in a Manufacturing Environment:
    - Defined: *costing in a manufacturing environment* would consist of 3 things: direct materials, direct labor and allocated overhead.
    - Direct materials & direct labor are fairly straight forward components of a product cost (with direct labor = assembly workers & their direct supervisors).
    - Allocating overhead can be trickier (ref: Construction Industry above).

- Retail Industry:
  - Defined: the *retail industry* is any store that sells directly to the public.
  - Things to discuss in the the retail industry include:
    - The difference between Cost of Good Sold (COGS) in Manufacturing vs. Retail Industries.
    - Estimating or calculating COGS in Retail.
    - Inventory & "Shrinkage"
      - Defined: *shrinkage* is a loss of inventory, typically due to theft.
  - Manufacturing vs. Retail Industries (re: COGS):
    - Calculating COGS in the Manufacturing Industry is vastly different than in the Retail Industry.
    - COGS (in Manufacturing Industry) = direct materials + direct labor + factory overhead.
    - COGS (in Retail Industry): Beg. Inventory + Purchases = Goods Available for Sale, - Ending Inventory = COGS.
  - In the Retail Industry - you can estimate COGS by way of Purchases (given that beginning and ending inventory levels are the same).

Chapter 8 - Industries (cont.)

- Retail Industry (cont.):
  - Inventory & Shrinkage:
    - Since COGS is needed for the Income Statement, accurate beginning & ending inventory levels are essential.
    - Therefore annual physical inventory counts will be paramount - in also determining how much shrinkage has occurred.

- Service Industry:
  - Defined: the *service industry* is one that does not involve a material product.
  - Examples include: child care, health care, legal and accounting industries.
  - Instead of COGS you use Cost of Sales (COS) Account, because there are no 'goods' being sold.
  - And since services are sold, the "direct salary expense" of those servicing the client (like a lawyer's salary) is the most major component of COS.

- Non-Profit Sector:
  - Is quite a different 'animal' and the only exception to "bookkeeping is bookkeeping" - no matter what the industry.
  - Major similarities & major differences:
    - Similarities: payroll, payroll taxes.
    - Differences: even the financial statements have a different look / name.
  - Learning on the job would be difficult at best.
  - Other books on the subject of bookkeeping for non-profits exist (see text for titles).

- Industry Audit Guides:
  - The IRS has made available the actual guides IRS auditors use in 40 different industries - including Retail and Construction.
  - This can help you know what's important (in an audit..).
  - They are available to view on-line.

Chapter 9 - Dealing(s) with the CPA

- Note: some of this information has been covered in previous chapters, buy may bear repeating.

- As the bookkeeper, you will probably have one or two things to do with a CPA - typically, Corporate Taxes & Quarterly Estimated Tax Payments.

- Corporate Tax Return(s):
    - Contact the CPA the first week in February to see what documents they will need.
    - Typical information is: financial statements, check registers, agings of payables and receivables, and a summary transaction listing.
    - Other items the CPA may need in detail include: "fixed asset" accounts, computer equipment, "draws" by the owner, & gifts/charitable.
    - Note: in addition to the Federal return, some states have a corporate income tax return due. The CPA should also produce this.

- Be sure to review reports for reasonableness (no gross errors) before giving to the CPA.

- Other year-end reports to the CPA?
    - Along with corporate tax items, your company's owner may want you to send:
        - Payroll tax reports (both federal and state).
        - Employee payroll report, listing amounts paid for the year.

- Quarterly Estimated Tax Payments:
    - Defined: *quarterly estimated tax payments* are 'installments' of the federal corporate income tax due.
    - Realize that you'll be making the deposits (electronically), but the CPA will determine any payment amount.
    - Due dates and contact dates:

Tax Due Dates	Contact CPA Dates
April 15th	April 1
June 15th	June 1
September 15th	September 1
December 15th	December 1

- Evolving Relationship is Possible:
    - The extent of your dealings with the CPA may depend upon several things:
        - How much your company's owner feels the need to use the CPA.
        - Your ability to complete bookkeeping tasks - which will probably evolve.
        - Your relationship with the business owner. As his/her confidence in you goes up, the owner's need to use the CPA decreases.

Chapter 10 - Bookkeeper as Management?

- Q: Should a full-charge bookkeeper think of him or herself as akin to management?
- A: Yes, for two reasons:
  - Dealing with money always has managerial importance, *and*
  - As a *full-charge* bookkeeper the company owner relies on you to handle the books without much, if any, supervision.

- Q: Should the bookkeeper "tread lightly"?
- A: Yes: no matter how much the owner entrusts the books to you, you wouldn't want to be telling the owner how to run his or her business.

- Q: So where should you "draw the line"?
- A: If it might/probably come back to "bite" you, as in the owner says, "Why didn't you mention *that*."

- There are several topics relating to management-type activities, including:
  - Having a watchful eye - over the books.
  - Supervisory situations.
  - Not taking on too much.
  - Fielding phone calls - regarding previous employees.
  - Whether you should sign checks (mentioned previously).

- Having a watchful eye - over the books:
  - This is a 'higher' function - maybe only taken on after significant experience.
  - Examples of things to bring to the owner's attention:
    - Shrinkage: if you become aware of a high amount of shrinkage, particularly in a certain area or certain items.
    - Cash Flow: if you observe a sharp decrease in cash flow from one quarter (3-month period) to the next:
      - Pull comparative financial statements.
      - Look at:
        1) sales (has there been a significant decrease?)
        2) expense categories (has any category spiked?)
        3) inventory levels (cash spent to raise inventory levels?).
    - Loose ends: any unaccounted for situations (example: video game tokens given, freely, to managers) may, treading lightly, warrant investigation.

- Supervisory Situations:
  - Two possibilities:
    - The full-charge position may report to someone other than the business owner.
    - You might have to supervise one or two employees,
  - If the full-charge position reports to someone else (may *not* be OK):
    - Example: like a Vice President of Finance.
    - It's been the author's observation that too many 'layers' in a department can create both waste and resentment.

Chapter 10 - Bookkeeper as Management? (cont.)

- Supervisory Situations (cont.):
  - If you have to supervise one or two employees (probably OK):
    - Example: like a payroll or billing clerk for a larger organization.
    - Would be best to start slowly:
      - First, a full-charge position - without supervising anyone.
      - Then supervise just one.

- Don't Take On Too Much:
  - Just because you may do some 'extra' administrative duties (like fielding calls), don't let the owner see you as the "catch-all" for any and everything else.
  - For instance:
    - Don't let them give you the title of H.R. Manager, or you'll probably end up being responsible for more than you'd like.
    - Be sure to outsource:
      - Networking of computers, *and*
      - Any web-site development.

- If you have to field phone calls regarding previous employees:
  - Administrative personnel in smaller companies are in short supply - so the bookkeeper may be the one to handle this human resource duty.
  - The bookkeeper should prepare for fielding these calls by:
    - Researching any state/local laws regarding privacy of information. For instance, you may only be allowed to confirm job title and dates.
    - Touch base with the owner, to see if (s)he has any preferences regarding what information is released, without exceeding any laws.
  - In the absence of laws or the owner's preferences, the best approach may be to just "verify" information the caller has, namely:
    - Job title.
    - Dates of employment.
    - Perhaps to confirm or deny the salary or wage if the caller can offer it.
  - For "persistent" callers reply, "I'm not at liberty to release that information."

- Does the owner want you to sign checks or possess a "signature stamp"?
  - Defined: a *signature stamp* is a rubber stamp possessing the signature of a signer on a bank account. A signature stamp can be used to sign checks.
  - As mentioned in Tasks > Accounts Payable, the author recommends against being a signer for multiple reasons.
  - If you do sign, someone other than you should reconcile that bank account.
  - However, possession of a signature stamp could, with precautions, be useful.
    - For instance, if the owner is to be out of town.
    - Precautions include:
      - Owner maintaining possession until it's needed,
      - Having another manager's initials on the check when stamp is used,
      - And keeping blank checks separate from the signature stamp. ///

Chapter 11 - A Word about Professionalism & Ethics

- Can you imagine a bookkeeper who is always late to work? Not very professional!

- Professionalism:
  - Includes:
    - Timeliness
    - Keeping organized, accurate records
    - "Due diligence"
      - Defined: *due diligence* is a way of saying - put forth the appropriate amount of effort for a particular situation.
      - Example: while being $40 out of balance warrants a good search, being 1 cent out of balance is not 'material' (or relevant) enough to spend gobs of time looking.
  - Timeliness:
    - Be 10 minutes early to work each day.
    - Timely completion of tasks (like payroll tax reports).
    - Don't leave things half done or undone as a rule.
  - Keeping organized and accurate record reflects on your professionalism and competence as a bookkeeper.

- Ethics:
  - Defined: to be *ethical* is to do what is legal and right.
  - Honest bookkeepers should know that some business owners may intend to operate "below board".
    - Defined: *below board* essentially means to operate outside the law.
    - Example: if the business owner intends not to pay time and a half for overtime.
      - Not only is that outside of federal law, but that puts you the bookkeeper in a 'sticky' situation.
      - How hard would it be hard for that same owner to say you were told to pay overtime, setting you up as the law-breaker?
    - Author's advice - take a hard-nosed approach:
      - Don't go to work for a law breaker.
      - If you are unaware when hired, take steps to protect yourself:
        1) Don't sign reports - like payroll tax reports, particularly if you're not completely comfortable with the information.
        2) Consider finding other employment, to protect your integrity.

Chapter 12 - A Word about "Audits"

- What is an "audit"?
  - Defined: an *audit* is an examination of some aspect of the company you work for.
  - Examples include:
    - An audit of the books by the IRS.
    - An audit of your company's operations by a state environmental dept.

- Bookkeepers need to be aware audits exist - in order to be prepared, should one come.

- Audits are typically prompted by something.

- *Reasons* or prompts for an audit include:
  - Non-payment or slow payment of taxes => IRS audit of the books.
  - Bank loans - loan covenants typically require an audit of the books => CPA firm audit of the books.
  - Insurance audit - to adjust, annually, worker's compensation insurance rates => insurance company audit (more below).
  - Company owner - if s/he wanted to have a CPA examine the books.

- *Sources* of an audit:
  - Federal Level:
    - IRS - of the books
    - FBI - if a non-bookkeeping issue.
  - State Level:
    - Your state's Department of Tax & Revenue or equivalent.
    - Or another Department within your state's government if there are any operational issues (eg. State Environmental Department).
  - Other:
    - Insurance Audit
    - Company Owner

- *Types* of audits:
  - Audit of the books
  - "Operational audit" (defined below)
  - Insurance audit

- Insurance Audit:
  - Worker's Compensation Insurance rates are often based on an annual audit.
  - They look at the number of employees and type/s of work each employee does.
  - The insurance company will either call to schedule it, or in some cases allow you to "self-audit" per their form.
  - Defined: a *self-audit*, here, is the insurance company allowing you to provide them the information they need by filling out their form, instead of a visit.

Chapter 12 - A Word about "Audits" (cont.)

- Operational Audit:
  - Defined: an *operational audit* is not of the books, but an audit of some other aspect of the company you work for.
  - Example: if your company transports or stores hazardous waste, your company might get audited by your state's Environmental Department.
  - Your responsibility as bookkeeper: to answer whatever questions come your way honestly and to the best of your ability.
  - There probably won't be very many questions about the books. For instance, they might ask about manifests (paperwork required to transport waste).

- An Audit of the Books:
  - Similar to an operational audit, answer whatever questions honestly and to the best of your ability.
  - It doesn't matter from where an audit comes, just keep the books "clean" and comply with the audit.
  - The best way to keep the books clean is to:
    - Do things the way they're supposed to be done. Example: filing payroll tax reports on time.
    - And, have adequate records or a good "paper trail" showing that things were done correctly (like: copies of payroll tax reports).
    - Defined: a *paper trail* is the records showing how things were done or that they were done correctly.
  - If your company's owner has a CPA audit the books, the typical goals are:
    - To provide reasonable assurance that the financial statements are "presented fairly" (defined below).
      - Defined: *presented fairly* refers to financial statements - saying that they are free from "material" error.
      - Defined: *material* is another way of saying "relevant". And what is relevant is what would change a decision maker's mind - when looking at financial statements.
    - To observe if anything funny has been going on with the books (eg. any findings of fraud).

- Audit Ready:
  - Doing things correctly, and
  - Having an adequate paper trail to display/prove that it was done correctly!

- Audit Guides (A Potential Useful Resource):
  - The IRS publishes "Audit Technique Guides", which are the actual guides IRS auditors use for specific industries like retail & construction.
  - They are available online.//

Full-Charge Bookkeeping

STUDY OUTLINE
FOR THE APPENDICES

by
Nick J. DeCandia, CPA

Copyright 2015
All Rights Reserved.

STUDY OUTLINE FOR APPENDICES
Preface

After significant deliberation, I (author NJD) consider it necessary for Certified Full Charge Bookkeepers (CFCB's) to know most of the material in Appendix D - Accounting 'Basics'. Inventory and Cost of Goods Sold is about the only topic in Appendix D that I provide more coverage in the book than will be tested - in the CFCB exam. Don't misunderstand. There will be material tested there, but I will cover what you need to know in this Study Outline - for the Appendices. Finally, there is some material in the other Appendices (A, C, & E) to cover, as well. The only form, that presents material to cover is the FUTA/SUTA spreadsheet design form. The other forms, for obvious reasons, do not present material that needs to be covered.//

Note: Appendix B material relating to the Chart of Accounts is covered in the >Tasks >General Ledger chapter.

Table of Contents

Appendix A - Master Calendar .... pg. 157
Appendix B - Chart of Accounts .... pg. 157
Appendix C - Financial Statements .... pg. 157
Appendix D - Accounting Basics .... pg. 158
    1) Accounting Equations .... pg. 158
    2) Accounting Methods .... pg. 158
    3) Closing A Year .... pg. 158
    4) Depreciation .... pg. 158
    5) Draws Taken By Owner.......................... pg. 159
    6) Inventory... pg. 159
    7) Office Supplies (Expense?) .... pg. 159
    8) Relationship Between Financial Statements &
        Chart of Accounts .... pg. 160
    9) Retained Earnings ....pg. 160
    10) "Writing Off" a Receivable .... pg. 160
Appendix E - Forms - FUTA/SUTA Design .... pg. 160

Note: there really is not quite enough material in the Appendices to issue separate practice Questions, in addition to the Certification Exam questions.

Appendix A - Master Calendar

- A Master Calendar (Schedule) is a complete listing of all full charge bookkeeping tasks (including payroll tax reports, etc.).

- It includes your state's specific requirements.

- It will help you never miss a deadline.

- - -

Appendix B - Chart of Accounts: is covered in the >Tasks >General Ledger chapter.

- - -

Appendix C - Financial Statements

- Balance Sheet:
    - Current Assets & Liabilities
        - "Current" is referring to anything that is less than one year.
        - For example: a payroll tax liability that's accrued, and then paid at the end of the quarter.
    - Long-Term Assets & Liabilities:
        - "Long Term" is referring to anything greater than one year.
        - Long-Term Assets are generally referred to as "Fixed Assets" (Property & Equipment).
        - An example of a Long Term Liability would be a Note Payable - due in five years.

- Income Statement:
  Note: in addition to what is covered in the >Tasks >Financial Statements or Monthly Reports chapter, a Certified Full Charge Bookkeeper should be familiar with the following Income Statement terms:
    - Net Sales = Sales - Returns - Discounts.
    - Gross Profit = Net Sales - COGS.
    - Cost of Goods Sold (COGS): the goods your company sold customers, what did they cost your company (to either make or buy).
        - Costs to make a product typically include:
            - Raw materials,
            - Direct labor (like factory workers) &
            - Some "overhead" (for example the factory lights, etc.).
    - Service Industry: COGS is different for a service business and can include the direct labor of workers performing the service. And, instead - it's referred to as Cost of Sales!

- - -

Appendix D - Accounting Basics

Introduction: students who become certified in full charge bookkeeping will be held to a higher standard on the job, and in the workplace. Hence, to become "Certified", your knowledge level will need to reflect that. So, the material covered in the Appendices (particularly Appendix D) becomes essential within the certification process.

1) Accounting Equations:
   - Assets - Liabilities = Owner's Equity.
   - Revenues - Expenses = Net Income.

2) Accounting Methods:
   - Cash Method: revenues and expenses are only recognized when cash is received or paid.
   - Accrual Method: revenues and expenses are posted when bills are sent or received (incurred), regardless of when they are actually paid.
   - Note: the Accrual Method is more widely used & accepted. In fact, there's a term: Generally Accepted Accounting Principles (or GAAP). Accrual Method is GAAP.

3) Closing A Year:
   - The Balance Sheet is a "snap shot" in time of the balances in those accounts, as of the last day in the year (or month).
     - The Balance Sheet year ending (or month ending) balances, by definition equal the next year's (or next month's) beginning balances. Makes sense, right?
   - The Income Statement reflects what happened in the business over a period of time (for the entire year or that month).
     - Since the Income Statement reflects what happened over a certain period of time, it stands to reason, that you would have to start from zero, at the beginning of the next period.
     - So, all Revenues and Expenses get "closed" to Net Income - for the period.
     - Net Income gets closed to the Balance Sheet account entitled "Retained Earnings".

4) Depreciation:
   - Depreciation Expense is the expense associated with using-up an asset, during its "useful life".
   - Useful Life is how long an asset can be expected to produce, or be able to be used.
     - The IRS determines the "useful lives" of assets, depending on the type of asset (like vehicle or office equipment).
       - Your company's CPA can be a source, to determine the useful lives, or
       - You can also reference IRS Instructions to Form 4562 ("Depreciation.."), >"Classification of Property".
   - To keep track of how much depreciation has been accumulated over time, the account entitled, "Accumulated Depreciation" is used.
   - So, the Journal Entry to post depreciation is as follows:
     DB: Depreciation Expense $$$
         CR: Accumulated Depreciation $$$

Appendix D - Accounting Basics (continued)

4) Depreciation (cont.):
- Accumulated Depreciation is known as a "contra-asset" account. Which means it subtracts from the asset amount to give you something called "book value" of the asset.
    - Book Value of the Asset = Asset (Original Cost) - Accumulated Depreciation.
    - When the Accumulated Depreciation $$'s = the Original Cost $$'s, the asset is deemed to be "Fully Written Off".

5) Draws Taken By Owner:
- A draw is a removal of cash from the business, beyond the owner's salary (~a dividend).
- "Owner - Draw" is an equity, actually contra-equity account (decreases equity).
- Journal Entry:
    DB: Draw - Owner $$
        CR: Cash $$

6) Inventory:
- For inventory, we're just going to cover the basic journal entries for buying inventory and then selling it (in the Retail industry).
- Journal Entry - When Buying Inventory:
    DB: Inventory $$
        CR: Cash or A/P $$
- Journal Entry - When Selling Product (Inventory):
    DB: Cash or A/R $$ [for the amount it sold for]
        CR: Sales $$ "
    DB: COGS $$ [for the cost of the inventory]
        CR: Inventory $$ "
    Note: yes, two entries when selling it. Cost of Goods Sold (COGS) is an Income Statement account, that reduces revenue.
- Notes:
    - 1) At year-end, companies typically take a physical inventory count and adjust the inventory on the books to match the actual count.
    - 2) This will involve writing up or most likely writing down those Inventory account/s with an off-set to a Gain or Loss account.
        DB: Other Expense / Loss $$ (increasing expense)
            CR: Inventory $$ (decreasing inventory)
    - Some companies use an account entitled, "Inventory Shrinkage".

7) Office Supplies (Expense?):
- Although some may want to consider office supplies to be an asset - used up over time, in practice, it's not practical to, depreciate a $20 waste paper basket.
- Instead, things like that can be expensed.
- Note: companies typically have a "capitalization policy", listing the amount below which something is "expensed" versus treated as an asset and depreciated.

- - -

Appendix D - Accounting Basics (continued)

8) <u>Relationship between Financial Statements and the Chart of Accounts</u>:
   - Generally speaking there are more accounts in the Chart of Accounts than line items in the Financial Statements.
   - For example, all of the separate bank accounts (General, Payroll, Savings) would aggregate to give one line item = "Cash", on the balance sheet.

9) <u>Retained Earnings (RE)</u>:
   - The equation that describes how RE works is:
     - Beginning RE
     - + Net Income
     - - Dividends
     - = Ending RE

10) <u>"Writing Off" A Receivable</u>:
   - "Writing off" a receivable means taking it off the books.
   - The typical entry is:
     DB: Bad Debt Expense $$ (increasing expense)
       CR: A/R - Joe Default Company $$ (decreasing asset)
   - If you subsequently collect:
     - First reverse the above entry (adding Joe Default Company - back to A/R)
     - Then, show the collection of it:
       DB: Cash $$
         CR: A/R - JDC $$

- - -

Appendix E - Forms: FUTA - SUTA Spreadsheet Design

- The main point I'd like to make here is: be sure to do any State Unemployment Taxes first, because Federal Unemployment Taxes are generally reduced by the amount of state taxes paid.
- Reference: IRS, Publication 15, >Federal Unemployment (FUTA) Tax.

- - - - -

Full-Charge Bookkeeping

TEST BANK

by
Nick J. DeCandia, CPA

Copyright 2015
All Rights Reserved.

TEST BANK

Preface

I've written a number of short Questions and Answers (Q & A) per chapter or task, below. As mentioned in the Study Outline, you should first spend ~15-20 minutes reading the associated chapter/pages in the book. For instance, since I've divided the "Accounts Payable" chapter into two classes, you should read approximately half of that chapter. Next, spend ~10-15 minutes reviewing the bullet points (for that chapter / those pages) in the Study Outline. And, finally, spend another 10-15 minutes reviewing the associated Questions and Answers (Q & A) in the Test Bank, that follows the Study Outline. You may want to cover-up the "Answers" - with a half sheet of blank paper, to see what you know.

Table of Contents

Ch. 1 - Introduction	pg. 163
Ch. 2 - Tasks > Human Resource Administration	pg. 163
Ch. 2 - Tasks > Accounts Payable	pg. 164
Ch. 2 - Tasks > Accounts Receivable	pg. 164
Ch. 2 - Tasks > Collections	pg. 165
Ch. 2 - Tasks > Payroll	pg. 165
Ch. 2 - Tasks > Commissions & Bonuses	pg. 167
Ch. 2 - Tasks > Payroll Taxes	pg. 167
Ch. 2 - Tasks > Other Taxes	pg. 168
Ch. 5* - Debits and Credits	pg. 168
Ch. 2 - Tasks > General Ledger	pg. 169
Ch. 2 - Tasks > Fixed Asset Purchases	pg. 169
Ch. 2 - Tasks > Bank Reconciliations	pg. 170
Ch. 2 - Tasks > Petty Cash	pg. 170
Ch. 2 - Tasks > State-Specific Tasks	pg. 171
Ch. 2 - Tasks > Financial Statements or Monthly Reports	pg. 171
Ch. 2 - Tasks > Year-End Items	pg. 172
Ch. 2 - Tasks > Corporate Taxes	pg. 173
Ch. 3 - Authorities	pg. 174
Ch. 4 - Manual Bookkeeping	pg. 174
Ch. 6* - Computers	pg. 175
Ch. 7 - Insurance	pg. 176
Ch. 8 - Industries	pg. 177
Ch. 9 - Dealing(s) with the CPA	pg. 179
Ch. 10 - Bookkeeper as Management?	pg. 180
Ch. 11 - A Word about Professionalism & Ethics	pg. 181
Ch. 12 - A Word about 'Audits'	pg. 181

* Chapter 5 - Debits and Credits is purposefully out of sequence to provide that information before the General Ledger - Journal Entries.

Chapter 1 - Introduction

Q: What does a full-charge bookkeeper do?
A: All of the bookkeeping tasks of a small business, except for corporate taxes.

Q: State one of the questions should you clarify when getting hired.
A: 1. What will I be responsible for?
   2. Are there any areas that need more urgent attention?

Q: After getting hired & having the position defined, where should you start?
   Hint: what if payroll were tomorrow? [Extra/full credit name 3 items.]
A: 1. Current employees list for payroll.
   2. Are the human resource files in order?
   3. Get a handle on the company bills, and company receivables.

Q: Explain what "damage control" is, and how it relates to entering a bookkeeper's position.
A: Damage control is controlling the damage that may have been done by a vacant bookkeeper's position. If you enter a position that's been vacant for awhile, you'll want to check, for instance, that all payroll tax reports have been filed.

Chapter 2 - Tasks > Human Resource Administration

Q: Why might some human resource tasks fall to the bookkeeper?
A: Because smaller companies don't have many "administrative" personnel.

Q: What two documents should be filled out when hired, in addition to the employment application?
A: Form W-4 & Form I-9.

Q: How does Form W-4 relate to payroll?
A: Form W-4 lists the number of withholding allowances which helps determine how much tax is withheld.

Q: What's the purpose of Form I-9?
A: Form I-9 determines if a worker is legal to work in the United States.

Q: How should the Human Resource files be organized?
A: Terminated employees' files should be separated from active employees' files, and both sections should be alphabetized by last name.

Chapter 2 - Tasks > Accounts Payable

Q: What's a packing slip, and what should you do with it?
A: It represents receipt of goods, and should be matched to the vendor's bill.

Q: What is a purchase order, and what should a bookkeeper do with it?
A: A purchase order shows the price(s) agreed to and should be verified against the bill (invoice).

Q: What should a bookkeeper do with a statement from a vendor?
A: Balance your company's books to it, post any finance charges, and file it with the unpaid vendor's bills.

Q: What is an accounts payable aging?
A: An accounts payable aging displays all outstanding bills, their dates and dollar amounts, organized by vendor name.

Q: If your company doesn't pay timely, what will the bookkeeper need to do?
A: The bookkeeper will need to keep a list of incoming calls and communications from vendors - looking for payment, and give that to the owner.

Chapter 2 - Tasks > Accounts Receivable

Q: What are accounts receivable?
A: Accounts receivable are what customers owe your company.

Q: How should accounts receivable invoices be organized?
A: Separate "paid" from "unpaid", and file them by customer/company name, *not* month of sale.

Q: When and why send statements of account?
A: When: once per month (typically at the end or beginning of the month).
Why: It helps keep accounts straight between you and your customer, and it also is a way of letting them know they owe you money.

Q: What is "factoring"?
A: Factoring is selling accounts receivable to another company.

Chapter 2 - Tasks > Collections

Q: What are "collections"?
A: Collecting accounts receivable from customers who are not paying timely.

Q: What's the first thing you need to do before starting any collection activity?
A: Get your boss (the company owner's) approval.

Q: What's the first approach to take with a customer, when calling about a past due bill?
A: Start softly - as your customer may have not received that bill.

Q: What's the "next approach" - after a soft call?
A: Continue to pursue - with "steady determination" or mail a "past due notice".

Q: Name one of the two reasons you should document your collection activity.
A: 1. It's the best way to keep on top of collection activity.
   2. It also enables you to keep your boss apprised of your efforts.

Q: When might legal action be needed?
A: If they are no longer a customer or if all else fails.

Q: Do you always need an attorney to pursue legal remedy?
A: Not necessarily. Some legal complaints can be filled out and filed by company personnel.

Q: What might be an effective policy to help with collections?
A: A 60-day cut-off policy, applied to all customers. When their bills reach 60 days, either they pay or you don't ship product/service.

Q: What are typically the best days to call on a past due bill? And why?
A: Tuesday, Wednesday & Thursday. Mondays and Fridays people tend to be out of the office.

Chapter 2 - Tasks > Payroll

Q: What does payroll start with?
A: A current list of employees, their pay rates and withholding allowances.

Q: Name two of the three things should you know before doing any payroll.
A: 1. *Minimum wage*: the federal and your state's minimum wages.
   2. *Overtime*: to pay overtime for any hours worked over 40 in a 7-day period.
   3. *Record keeping*: to keep records of hours worked, wages earned, and identifying information (for hourly employees).

Chapter 2 - Tasks > Payroll (continued)

Q: In what year was the last federal minimum wage increase? 2007, 2008 or 2009?
A: 2009.

Q: In January 2015, how many states increased their minimum wage rates? 10, 15 or 20?
A: 20.

Q: How many states now have minimum wage rates higher than the federal? 9, 19 or 29?
A: 29.

Q: If your state's minimum wage is higher than the federal minimum wage, which rate applies - the federal or state?
A: Your state's minimum wage would apply.

Q: If Joe makes $8 per hour and worked 45 hours one week, what would Joe's "gross" wages be (before any deductions)?
A: $8 x 40 hours ('straight' wages)= $320
   + $12 x 5 hours ('overtime')   = $ 60
                                   = **$380**

Q: What is the % deducted from an employee's pay check for FICA tax?
A: 7.65%

Q: If Sally had $300 in "gross" wages, $40 in federal withholding (excluding any state taxes) what would be Sally's correct net wages? Don't forget FICA.
A: $300   Gross wages
   <$ 40> Federal Withholding
   <$ 22.95> FICA   [7.65% x $300]
   $237.05

Q: If George had $375 in gross wages, 10% Federal Withholding, and 5% in state taxes what would George's net pay be (don't forget FICA)?
A: $375   Gross wages
   <$ 37.50> Federal Withholding (10%)
   <$ 18.75> State Withholding (5%)
   <$ 28.69> FICA   [7.65% x $375]
   $290.06

Q: Do you make any "payroll deductions" from an independent contractor's pay (& why)?
A: No deductions, because an independent contractor is self-employed and they pay their own payroll taxes.

Chapter 2 - Tasks > Commissions & Bonuses

Q: Are commissions & bonuses taxable? If so, what taxes are they subject to?
A: Yes, they are taxable and subject to federal withholding, FICA, and FUTA.

Q: True or false? Commissions and bonuses should *not* be included in employees' pay - reported on their W-2's at year-end.
A: False.

Q: If Sally earns 12% commission on all sales she makes, and she sold $2500 worth, what would her commission be?
A: $2500 x 0.12 = $300.

Q: Harry gets paid 15% commission on the 1st $1000 in sales, and 10% for every dollar sold over $1000. If Harry sold $2500, what would his commission be (show your work)?
A: $1000 x .15 = $150
   $1500 x .10 = $150
                 $300

Chapter 2 - Tasks > Payroll Taxes

Q: What is meant by employer's matching payroll tax?
A: For every 7.65% FICA deducted, the employer must match that 7.65%.

Q: If you had $2000 in gross wages for a payroll and $250 in Federal Withholding, what would be the amount of your federal payroll tax deposit?
A: ($2000 x 0.153) + $250 = $556

Q: Name one of the two federal payroll tax items to file quarterly.
A: (1) Form 941, & (2) payment of FUTA (Federal Unemployment Tax).

Q: What is the only federal annual payroll tax report to file?
A: Form 940, "Employer's Annual Federal Unemployment (FUTA) Tax Return"

Q: True or false? The amount of State Unemployment Taxes (SUTA) paid typically reduces the amount of Federal Unemployment Taxes (FUTA) owed.
A: True.

Q: Name one of the two typical state payroll taxes.
A: (1) State Unemployment (SUTA) Tax, and (2) State income tax.

Chapter 2 - Tasks > Other Taxes

Q: Name one of the three typical other taxes a bookkeeper might run into.
A: (1) State sales tax, (2) property tax, and (3) a business license fee.

Q: What's the typical difference between state sales tax and "gross receipts" tax?
A: While state sales tax is typically levied on only products sold, gross receipts tax is generally levied on both products *and services* sold.

Q: Is it possible for some transactions to be exempt from sales tax within a state? If so, give an example of an exemption.
A: Yes, non-profit organizations.

Q: Is there a national sales tax?
A: No.

Note: knowledge of debits and credits are needed for the General Ledger, so Chapter 5 is taught before proceeding to Tasks > General Ledger.

Chapter 5 - Debits and Credits

Q: Why does a bookkeeper need to know debits & credits?
A: To be able to do journal entries for things like petty cash & depreciation.

Q: Describe what is meant by a "dual entry system". Give an example.
A: It means that each transaction affects two accounts. For example when you buy equipment, your cash account decreases, and your equipment account increases.

Q: What is the name of the listing of all accounts?
A: Chart of Accounts.

Q: Assets - Liabilities = ?
A: Owner's Equity or Equity of the Owner

Q: True or false? All debits need to equal all credits in a journal entry.
A: True.

Q: To increase assets _____ them.
A: Debit.

Q: To decrease assets _____ them.
A: Credit.

Q: To increase liabilities & owner's equity _____ them.
A: Credit.

Chapter 2 - Tasks > General Ledger

Q: What is the place or module, in the computer called where all transactions (debits & credits) get posted?
A: General Ledger.

Q: True or false? Most transactions entered into the computer will automatically post to the General Ledger.
A: True.

Q: Give an example of a transaction that will not automatically post to the General Ledger.
A: Petty Cash.

Q: What is a "journal entry"?
A: A journal entry is debits and credits in balance describing a transaction.

Q: What is a "transaction listing"?
A: A transaction listing lists all of the transactions (debits and credits) for selected accounts, over a specified period of time.

Q: Should accounts, typically, be deleted from the Chart of Accounts? Why?
A: No, because accounts will typically have balances attached or associated with them (amounts posted to them) and therefore should not be deleted.

Q: What does it mean for the General Ledger to balance?
A: The general ledger balances when all debits posted equal all credits posted.

Chapter 2 - Tasks > Fixed Asset Purchases

Q: What's another name for "fixed assets"? Hint: you find them on the Balance Sheet.
A: Property, plant and equipment.

Q: Give some examples of fixed assets.
A: Land, buildings, vehicles, furniture, fixtures and equipment.

Q: Name one of the three things a bookkeeper's responsible for regarding fixed asset purchases.
A: 1. Track fixed assets purchased during the year.
   2. Post those assets to the General Ledger.
   3. And communicate this information to the CPA at the end of the year.

Chapter 2 - Tasks > Bank Reconciliations

Q: Is a corporate bank reconciliation very different from a personal bank account reconciliation? Yes or no?
A: No.

Q: What is a paper trail?
A: A paper trail shows how things were done or that they were done correctly.

Q: What "powers" do you have and should you use to locate an outage?
A: "Analytical" powers.

Q: True or false? You should spend 4 days looking for one penny.
A: False.

Q: What does it mean to "leave no stone unturned" when working an outage?
A: It means to look in every single place, even if you think it certainly is not "there".

Q: Name the two tips for finding an outage.
A: The divide by 9 tip, and the divide by 2 tip.

Chapter 2 - Tasks > Petty Cash

Q: What is petty cash?
A: A small amount of cash kept on hand for incidental items.

Q: Where should petty cash be kept?
A: In a locked box.

Q: Who (at most) should have access to petty cash?
A: The bookkeeper and business owner.

Q: What are the first and second steps in the use of petty cash for a purchase?
A: 1. Approval from the company owner (verbal is ok).
   2. Signed petty cash receipt from those receiving cash.

Q: What does a bookkeeper need to do with petty cash at the end of the month?
A: 1. Balance petty cash.
   2. Post it to the general ledger.
   3. Store receipts.

Q: What does it mean to "balance petty cash"?
A: Balancing petty cash means that the beginning cash in the box less receipts equals what cash is left in the box.

Chapter 2 - Tasks > State-Specific Tasks

Q: What does the Personal Responsibility and Work Opportunity Reconciliation Act require of employers?
A: It requires employers to report new-hires and rehires to a state directory.

Q: What's the point of reporting new-hires and rehires?
A: It helps facilitate child support payments for parents who change jobs frequently.

Q: True or false? PRWORA is certainly the *only* state-specific task out there.
A: False.

Q: Why do state-specific tasks typically fall to the bookkeeper?
A: Because smaller companies do not have many "administrative" personnel working for them.

Chapter 2 - Tasks > Financial Statements or Monthly Reports

Q: What are the two main financial statements?
A: Income Statement (or Profit & Loss) and Balance Sheet.

Q: What does a Balance Sheet show?
A: A Balance Sheet lists assets, liabilities, and "owner's equity" as of the last day in the period.

Q: Before printing financial statements what do you need to do?
A: Make sure all data is entered for the month.

Q: Do computer bookkeeping programs (like QuickBooks and Sage 50) typically have preloaded financial statements? Yes or no?
A: Yes.

Q: In addition to financial statements, name two other reports that typically get printed monthly.
A: Aging of Payables, Aging of Receivables, Check Register(s) and/or General Ledger Transaction Listing.

Q: What does an Income Statement show?
A: An Income Statement subtracts expenses from revenues to arrive at net income for the period.

Chapter 2 - Tasks > Year-End Items

Q: Name two of the four "year-end items".
A: 1. W-2's
   2. 1099's
   3. Record retention
   4. Gathering year-end reports for corporate taxes.

Q: What's a W-2?
A: W-2's are the forms mailed by companies at the end of the year, indicating each employee's wages and taxes paid, for the calendar year.

Q: How many copies of each W-2 should you make? Name two.
A: At least 4.
   1. Federal
   2. State
   3. copy for employee
   4. copy for bookkeeper

Q: What are 1099's (MISC) for?
A: To document wages paid to contract labor. It helps the government keep track.

Q: If your company pays an independent contractor $500 in one year, are you required to issue that person a 1099? Why?
A: No, because there is a $600 threshold. Anything less than $600 and no 1099 is required.

Q: Name one of the three sources to obtain blank W-2's or 1099's.
A: (1) Office supply stores, (2) bookkeeping software companies and (3) the IRS.

Q: What is a record retention schedule? Give one example.
A: It is a list showing how long to keep what types of files.
   Example: A/P - 5 years.

Q: When should you contact the CPA about the corporate tax return?
A: In early February.

Q: Name one of two of the "other year-end reports" to gather for the CPA.
A: 1. Copies of payroll tax reports.
   2. Employee payroll reports - showing summary amounts paid.

Chapter 2 - Tasks > Corporate Taxes

Q: What's typically the only bookkeeping task that a bookkeeper FCB "outsources"?
A: Corporate taxes.

Q: Give an example of a "fiscal" year (that's not a calendar year).
A: [Any 12 months other than January 1st - December 31st]

Q: What is the bookkeeper's responsibility regarding corporate taxes?
    Hint: there's two items.
A: 1. To provide to the CPA the needed information to produce the return/s.
    2. To make quarterly estimated tax payments.

Q: What are quarterly estimated tax payments?
A: They are "installments" of federal corporate income tax.

Q: Name two of the four *typical* corporate tax items.
A: 1. Financial statements
    2. Check register/s
    3. Summary agings of payables & receivables
    4. General Ledger - summary transaction listing.

Q: Name two of the four *additional* corporate tax items. Hint: detailed transaction listings of these items.
A: 1. Fixed assets account(s)
    2. Computer equipment asset or expense account
    3. Charitable contributions / gifts account
    4. "Draws" by the Owner - account

Q: True or false? States *never* have a corporate income tax return due.
A: False.

Q: What is the only method or way to deposit estimated taxes?
A: Electronically.

Chapter 3 - Authorities

Q: Who is the only federal authority used *frequently* by a full-charge bookkeeper?
A: IRS.

Q: What is IRS' Publication 15 (Circular E) entitled?
A: Employer's Tax Guide.

Q: True or false? Generally speaking, each state is different in what taxes it collects & how it collects them.
A: True.

Q: Name two of the three typical state taxes.
A: 1. State Unemployment Tax (SUTA)
   2. State sales tax
   3. State income tax

Q: True or false? It is possible for your state to have more than one taxing authority.
A: True.

Chapter 4 - Manual Bookkeeping

Q: True or false? There's absolutely no point of learning manual bookkeeping.
A: False.

Q: True or false? Bookkeeping is best learned in the following order: manual bookkeeping, debits & credits, followed by computer bookkeeping.
A: True.

Q: True or false? There is not much a business owner can do bookkeeping-wise, without a computer or debits and credits.
A: False.

Q: Name two of nine bookkeeping tasks a business owner can accomplish without debits & credits or a computer.
A: A/P, A/R, Payroll, Payroll Taxes, Commissions, Other Taxes, Bank Reconciliations, Human Resource Administration, & Petty Cash.

Q: Name one of three "next steps" for a business owner - regarding bookkeeping.
A: 1. Get a computer.
   2. Get an outside accountant (to generate an Income Statement).
   3. Hire a full-charge bookkeeper.

Note: since debits and credits are needed for the General Ledger, Chapter 5 is taught out of sequence, and can be found just before Tasks > General Ledger.

Chapter 6 - Computers

Q: What's an easy way to learn a computer bookkeeping program?
Hint: it's typically built right into the program.
A: The tutorial/s.

Q: Name one of the two most popular small business computer bookkeeping programs out there.
A: 1. QuickBooks
   2. Sage 50 Accounting

Q: Are there different versions of QuickBooks out there? If yes, give an example.
A: Yes. Example: QuickBooks versus QuickBooks Pro.

Q: A potentially good system for customer / vendor ID numbers is?
Hint: Federal Express Corporation.
A: Four letters followed by two numbers. Example: FEDE01.

Q: How often should you "back-up" your work?
A: Every day.

Q: Is it a good idea to keep a back-up copy "off premises"? If yes, why?
A: Yes, in case of a catastrophe at work - like fire/flood.

Q: Name one of the two types of programs included in "office" software.
A: 1. Word processing
   2. Spreadsheet

Q: Give one of the two situations when a computer consultant would be needed.
A: 1. Networking of the computers
   2. Web-site work.

Q: True or false? You may need to update your payroll tax tables.
A: True.

Chapter 7 - Insurance

Q: True or false? Health insurance is required for ALL companies to carry.
A: False.

Q: True or false? Health insurance is subject to state laws & insurance company requirements.
A: True.

Q: What does HIPAA require of plan administrators / bookkeepers?
A: To be sure a certificate of prior health coverage was issued to terminated employees who had health insurance.

Q: What does COBRA do for terminated employees?
A: Allows them to continue health insurance coverage.

Q: Does COBRA apply to all companies? Explain.
A: No. It doesn't apply to companies with less than 20 employees in the prior year?

Q: What is worker's compensation insurance for?
A: In case an employee is injured on the job.

Q: True or false? Worker's compensation insurance is widely required to be carried.
A: True.

Q: What are worker's compensation insurance rates often based on?
A: An insurance audit (of number of employees and type/s of work they do).

Q: Give an example of something that might affect your worker's compensation insurance rate.
A: 1. the number of employees in your company
2. the type(s) of work your employees do.

Q: What do you need to obtain from an independent contractor - working for your company? Why?
A: Obtain a certificate of worker's compensation insurance from him/her.
Why: because if you don't have it, your insurance company will raise your rate to cover them.

Q: What is corporate liability insurance for (give an example)?
A: It is general coverage for things like fire/flood.

Chapter 8 - Industries

Q: True or false? Bookkeeping is essentially bookkeeping - no matter what the industry.
A: True.

Construction Industry

Q: What's a simple way to set-up job costing for a construction job?
A: Set-up a clipboard for that construction job.

Q: Should your company have to wait until you complete the entire construction project before getting paid? Explain.
A: No. Progress billings, depending on the contract, are there so you can be paid for work done to date.

Q: If you have a sub-contractor or independent contractor working for your company, what should you obtain from them (hint: re: insurance)? Why?
A: A certificate of worker's compensation insurance from their insurance company. That way you won't have to list them on your insurance.

Q: What is a lien for?
A: A lien represents a legal right to property and will help you get paid for construction work done.

Food & Beverage Industry

Q: How does a wait person's minimum wage work?
A: They are allowed to be paid as little as $2.13 / hour, as long as their tips make up the difference to get to the federal or your state/local minimum wage, if that's higher.

Q: Is it the employ*ee's* or employ*er's* responsibility to keep initial track of tips earned?
A: It is the employee's responsibility.

Q: True or false? It's ok for a wait person to *report* tips only once per month.
A: True.

Q: Should bookkeepers calculate taxes on just the wait staff's base wage ($2.13/hr)? Explain.
A: No. Bookkeepers need to add tips to the base wage in order to calculate taxes.

(continued next page)

Chapter 8 - Industries (cont.)

Manufacturing Industry

Q: How often do companies typically take a physical inventory count?
A: Once per year.

Q: Explain what is meant by a "tax-free wholesale".
A: In some states, the wholesaler may not be required to charge sales tax (to avoid double taxation) since the retailer will be charging tax.

Q: What are the 3 components of any cost analysis, in manufacturing?
A: Direct materials, direct labor & overhead.

Q: Why are accurate beginning & ending inventory levels important?
A: In order to calculate Cost of Goods Sold, needed to produce an Income Statement.

Retail Industry

Q: Define the Retail Industry.
A: Any store/company that sells directly to the public.

Q: What is shrinkage?
A: Loss of inventory, typically due to theft.

Q: True or false? Calculating COGS in the Manufacturing Industry is vastly different than in the Retail Industry.
A: True.

Q: COGS in the Manufacturing Industry = ?
A: Direct materials + direct labor + factory overhead.

Q: COGS in the Retail Industry = ?
A: Beginning inventory + purchases = goods available for sale, - ending inventory = COGS.

Q: True or false? In the retail industry you can estimate COGS by way of purchases.
A: True.

Q: True or false? In the retail industry, accurate beginning and ending inventory levels will help you accurately calculate COGS.
A: True.

Q: True or false? In the retail industry, shrinkage will always have no affect on your ending inventory level/s.
A: False. Shrinkage can certainly impact ending inventory levels.

Chapter 8 - Industries (cont.)

<u>Service Industry</u>
- Q: What is the service industry [or what is it not]? Give an example.
- A: The service industry doesn't involve a material product to sell. Examples include: child care, health care, legal and accounting services.

- Q: Instead of the Cost of Goods Sold account, what account name does the service industry use? Why?
- A: Cost of Sales, because there are no "goods" being sold.

<u>Non-Profit Sector</u>
- Q: True or false? To learn bookkeeping for non-profits look at another book.
- A: True.

<u>Industry Audit Guides</u>
- Q: True or false? IRS industry audit guides exist and are available for approximately 40 different industries.
- A: True.

Chapter 9 - Dealing(s) with the CPA

Q: True or false? There is a chance you will have one or two things to do with your company's CPA.
A: True.

Q: When should you contact the CPA to see what s/he will need to produce the corporate tax return?
A: Early in February.

Q: True or false? In general, a CPA may have to generate a state corporate tax return, also.
A: True.

Q: Typically, will the CPA or will the bookkeeper be making the quarterly estimated tax payments?
A: The bookkeeper will.

Q: Will the bookkeeper or will the CPA determine the amount of the quarterly estimated tax deposit?
A: The CPA will determine the amount.

Chapter 9 - Dealing(s) with the CPA (cont.)

Q: What is the only acceptable method of depositing estimated corporate tax payments?
A: Electronically.

Q: Name one of the three things that could cause an evolving (or growing) relationship between the bookkeeper, the business owner, and the CPA?
A: 1. How the company owner feels the need to use the CPA,
    2. The bookkeeper's ability to complete bookkeeping tasks,
    3. The bookkeeper's relationship with the business owner - as far as confidence goes.

Chapter 10 - Bookkeeper as Management?

Q: Should the bookkeeper think of him/herself as akin to management? Why?
A: Yes, because dealing with money always has managerial importance, and as a full-charge bookkeeper, the owner relies on the bookkeeper to handle the books with little or no supervision.

Q: Should the bookkeeper tread lightly? Why?
A: Yes, because you wouldn't want to be telling the owner how to run his or her business.

Q: Name one of the two supervisory possibilities that a bookkeeper might be subject to.
A: 1. The full-charge position reports to someone other than the business owner.
    2. The bookkeeper might have to supervise one or two employees.

Q: True or false, and why? The bookkeeper may need to field calls regarding previous employees.
A: True, because smaller companies don't have many administrative personnel.

Q: In the absence of laws, describe the best approach to a caller about a previous employee.
A: Bookkeeper should simply verify information the caller has, such as job title, dates of employment, and perhaps the wage if caller can provide it.

Q: What is a "signature stamp"?
A: A signature stamp is a rubber stamp possessing the signature of a signer on a bank account. A signature stamp can be used to sign checks.

Chapter 11 - A Word about Professionalism & Ethics

Q: True or false? Being late for work is unprofessional.
A: True.

Q: Name two of the three ways to demonstrate professionalism.
A: 1. Timeliness
   2. Due diligence
   3. Keeping organized and accurate records.

Q: Name one of the three ways to demonstrate timeliness.
A: 1. Be 10 minutes early to work each day.
   2. Timely completion of tasks (like payroll tax reports).
   3. Not leaving things half done or undone, as a rule.

Q: What does it mean to be ethical?
A: To do what is legal and right.

Q: What does it mean to operate "below board"?
A: To operate outside the law.

Chapter 11 - A Word about Professionalism & Ethics (cont.)

Q: Name one way to deal with an owner who intends to operate "below board"?
A: 1. Don't go to work for him or her in the first place.
   2. Protect yourself: don't sign reports you're not comfortable with.
   3. Seek other employment.

Chapter 12 - A Word about 'Audits'

Q: What is an audit?
A: An audit is an examination of some aspect of the company you work for.

Q: True or false? Audits are typically prompted by something.
A: True.

Q: Name one *reason* or prompt for an audit.
A: 1. Non-payment or slow payment of taxes.
   2. Bank loan covenants.
   3. Insurance audit - to adjust worker's compensation insurance rates.
   4. Company owner - if s/he wanted to have a CPA examine the books.

Q: Name one *source* of an audit (from where or whom an audit can come).
A: 1. Federal level: IRS or FBI.
   2. State level.
   3. Insurance company.
   4. Company owner.

Chapter 12 - A Word about 'Audits' (cont.)

Q: Name one *type* of audit.
A: 1. Audit of the books.
   2. Operational audit.
   3. Insurance audit.

Q: Why do bookkeepers need to be aware audits exist?
A: In order to be prepared should one come along.

Q: What's an operational audit?
A: An audit, not of the books, but of some other aspect of your company.

Q: What are the two components to keeping the books "audit ready"?
A: 1. Doing things the way they're supposed to be done, and
   2. Having adequate records or a "paper trail", showing that things were done correctly.//

Note: now that you have completed this course, consider taking it to the next level - Certification (see Preface), or visit: www.Full-ChargeBookkeeper.com/Certification.

Index

A Word about Audits .... pg. 64
A Word about Career Advancement .... pg. 94
A Word about Professionalism & Ethics .... pg. 63
Accounting Basics .... pg. 73
    Accounting Equations .... pg. 73
    Accounting Methods .... pg. 73
    Closing A Year .... pg. 73
    Depreciating Assets .... pg. 74
    Draws Taken by the Owner .... pg. 75
    Inventory and Cost of Goods Sold .... pg. 75
    Office Supplies (Expense?) .... pg. 78
    Relationship Between Financial Statements and
        the Chart of Accounts .... pg. 78
    Retained Earnings .... pg. 79
    Writing-Off a Receivable .... pg. 79
Accounts Payable .... pg. 11
Accounts Receivable .... pg. 15
Authorities .... pg. 44
Balance Sheet .... pg. 72
Bank Reconciliations (Including Finding Outages) .... pg. 32
Bookkeeper as Management? .... pg. 60
Career Resource Binder Kept At Home .... pg. 96
Chart of Accounts (Sample) .... pg. 68
Commissions & Bonuses .... pg. 23
Computers .... pg. 49
Collections .... pg. 16
Corporate Taxes .... pg. 42
Dealing(s) with the CPA .... pg. 58
Debits and Credits .... pg. 47
Financial Statement (Samples) .... pg. 70
Financial Statements or Monthly Reports .... pg. 37
Finding Outages (Bank Reconciliation chapter) .... pg. 32
Fixed Asset Purchases .... pg. 31
General Ledger .... pg. 29
Getting Started and Organized When Hired .... pg. 8
Human Resource Administration .... pg. 10
Income Statement .... pg. 71
Industries .... pg. 54
Insurance .... pg. 52
Manual Bookkeeping .... pg. 46
Master Calendar (Schedule) .... pg. 66
New Job Checklist .... pg. 9
Other Taxes .... pg. 28
Payroll .... pg. 18
Payroll Taxes .... pg. 24
Petty Cash .... pg. 34
Resources & Bibliography .... pg. 97
Sample Forms .... pg. 80
    Collection Form .... pg. 81
    Commission Spreadsheet Form .... pg. 82
    Fax Cover Sheet .... pg. 83
    FUTA - SUTA Spreadsheet Design .... pg. 84
    HR - Employee Request for Time Off Form .... pg. 86

Index (continued)

Sample Forms (continued)
- HR - Employee Update Information Form .... pg. 85
- HR - Employee Warning Notice .... pg. 87
- Past Due Notice .... pg. 88
- Petty Cash - Change Order .... pg. 90
- Petty Cash - Receipts .... pg. 89
- Record Retention Form .... pg. 91
- Time Sheet for Employees .... pg. 92
- Travel Mileage Form .... pg. 93

State-Specific Tasks .... pg. 36
What is Full-Charge Bookkeeping? .... pg. 8
Year-End Items (W-2's, 1099's, Record Retention) .... pg. 39

STUDY OUTLINE .... pg. 115

TEST BANK .... pg. 161

Made in the USA
Lexington, KY
24 August 2015